The Death and Life of Drama

DATE DUE

MAR – 2008		Arrival Date	

Previous Works

The Death and Life of Drama

Reflections on Writing and Human Nature

LANCE LEE

UNIVERSITY OF TEXAS PRESS *Austin*

Requests for permission to reproduce material from this work should be sent to:

Permissions
University of Texas Press
P.O. Box 7819
Austin, TX 78713-7819

www.utexas.edu/utpress/about/bpermission.html

⊚ The paper used in this book meets the minimum requirements
of ANSI/NISO Z39.48-1992 (R1997) (Permanence of Paper).

LIBRARY OF CONGRESS CATALOGING-IN-PUBLICATION DATA

Lee, Lance, 1942–
The death and life of drama : reflections on writing and human nature / Lance Lee—1st ed.
    p.   cm.
  ISBN 0-292-70532-8 (cloth : alk. paper) — ISBN 0-292-70964-1 (pbk. : alk. paper)
  1. Motion picture authorship.   2. Playwriting.   1. Title.
  PN1996.L387 2005
  808.2'3—dc22

                                                        2004027264

to my wife, Jeanne
and to John Matthews, mentor

Contents

Preface

OFTEN I ask screenwriters, Why not abolish the entire film and dramatic enterprise which consumes billions of dollars a year and endless hours, to say nothing of the money involved in related industries, and use all that money, time, and effort for the elimination of poverty, say, in Africa? Or Appalachia? Why not take all that money and invest it in the elimination of a particular killer disease? Wouldn't that be morally better and a far more humane activity than writing another screenplay or producing another film? Wouldn't relieving the suffering of one child be reason enough to abolish an industry whose only widely accepted function is entertainment? To their credit a few writers in a given discussion group vote to do just that.

Most do not, although even the arguments offered after we get past easy and cynical responses are unconvincing. One response that emerges repeatedly is that abolishing the film and entertainment industry for these purposes wouldn't work: creating drama and all that entails by way of production and dissemination would start again from the ground up. There is something necessary about this creative activity, hard as it may be to put that necessity into words.

The nature of that necessity certainly cannot be found by writing another screenwriting manual or reviewing the literature within the field. Drama, which includes the continual creation of new dramas, occupies so pervasive a position in our culture and one so caught up within the argument modern culture is having with itself that to understand its role demands perspectives that go beyond those discussed within the field into broader cultural, psychological, and philosophical areas. This is also true for understanding what we must do when we believe we are caught up in purely technical writing problems, for a continuous theme here is how dramatic structure roots in psychic structure.

These reflections led me to adopt the more personal essay style. This does not imply these are essays of aesthetics or criticism. I hope writers will get as much real use out of these essays as any more traditionally specialized text, for the goal is to give them a better understanding of what the various technical tools they use are for. Much of what is offered here has grown from reflection based on long experience as a writer and teacher, although any necessary documentation is given in the notes.

I use the term "drama" broadly, applying drama equally to stage and film. And like the ancient Greeks, I include comedy within drama as one of its two great divisions in treating human nature and experience. Tragedy may have its suffering mask, comedy its laughing, but if we look at traditional renderings we can find ourselves struggling to distinguish between the pain in either mask, just as in life it can be hard to tell tears of joy from tears of grief. Yet both are part of the great river of drama on which we so strongly float.

Including screenwriting as "drama" seems obvious on the face of it, although I suppose some don't realize writing drama for the stage or film is the same, allowing for the adjustments caused by using the different production mediums. A production medium makes for a variety in the art of drama but is not drama itself, not the exploration of the human spirit through the guise of dramatic action.

Beyond this, the dramatic impulse has moved powerfully to film in the last sixty years. If we reach for an illustrative dramatic example for some point we are making, we are far more likely to do so from a film than stage drama, including filmed versions of notable dramas such as the multitude of filmed versions of Shakespeare. Even in England the example reached for is far more likely now to stem from a filmed version of Shakespeare than ever before, with arguments over whether Olivier got Henry V right in *Henry V* or Branagh, in their *film* versions, or whether Olivier or Branagh got Hamlet right in their *film* versions.

I will think of this book as a success if the reflections offered here, however sure or tentative, spark further reflection and help some writer give a screenplay that extra dimension that ensures success and meaningfulness.

The Death and Life of Drama

PART I

Immediate Issues

CHAPTER 1

By the Ocean of Time

Time

THE title for this essay is taken from a chapter in Thomas Mann's *Magic Mountain* where he reflects on some of the paradoxes we encounter in our experience of time.[1] Nothing is more commonplace or harder to understand or more likely to make us feel we are in Plato's cave watching shadows we confuse with reality. Often we feel a nagging sense, like Neo in *The Matrix,* that there is a truer reality above or below or beyond what we experience, and that if our immediate experience is an illusion so too is our perception of time, for that is inextricably bound up with our experience of reality. When time drags, experience drags. But it is not easy to say what makes time drag even in the case of dramatic action, which is just a special instance of our larger experience of time.

Mann writes that if we fill time up with activity, as a drama is supposed to do with action, such that one day after another is full of our doings, cumulatively time seems to go very slowly, even though each day flies by. A week feels like it stretches out, in comparison to others with little activity, and feels full as opposed to empty. Something of our sense of childhood is built into this experience of time, those days of continual activity whether of school or with friends that seem eternal while we are in their midst. Yet if that activity accumulates over a long stretch of experience, suddenly we feel that time has abruptly fled: "Where has it all gone?" we wonder. What was it we were doing? Was it anything at all? What happened to childhood? Or youth? Or . . . ? The answer "We were living" immediately gives rise to the response "Was that all there was to life?"

Paradoxically, the opposite experience of time brings us here too. Oblomov's days pass in almost dreamlike withdrawal and inactivity in Goncharov's novel *Oblomov.*[2] Each day feels impossibly long and dull, yet the cumulative lapse of boredom is also one day felt as fast, as Oblomov feels in the moment of his awakening to love. He too wonders, "Where has it all gone?" However our days seem to pass, one day we look back as if suddenly waking and they appear like a fading dream: what seemed so full or eternal turns into shadows.

Drama makes use of parts our fluid time sense, of how a good deal of action can make time seem to fly and life be full, and also how with little dramatic action life feels empty and drags. But we do not get to the paradox in a dramatic story as a matter of story handling of how inactive, time-filled days at first seem slow but then, after some indefinable point, to have flown: a story that drags in any sense loses us before it can ever seem cumulatively fast, even if our experience of it, so soon dismissed as we walk out of the theatre, slides into some of these paradoxes.

A peculiarity of all these different ways of experiencing time is time's *nowness*, whether of experience dragging or speeding or ending up in the same place from different directions. The only time we ever have to experience is the one we experience *now*.

Complicating this further in an everyday sense is how time is experienced differently by individuals. There is the clock: the two hours that we see elapse drag for me but fly by for you. Characters in our stories are constantly in different temporal spaces. That is one of the inherent expressions of conflict.

Look how Hamlet twits Ophelia as the play-within-a-play scene begins in *Hamlet*. He tells her only two hours have passed since his father's death: she swiftly corrects him, saying that *twice two months* have passed.[3] Ophelia is not suffering from a loss, however, like Hamlet: her experience of reality and hence time are largely conventional. Her troubles with Hamlet can be seen from her point of view as upsetting but romantic. But Hamlet is trapped within his grief over his father's death and paralyzed by his father's demand for vengeance: he is in a single emotional— hence single temporal—space, like Oblomov dreaming away his life on his couch.

Or think of Edie and Terry in *On the Waterfront* as she urges him to leave the docks, after his failure to unseat Johnny Friendly by going to court has become apparent. She is urgent, her emotions hammer at Terry: "Let's go, let's go now, let's go upstate and farm, let's not deal with Johnny Friendly and his thugs and the longshoremen who are now ostracizing you: let's have a life away from all of this." Terry is silent, thinking, marking time deliberately and almost literally with the way he plays with his longshoreman's hook. They are experiencing reality in radically different ways and so experience time differently, urgent vs. reflective, fast vs. slow, fleeting vs. rooted in place and milieu, for Terry's final decision is to go down to the docks and get his rights. As in *Hamlet*, we experience both times simultaneously through these characters.

Flashback is based on this fluidity of our temporal consciousness, namely, that we can go back and relive time, *we* being the audience as well as the characters whose memories we relive through them. We think of flashback as a writing convention, but it could not exist unless it accorded with how our minds work and experience memory, or with the way in which we live daily in a stream of experience that interweaves many different senses of time. What's more, when we do use flashback in drama, that relived past is experienced as *now,* for our experience of time is always *now.* Language may begin to break down into paradox when we put "past" and "now" together, *but not our experience of reality.*

Various forms of psychotherapy, which many of us have experienced directly, take us back in time as we recall and rethink events, even find what we had forgotten, and thereby change our perception of the past. In doing so we know that in some sense we alter that past too. We discover that time past and time now are far less divided than conventionally thought. Even outside the framework of psychotherapy, all of us routinely relive events in memory and, as time passes in our lives, start to see some of those events differently. Suddenly we are in the middle of paradox: what should have been past is not past but still undergoing immediate change. Take away our ability both to remember and to alter the meaning of memory and we cease to be human or become frozen in our response to experience.

What do we mean by calling something past, then? If the experience of our lives changes even those parts we thought past, if characters' experience changes in dramas the same way, and this is all experienced in the *nowness* of immediate experience, how can we ever maintain a purely conventional sense of experience or time at all except as a convenience of discourse? Granted we and the characters in our dramas don't live on this level of awareness all the time, yet it hovers continually just below consciousness. Only a little reflection makes us feel an illusory quality to our experience and sense of time, like Neo in *Matrix* or Hamlet in *Hamlet* or as in Plato's haunting cave image.

A film like *Rashômon* depends on our underlying sense of time's fluidity and brings me another step in this reflection. Our experience of the film goes well beyond understanding each individual storyteller's tale or reflecting on the ultimate unknowability of experience as we sort through their contradictory stories, told largely in flashback, each in turn as convincing in its detail and sense of *nowness*. It breaks in on us that there is *no limit for the mind* in how often an experience with its associated time frame can be *now,* relived and changed. That realization comes with a shock of familiarity: "This was always true," we think suddenly, as some intense memory fills our mind.

This is the part of our fluid sense of time, with which all screenplays deal. Hamlet's father may be dead in *Hamlet,* but what to make of that death, how to judge whether his father's ghost is the real thing or a devilish deception and his tale of murder a lie, and what to do about Claudius are all living questions. Time is not just a date in a chronology but the experiences that go with that event: to speak of an event as *set* is to say that those experiences and the experience of time they embody are equally set, which is not the case in drama generally or *Hamlet* specifically, any more than for *Rashômon* with regard to the husband's death, the wife's motivation, or the bandit's character. Everything is up for grabs; it is all still *now.* Even the husband is experienced in the present through the medium, as well as variously in flashback.

Modern psychoanalysis and analytic psychotherapies offer an interesting variant. We refer to a behavioral pattern developed to deal with a past trauma that we keep applying to *present* experience when we speak of neurosis. Hamlet can be seen as neurotic because he continues to treat new experience in the same way in which he coped with his father's death. He continually recoils from that experience and the ghost's demand for action as though death made him see the wholly illusory nature of immediate experience/action, like a kind of Buddha or Neo in *The Matrix* discovering that reality is a programmed illusion. This fixed pattern of imposing past behavior on the present forms an essential part of the transference in psychoanalysis, as we act now toward the analyst as we have toward key others in our lives as if the circumstances that first gave rise to our arrested behavior still endure.

This kind of behavior has a fixity to it. In reality, it leads to a great deal of suffering and stunting for an individual who cannot move past temporally frozen responses. Once we recognize such a pattern in a *character*, we know we are in for a radical change or, if not, for a defeat or a death. This fixity of experience and time is the opposite of what we mean by living creatively and of what we expect from a dramatic hero or heroine, who must overcome the conflict he or she is engaged in and defined by—unless the story is a tragedy, in which case the larger community, even if an antagonist's, transcends the conflict.

But time and the nature of experience are not settled either in absolute or relative terms beyond the habit of conventional definition; worse, their natures are caught up in the argument our culture is having with itself and in which our drama takes a side.

The Argument We Are Caught In

Time has been conceived with enormous variation in history—governing the day with clocks only begins in the later middle ages. The measurement of time permits navigation; its relativity in Einstein has colored our culture. Societies are characterized by their assumptions of time. We think of time as a linear experience in which things get steadily better. Other societies have thought of time as characterized by great, repetitive cycles, as in Hinduism, or progressive, so that societies move forward, even to a state of perfection (see modern variants in Hegel, for whom it was the Prussian State, or Marx, with his utopian proletarian dream). The Greeks and Romans pictured time as a steady descent from a golden age; Christians and Jews, from Eden and innocence. Christianity sees the world as a stage for the soul's salvation in which history will end in the Last Judgment, just as for a Marxist in a communist utopia.

But to understand what time means to us and how every screenwriter uses it in our films inevitably draws us into the central argument characterizing our own culture. That argument begins with the prudent move of Rene Descartes from restrictive, Catholic France to tolerant Holland in order to think freely and to understand himself, both radical ideas given our medieval heritage. In that age we were certain we had a soul, what that was, and what rewards awaited us, through God's grace and good works, or punishments if we fell into temptation. Descartes no longer knows these things: a century of warring faiths opened the door to his rare, inquiring mind. Systematically in his *Meditations* in his candlelit room in a

Dutch inn, he pares away all elements of his experience that can be contested until he reaches his rock of certainty, his *cogito, ergo sum* "I think, therefore I am."[4] Nothing of sense experience is left but some abstract qualities, while we become a thinking machine in his vision. Our seeing the computer as an analogy of mental functioning descends directly from Descartes' musings, as well as our periodically remarked alienation, as in Riesman's *The Lonely Crowd* in the 1950s.[5] If only the individual thinking "I" exists, everything else is secondary, not part of the soul, or exploitable, whether reduced to "other" or "producer" or "consumer." Dehumanization is the inevitable gift of the lonely self.

Descartes knows, as do most philosophers, that once he reaches his extreme position he must find some way back to explain our immediate experience, whether as some form of illusion or not. Descartes' exit from his "lonely I" is embedded in abstract thought, suitably enough for him: he examines the qualities attached to his idea of God, establishes to his satisfaction they can only have come from God, for nothing in experience could give rise to them, and concludes God exists. Moreover, he affirms God is not a liar about the creation, as later Einstein would believe God does not play a game with the universe: reality adds up, in other words. Thus our immediate sensual experience for Descartes, even if reduced to broad characteristics like extension, texture, or weight, is real.

Nonetheless, a severe dualism results between the abstract, thinking "I" *and* sense experience, between "me" and "not me," the realm of which any other "I" is part. This dualism is our modern fatality against whose atomism and solipsism we have been arguing ever since, largely futilely, in the name of a broader sense of self and a wider, more encompassing sense of reality. Drama is as deeply caught up in this struggle as it is possible to be, because it argues reality is not described by a "me vs. not me" description.

Time, in the Cartesian realm of thought, however defined, is part of the experience guaranteed by God for the lonely thinking machine. The same is true for the experience of space or of a quality of experience like causality: these all apply to the "not me" world the atomistic, alienated "I" of dualism reflects on as external to itself.

Needless to say, Descartes' tortuous thinking justifying a divine guarantee of the reality of immediate experience beyond the certain "I" was soon dispensed with, leaving just a "me vs. not me" way of conceiving reality. Philosophy split after Descartes between idealism and empiricism, between the idea that what is real exists above and beyond immediate experience vs. the idea that what is real arises from actual experience and our thoughtful evaluation of it. The Cartesian "I" continued in triumph in both—until subjected to David Hume's withering attack a hundred years later in his *Treatise on Human Nature,* which left thinking about knowledge for anyone, empiricist or idealist, in shambles.[6]

Hume is one of those rare, readable philosophers able to communicate what he means without tortuous circumlocutions and not afraid to be understood. He is a figure of the Scottish Renaissance, a man who enjoyed his friends, humor, and a good meal. Yet after he examines our experience meticulously, he destroys the Cartesian framework for understanding reality. Since that is the ur-ground of modern thought, its destruction left modern thought in pieces without apparent repair. He observes that the same thinking experience Descartes examines, if examined more carefully, provides no proof of an "I" whatsoever. There are simply associated states of experience with no guarantee of reality or persistence we conveniently label "I." "I" is no more than a bad intellectual habit. This goes far beyond correcting Descartes to say "it" thinks instead of "I" think: it leaves instead an assemblage of associated conscious states which have no more than an accidental coincidence.

Hume turns the same spotlight on time and ends with mere sequence and, as if anticipating quantum mechanics, proves causality does not exist: only a certain degree of probability can ever be attributed to one event "causing" the same result again. Similarly, he destroys the conventional idea of space. There is space in the sense of mere immediate extension, the area we occupy, but something called, absolutely, space? Something that exists apart from our all-too-human experience? What would that be? Where would it be? All that is left of humanity and reality for Hume is a being governed by habit, indulging in illusion, with sensations whose source is unknowable.

As the great contemporary British psychoanalyst D. W. Winnicott observes, and as we all intuitively know, and as every dramatist knows in his or her bones creatively, we and the characters we invent live in a space-time continuum characterized by, among other things, causality and necessity.[7] We insist on those qualities in good writing and conventionally, echoing Aristotle, consider that such storytelling imitating an action embodies reality. Certainly Hume's friends, unable to disprove him, were concerned about this destruction of the meaningfulness of experience: How could he get on with his life, they demanded?

Unrepentant, Hume reminded them he enjoyed good conversation and meeting his friends for a convivial drink and meal, and otherwise had no trouble going about his business. What he implies is that understanding the nature of life and reality just doesn't matter nearly as much as everyone likes to think. He's dazzling: some part of myself would like to think we could dance so lightly through life, but little in our long, lamentable history supports such an idea.

Even as silly a story as Billy Crystal going west to herd cattle in *City Slickers* as he tries to find his smile is impossible to conceive in a Humean universe, let alone Curly's actually knowing the meaning of life, even if, like a good modern citizen, the meaning he finds is relative to each individual. The Humean ludicrousness of an art form dealing more substantially with the meaning of our actions, as in a film like *Schindler's List,* is apparent: certainty in life cannot be found, while an art dramatizing a rise to knowledge in a character is inherently a fraud in Hume's universe. Drama wouldn't exist if we actually shared Hume's ideas. If this exaggerates Hume, then it serves to drive home how radical and dismissive his thought is and to what an extent *we live and practice within a society's underlying assumptions about time and reality.*

Worrying about dualism in a Humean universe certainly makes little sense—skepticism makes worrying about the nature of reality absurd. Yet we do so nonetheless: a movie series can be made about the nature of reality and make a huge profit, like *The Matrix* and its sequels. It remained for the Prussian thinker Immanuel Kant to pick up Hume's gauntlet. Kant knew knowledge and self-conception could not be left in a Humean state, even as he found Hume's views electrifying. He saw *everything* was at stake.

Immanuel Kant was a man of such regularity that housewives in late-eighteenth-century Konigsberg in East Prussia set their clocks as he walked to and from the university. He might have remained a minor German thinker of impenetrable prose if he had never encountered Hume, for no one will claim Kant is readable like Hume or possesses Nietzsche's aphoristic glitter.

Kant realizes most people live perfectly well without worrying about what philosophers think, but he understands that a culture's root assumptions about how we think and believe, conscious or not, ultimately condition what we do and fail to do individually and as a society. He also knows we cannot live in a skeptical universe: people never have and never will. We approach our lives with a commonsense assurance that our actions have varying merits and our experience is real, including time, space, and causality. Philosophies themselves are never disproved: their times come and go as our broad cultural experience and expectations alter and evolve. We no longer worry much about what troubled the medieval scholastics.

In another sense, philosophy hardly ever alters. It has long been divided between those like Plato who argue our immediate experience is deceptive and true reality is something above and beyond or below it, and those like Aristotle and the practitioners of modern science who maintain that experience is indeed real, although there are formative forces working within it that careful discrimination can lay bare. Kant falls into the latter camp but gives it a spin that forms the modern cornerstone of our conception of reality. He is *the* essential thinker.

Kant agrees with our commonsense approach to reality in the sense that he bluntly asserts all knowledge rises from experience. Thought may move into abstract realms trying to understand experience's nature in outer reality (physics) or inner (psychology), but its root in the reality of immediate experience is essential.

He also knows very well that even though we all take time, space, and causality for granted, there is no certain way to refute Hume. A revolution was called for in our understanding in order to move beyond Hume and make him not wrong but irrelevant. So Kant takes for granted the reality of the elements in dispute and shifts the ground of argument. He points out that having experience *at all* depends on the presence of our senses of time, space, causality, and the self. In other words, time, space, causality, and the sense of self, or ego as we might say, are a priori ordering principles of the *mind*.[8]

We take this way of thinking for granted now. We know our bodies have evolved over millennia, so that much that characterized the australopithecine called Lucy is still with us, if much developed and refined. Some of us up on the literature know that despite all our evolution, the difference between our gene pool and a chimpanzee's is minute. We know that embryonically we recapitulate an even longer period of evolution, at one point even possessing prototypical gills. Hearing and sight, we know, refine a sensory stream into the particular sounds and sights we "hear" and "see." Kant lays the groundwork for thinking the mind comes into the world with a similar ordering structure.

Saving time, space, and causality as forces of mental structuring that make experience comprehensible comes with a deep price, however. It plunges us even deeper into ourselves than Descartes: the "me vs. not me" split is profounder, thanks to Kant. We may all share these ordering characteristics of the mind and the sense of the reality of experience they make possible, but ultimately we can never know *in itself* what it is that gives rise to experience, what Kant calls *the thing in itself.* I can't be you or, more simply, a table: I can only deal with how either impacts "me." This is something so obvious my, and I'm sure your, reaction amounts to, so what? But this way of thinking isn't obvious at all—it's a prejudice of modern self-conception, and one with which I have said drama is profoundly at odds; in fact, part of drama's enduring hold on us is its provision of another view of reality altogether.

But we can highlight one beneficial consequence of this revolution in thinking, namely, that our experience of time is a mental activity, a construct. Good writers make creative use of this built-in sense of time's fluidity, as we saw in *Hamlet* and *On the Waterfront;* poor ones use it prosaically and conventionally. Every dramatist as she or he begins a screenplay or, more widely, drama, establishes the reality of that story—where it is, who is there, what problem they have, and how that reality is handled temporally.

Are we in for straightforward narration, as in *Indiana Jones*? Are we going to do a realistic narrative with key use of flashback, as in the classic chestnut *Suddenly Last Summer*? Or is time going to be almost hopelessly fluid, the protagonist mired in a life in which he or she can remember no more than the last twenty minutes, as in *Memento*? Are the characters of a given story delusively repeating themselves, blindly under the past's sway, contrary to the apparent immediacy of the action? Is that why so often an event comes along to jar the heroine or hero, and so ourselves, into an awareness of error that also alters our sense of the nature of the time being experienced? All of these and more are possible because of the internal, fluid nature of time itself.

Perhaps the deepest insight Kant yields of relevance here is that *experience itself is creative:* by the time we are aware of whatever is holding our attention at a given moment, it has already gone through a physiological filtering and, crucially, a mental structuring in order to be perceived as what it is in the first place. Imagine, briefly, if this was not true and we were mired in a flood of sensation from which only indifference and habit could save us. The question of abolishing the entertainment industry for a higher activity could never be asked: there would be no creative industry to abolish.

Modern psychology is inconceivable without this Kantian perspective, however it refines Kant's views. We accept, with many an argument over what it means, that the mind has conscious and unconscious parts, and perhaps possesses an intermediate subconscious area as well. Both Freudian psychoanalysis and Jungian analytic psychology, for all their divergences, agree on certain characteristics of these parts of the mind. The conscious mind, which we commonly call the ego, deals with immediate experience and is, somehow, the seat of awareness. The unconscious mind is the home of dreams, instincts, all that is repressed, and other elements, and is only indirectly accessible to the ego. Freud wrote of dreams as the road into understanding the unconscious, and most psychotherapeutic practitioners agree to some extent.

There are more profound differences between the conscious and unconscious parts of the mind, however. As Freud and others soon noticed, *conscious time* works in a more or less linear way. Consciously, opposites are experienced as opposites and experience is governed by a sense of causality. All is different in the unconscious, where the opposite of one thing can stand for another, where distant and near are interchangeable and causal connections harder to find than hens' teeth. In the unconscious, *past and present are inseparable.* The differences become immediately clear to all of us if we contrast our waking experience and assumptions to our dreams or nightmares.

For the ego a thing is what it is, we are here and not there, now as opposed to then, and one thing follows another for determinative reasons. *Kant rescues only this conscious, linear way of thinking from Hume:* the a priori concepts are elements of the structuring of experience *the ego* imposes on our conscious experience to make it cohesive and usable.

Carl Jung made an interesting hypothesis as he wrestled with the bizarre implications of quantum physics. He wondered if the fluid, unpredictable sense of time and space characterizing the unconscious wasn't more in tune with reality than our conscious, linear presumptions. Unconsciously we could be in more than one place at a time, or we could know what was too distant according to the conscious mind to know, because unconsciously it was not distant at all. Emerson puzzled over how Swedenborg in Sweden could accurately know about a fire at the moment it happened a continent away: within the Jungian hypothesis such knowledge becomes explainable. Reality is much more strange than we realize. Experiments separating paired electrons conducted at CERN in Europe discovered that what was done to one, although removed from the influence of the other, *happened simultaneously to the other.*[9]

This brings us to one of the key elements of dramatic writing, for drama utilizes both senses of time: indeed, *drama allows us to experience both senses of time knowingly.* We may be caught up in a cause-and-effect sequence of action, but the time portrayed may be anything but straightforward. *Drama is a fundamental managing of time through the management of the experience the action.* Time and structure are inseparable in a screenplay because time and experience are inseparable, which means that dramatic writing structures the very experience it creates, just as our minds create our experience from the raw stream of sensations in reality.

Time and Drama

These aspects of time we struggle to give rational voice to and argue over philosophically and psychologically have been known to drama for its entirety. What seems peculiar in modern science is commonplace in a screenplay. Einstein noted that if we set off at light speed and come home a few years later, we will experience time conventionally yet find those we come back to far older. Recently some physicists have shown that we needn't go off at light speed and return to have this experience:[10] time can be experienced differently, depending on how one is positioned to view an event, as we saw with Hamlet in *Hamlet* and Terry in *On the Waterfront* earlier. Dramatic conflict always positions characters differently: one of its characteristics is the effort of protagonists to position themselves through the action so that their perspective on experience prevails for all. In so doing they invariably alter the nature of the time and experience characters think themselves within.

Quantum physics is even more radical, and closer to Hume than to Kant. Probability replaces cause and effect in the quantum world: electrons can't be placed for sure in a given space and time. Reality is indeterminate, an idea of Heisenberg's that some have erected into a way of looking at all reality. Certainly in *any* drama some characters think they have a handle on the nature of the truth—i.e., of their experience—at any given moment, only to discover as the conflict arises and changes them that their certainty was misplaced. *Before* the hero's triumph, time and reality are up for grabs.

Even odder, in quantum physics space can be envisioned as not empty but filled with ghost particles flashing in and out of experience. Theoretically, there is nothing to prevent such a minute piece of space from suddenly experiencing a cascade into a large act of creation. In drama, characters discover the space and time they occupy are full of elements they hadn't guessed or had forgotten or misunderstood: ghost particles, if you will, of past actions and conflicts, temporally and story bound. The *inciting event* in drama forces these ghosts into the light, where they have a critical impact on the action.[11]

This brings us to an essential characteristic of time in drama, for in drama conflict reaches an end, by which we mean the issues that are raised in a dramatic story are resolved one way or another. Even if that resolution is ambiguous, we feel that ambiguity is the end to a given story. The time which seemed unsettled—not past, not set, but available for reexperiencing and rethinking—has indeed been rethought and reexperienced and reached resolution, whether of Hamlet dying and Fortinbras taking over in *Hamlet,* or Verbal in *The Usual Suspects* being revealed finally as the devil incarnate, or Terry leading the longshoremen to work after the overthrow of Johnny Friendly in *On the Waterfront.*

Moreover, at the end we see the dramatic action as a whole, and one that is wholly understood. There is a good reason why Tarkovsky called his book on film *Sculpting in Time.*[12] We "sculpt" or structure the story in our fluid, attending minds as audience through the fundamental story pattern as realized uniquely in each screenplay.

That pattern is worth reviewing briefly here for future use. It is not a formula for a dramatist to use, but rather an observation that dramatic stories fall into five parts. First is the past, everything of the characters' lives before the actual beginning of the action. Usually that past, at the Beginning, is assumed to be past by ourselves and the characters, in the sense of being a set time. But that time is found through the immediate action to be far from set, for in this past reside long-simmering problems awaiting their chance to emerge and finally be dealt with. Characters may be in ignorance of these problems, or may know of them but have dealt with them in some wrong, inconclusive way which continues to condition their present lives. This ignorance or false solution of past problems, however, is the root of the modus vivendi a writer establishes at the start of an action.

Think of Terry in *On the Waterfront* who at the start calls out his friend Joey, not expecting Johnny Friendly's thugs will actually kill him. Although Terry feels guilt over the outcome, he is fobbed off by Johnny Friendly with a cushy job and money. Terry is living a lie, and we discover that lie is rooted in the past when he took a dive in a critical fight he could have won so Johnny Friendly and Terry's brother, Charley, and their friends could make some money. He has not been the same since but, far from rebelling, has simply accepted the compromising milieu he is in, as he does again with Joey's death.

Acts 1–3—the Beginning, Middle, and End—are the second, third, and fourth parts of the fundamental story pattern. Terry first shows the false modus vivendi he is caught in, then falls in love with Edie in Act 1 even as she pleads with him to help her find Joey's murderer, not realizing Terry's role in her brother's death. When Terry equivocates and tells her a man should simply look out for himself and the hell with others, she turns on him in a rage and calls him a bum. If he wants Edie, he must begin to acknowledge and sort out his conscience, which he has buried for years. But he can't demand a place, a mental space, for his conscience without acting against Johnny Friendly, who was the cause of his fall. Terry is torn but flattens one of Friendly's thugs as Father Barry delivers his great peroration in the ship's hold over the rebellious Dugan's body. Then he defies Friendly by taking Edie and all she represents into his arms after being told to forget her. In doing so, Terry reveals he has decided to stand up for himself.

This is typical of Beginnings, or Act 1s: the hero discovers his modus vivendi amounts to a living lie when he is confronted with an urgent, present problem whose solution demands abandoning that lie, which is the false, continuing solution of his past problems. In *On the Waterfront* that is Edie's plea coupled with Terry falling in love with her. Typically, at the end of the Beginning the hero or heroine chooses or stumbles into a line of action he or she thinks will help resolve the dual problem—in *On the Waterfront,* when Terry embraces Edie, we understand they will now act together.

Act 2, or the Middle, is the history of that action chosen or fallen into at the end of Act 1. In Terry's case, his demand to sort out his conscience puts him on the side of Father Barry and Edie, involving him in accumulating conflict with Johnny Friendly and his brother, Charley, who, in the famous scene where Terry laments he could have been someone, even a contender, lets him go and so is killed himself. Terry discovers he can't sort his conscience out however he might like: Friendly won't let him. The Middle ends, then, with the crisis—referred to as the *crisis* henceforward— which is the failure of that effort begun at the end of the first act.

Act 3 sees, finally, a climactic resolution, referred to as the *climax* henceforward. For Terry it means the discovery that testifying against Johnny Friendly in court wasn't sufficient to unseat him, or make his own life or Edie's safe, but that he has to confront Friendly directly. He does so in a head-to-head confrontation that first involves arguing over the nature of the past and what to make of it, and then in a direct fight with Friendly that Terry is winning until Friendly's thugs overwhelm him. Even then Terry still wins: he has Father Barry help him to his feet when told Johnny Friendly is laying bets he won't get up, just like he didn't get up when he took the dive that first compromised him years ago. Now he leads the longshoremen to work, breaking Johnny Friendly's power. Past and present have come together and been resolved. Time is set.

The fifth part of the fundamental story pattern follows from here: the New Beginning. It is the future we glimpse but don't enter unless in a sequel, usually to the story's cost and that of our patience. In the New Beginning the audience through the hero experiences the possibility of a new, unconflicted life freed from the past. If we lack that sense of a New Beginning, inevitably we feel a story has not ended: there is a structural problem with Act 3 that leaves us unsatisfied and critical. The New Beginning, being free of the past, represents a true *now*—moreover, one we often see in terms of "they lived happily ever after."

Clearly the hero's role is at times carried out by a woman, as with Julie in *Blue* or Emilie in *Fanny and Alexander,* with famous examples as far back as Sophocles' *Antigone.* Our colloquial use of "hero" and "heroine" should not obscure, however, the *technically* different nature and function of the hero, as defined for the *dramatic* hero in Chapter 10, and the heroine, which is explored in many works here. Edie in *On the Waterfront* is a typical heroine. A burden of writing analytically about drama is this blur between the technical meaning and the looser colloquial meaning of its terms in common use, unlike the technical terms in the physical sciences. Usually what is meant is perfectly clear in context.

Moreover, as I reflect on the fundamental story pattern, we can distinguish between three ever-present time frames a dramatic action entails, with whatever additional times may be involved within the action: story time, the overall time involved in the entire story, past and present; dramatic time, the time involved in the actual dramatic story filmed; and running time, with its sense of causal propulsion. These are three very different times and can be used creatively by writers, as when Shakespeare sets dramatic time spinning against running time as Hamlet and Ophelia exchange words over how much time has passed since his father's death in *Hamlet.* We saw that the upshot of that exchange is to drive home how different is Hamlet's experience of time from that of others around him. Even more tellingly it bares the nature of action for Hamlet, namely, *that action is an illusion.* That should have made us feel the play was slow; instead, it exposes the active scenes we have lived through with Hamlet as *similarly illusive,* setting dramatic time spinning against running time *in us.* Thus we can experience Hamlet's relation to reality, as well as the others' more conventional relations, including, up to that moment, our own as audience. Time and experience are tellingly linked.

Slow vs. Swift

Now we can deal with what makes a screenplay feel slow or swift. Carrière and Kaufman's *The Unbearable Lightness of Being* and Foreman's *High Noon* will help here.

The Unbearable Lightness of Being (*Unbearable Lightness* henceforward) is admired by some, while others find it slow. *High Noon* is regarded as a taut classic, a western that casts a critical light on the conformity and

McCarthyism of the early 1950s as its hero finally stands alone for what is right despite the expedient behavior of those around him. Some, rather than finding it swift, cannot relate to it because they dislike westerns.

Film is a public art, and these kinds of reactions are equally valid: there is not some academic evaluation that has the right to override our individual emotional response to a given film. I say this so that if you fall into the admiring camp for *Unbearable Lightness* or the critical camp for *High Noon* you may apply what is offered here as an explanation of their slowness or swiftness to other films that have those qualities for you.

Tomas in *Unbearable Lightness* is a highly specialized and respected doctor, as well as a lover who will never stay the night. Any attractive woman will do, and many respond to him with avidity. Sabina has the wit to make no demands on him: she can play with him. Tereza, on the other hand, is an earnest young woman who follows Tomas back to Prague, makes impassioned love with him, and *stays*. There is a quality in Tomas that allows him to float: being is light for him. It is as if David Hume is his creator, not Milan Kundera. He's not an exploiter: life presents itself to him as a constant invitation to light-hearted pleasure, however intense a sexual encounter may be. In passing we see this is the period in Czechoslovakia that would collapse in 1968 as the USSR crushed Dubcek's attempt to develop a communism with a "human face." That plays merely as background through Act 1.

Tomas is nonplussed and enchanted by Tereza's naïve, earnest approach to life. He asks Sabina to help her, as Tereza is interested in photography and Sabina is an artist. Sabina makes the point to Tereza that she will not let herself get too attached to anyone, although she and Tomas continue their affair even after Tereza has moved into Tomas's apartment. Tension builds between Tereza and Tomas: she begins to have revealing dreams, like the one in which she tells Tomas, after her thrashing wakes them both, that she dreamed he made her watch him make love to Sabina.

The outside world intervenes only slightly in the war of music between party hacks and the young set at a dance hall. More important is that Tomas cannot keep his eyes off Tereza when she dances with another. Once they are home, he admits that upset him but won't call it jealousy, as Tereza teases him. But he cannot resist her plea to get married.

They do so before a priggish Communist official: life isn't easy, he warns them. They can't keep a straight face. Marriage, however, does not make

Tomas take life more weightily, although he publishes a piece critical of the Communist Party in the guise of an article on Oedipus. Typically, he also has a sexual encounter with a woman in the publisher's offices: nothing in his life has changed. Tereza is just the woman who is there at night. But his faithlessness is increasingly unendurable to Tereza. She imagines him with other women even when she goes swimming and finally, at the end of Act 1, asks Tomas to take her with him when he makes love with other women. It's an impossible request, betraying an anguish and an attitude to life incomprehensible to Tomas.

What are they to do?

We don't find out, although that has been the focus of the action to this critical point. Instead, Act 2 starts with the Soviet repression of Czechoslovakia. The initial shock of the Czechs is powerfully evoked, their peaceful initial response, then their increasing frenzy and violence, emphasized by the film reverting to black and white. Heroically Tereza flings herself into the midst of the event with her camera. She realizes the danger and gives her rolls of film to someone to get them out of the country. Then she is picked up. To her horror she discovers that many of her photos are being used to identify protesters for prosecution. Distraught, she persuades Tomas to leave Czechoslovakia, and they flee to Geneva, where Sabina has already gone.

This is all very interesting but structurally problematic. What was background in Act 1 has become foreground, and the Act 1 foreground of marital tension has disappeared, replaced by repression and flight and, once in Geneva, the attempt to build a new life in an alien setting.

Both are perfectly legitimate subjects for a screenplay, but here there is a disjunction: the story we are involved in and invited to follow in the Beginning is submerged in another in the Middle. One does not follow from the other. Tragically, history may have that effect all too often on our lives, but screenplays shape our experience into cause-and-effect sequences that invite us to expect the action will develop in a particular direction. The effect of this disjunction between the first two acts in *Unbearable Lightness* is to ask us to start over in the middle of the story. We're able do that: even a critic of the film like myself finds Tomas and Tereza appealing and their difficulties engrossing. It is just that we must take in a new conflict, with the older not followed through at a critical moment. The inevitable result is a story that feels like it has multiple starts, and that makes the overall film feel slow, however engrossing individual sequences of action may be.

Things do not improve structurally in Geneva. Sabina is already disenchanted with émigré gatherings, with their easy, merely verbal sentiments. She is already involved in an affair with another married man, Franz, who finds her as irresistible as she finds Tomas, though he is as earnest as Tereza. Nothing much has changed in her life except the setting; she, at least, is essentially consistent in handling.

Tereza finds her photos of repression are yesterday's news: for an assignment, she is reduced to photographing a cactus. Tomas resumes his affair with Sabina. When Franz makes a real commitment to Sabina, she—consistent with what she told Tereza in Act 1 about avoiding real entanglements—abandons him. He arrives, after having told his wife he was leaving her, to find Sabina's apartment stripped bare.

Sabina does not try to escape her feelings for Tomas or treat him like Franz, although she is prepared to leave him behind when she goes off to America. But then he is never willing to commit to her: more tellingly, she has a far more creative response to her experience than Tereza. Sabina finds ways to land on her feet, to create, to make life workable; Tereza cannot. In a key scene Tereza photographs Sabina; after a time, Sabina turns the tables. The camera in her hands is an invasive, appropriative force, but finally neither woman can penetrate the other, despite the loaded intimacy of the scene. What they stand for is incommensurate.

So Tereza leaves Geneva for repressed Czechoslovakia, explaining in her letter to Tomas how weak she is and how heavy life feels to her. Czechoslovakia is the homeland of the weak. Tomas resists following her, at first idly flirting: Tomas is like Sabina, not so much in his creative response to experience but in his ability to float over the weight of entanglement, except where Tereza is involved. I could say he loves and so follows her, but it is probably more accurate to say he senses her as his missing half, someone who is in an almost literal way indispensable and necessary. He follows her back to the homeland of the weak.

We are at the film's *crisis*, but that crisis is not related to the end of the first act and does not represent a failure of an effort to deal with their marital problems, as the end of that act left them, *but is the crisis instead of the second story*, that dealing with invasion and flight. There are elements of overlap: it is Tereza's intensity and inability to deal with the "lightness of being" that drives her home, just as it made her miserable with Tomas, while his continuing flirtations are as intolerable to her in Geneva as in Prague. But their personal problems at the end of Act 1 are still in the same state. We have been involved in a different story in Act 2.

However interesting, the film now feels very long. As we saw when looking at the fundamental story pattern, the direction we expect to follow at the end of Act 1 never materializes in *Unbearable Lightness,* where an organic line of personal development has been supplanted by an episodic overwhelming of the personal in Act 2. We can't add this up as one *dramatic story,* though we can certainly relate to it as a story in a novelistic way. This does not mean we are dealing with a problem caused by using a novel as a springboard: something like half of all screenplays filmed are adaptations—and no more or less successful than original scripts, which run into the same difficulties. The failing of *Unbearable Lightness* is a structural failure of the imagination, and revealing on that score.

Finally, in Act 3, Tomas takes on some weight of being. He won't retract his views in the article on Oedipus published in Act 1. Consequently he loses his position as a doctor and ends up cleaning windows. But he continues to have sexual escapades, the perfume from which Tereza can smell in his hair. She sinks into a depressing affair herself, then wonders if she has been exploited by a state agent and begs Tomas to leave Prague again, now for the country. They take up farming. Now, finally, their relationship thrives, if only because all temptations have at last been removed for Tomas. When they die in an accident after a moment of romantic happiness, we are done.

Nonetheless, it is hard to feel any sense of dramatic closure: the accident ends the story like a deus ex machina.

Not only does the film feel slow, *time feels congested.* Running time is presumed to carry one dramatic time, but the lack of a sense of closure to any of the stories in *Unbearable Lightness* leads to a sense of several left in limbo, with no New Beginning. Moreover the ending, so accidental in nature (no pun intended) deliberately undercuts our sense of the cause-and-effect development of the conflict(s) and our demand, ever deeper with ambitious writing, that events in such a causal sequence appear necessary and probable to us.

These are demands of drama, not of life; arguing from life to excuse dramatic faults is commonplace but entirely misses the point. A film is a construct, entirely symbolic: in the usual hour and a half to two hours of running time, everything in a story must bear on creating that sense of lives in conflict in a clear space-time continuum where their conflict is coherently developed and dealt with definitively. That is what we mean by dramatic action, and of the fourth part of the fundamental story pattern being the End. Not simply a ceasing, but a resolving. Cause-and-effect writing makes us *feel* that one action leads to another; necessary and probable make those actions *feel* likely and inevitable; our emotional response to those actions through the characters' suitable emotions makes us *feel* those actions are real; and by identifying with the characters, we feel their dilemmas and resolutions *are our own*.

Contrast *Unbearable Lightness* with Carl Foreman's *High Noon*. Amy and Will Kane are happily getting married in the Beginning when news arrives Frank Miller is out of jail and coming back to town. Nonetheless, Will is sent off with Amy to start a new life: the town will survive for a day, the mayor assures them, before a new marshal arrives. They leave, only to have Will turn back on the prairie over Amy's protests: Miller is coming for vengeance against him, and Will doesn't want to be tracked down on the prairie; besides, going back is the right thing to do. But Amy makes it clear she won't stand by him.

Swiftly we see the result of his return, for Will has a clear agenda: he wants help in dealing with Miller and his cronies. Amy, however, abandons him and waits for her train in the hotel lobby. Harvey, his deputy, won't help unless Will supports his becoming marshal. The judge is leaving, rather than face Miller, whom a verbal flashback lets us hear vowing vengeance. This is just a "dirty little village of nowhere," the judge tells Will.

Harvey provokes Helen—Will's former mistress and, before him, Miller's—into dismissing him: there's more to being a man than having broad shoulders, she informs Harvey after they argue over Will. But Helen too is selling out: she intends to leave rather than face Miller and won't offer assistance to Will.

There are several stories here, as in *Unbearable Lightness,* but the subplots are subsumed into the main action and bear directly on the issue of helping Will.

Amy discovers through the hotel clerk there is a lot of dislike for Will; sure, he cleaned the town up, but business was better with Miller around.

Will discovers much the same: those in the saloon he goes to for help refuse to become deputies. His friend Sam tells his wife to lie when he sees Will coming; he won't help either. He's "not in." When Will turns to the townsfolk in church, the initial enthusiasm of some is throttled by the mayor, who argues the inexpediency of having blood on the streets for the respectable image of the town. Let Miller have his way, there will be a replacement for Will shortly. Will is abandoned by them too.

Thus Act 2 starts with the question in our minds, which is the question in Will's: *what can he do?* He goes for advice and help to his predecessor, Martin, but Martin too advises him to leave, and points out justly that with arthritic hands he would be a liability in a gunfight. Helen and Amy meet, for Amy mistakenly thinks Will is still involved with her: she saw him in Act 1 go to see Helen, not realizing he was simply warning her to leave. Helen can't understand Amy not being supportive, and Amy explains finally that she lost a father and brother to violence, is a Quaker, and cannot face the prospect of violence again. This would be a credibility problem for her relationship to Will except for the fact he was giving up a life of violence as they married.

Harvey is taunted in the saloon, leaves, and assaults Will in the stable to force him to leave, his guilty conscience pathetically evident. He loses, and the one recruit Will had made abandons him when he discovers there are no others. Only a boy is willing to help, and Will won't let him. The omnipresent clock nears high noon, when Miller's train is due in. Will licks down the flap of the envelope with his will, pulls himself together, and steps outside into the blazing light as Helen and Amy drive past on their way to the train station. Will is left alone in the street to face his fate. The question "What can he do?" asked at the end of Act 1 is answered with "He will do this alone." It is his duty, it is right, and it is necessary.

The Act 3 shoot-out follows, with Amy's last-minute intervention as she shoots one of Miller's cronies in the back, then scratches and breaks away from Miller, who has seized her, so Will can kill him. In a famous scene as the boy brings their buggy and the townspeople swarm into the street, Will shakes his hand, helps Amy up, eyes the townspeople with contempt, tosses his star in the dust, and drives off.

Clearly we are dealing with a much tighter structure than in *Unbearable Lightness*. As clearly the problems generating conflict are carried through: we do not enter alternate stories with alternate problems. I say this because an episodic plot, like that of *Raiders of the Lost Ark*, can flow just as swiftly as one as tightly integrated as *High Noon*'s, so long as we feel the necessary and causally interrelated drive of the story's segments, however stylistically or structurally varied. Time handled in this causal, consequential way moves swiftly: time handled acausally, or in a framework that feels multistoried, feels slow.

Rashômon, for example, has one story in it; the difficulty is deciding which one is the true version, until finally we reach the conclusion all are partly true, partly contradictory, *and we can never finally be sure which, for the truth is beyond us,* the key point of the film. *The Usual Suspects* has one story in it also, Verbal under pressure of the interrogation recalling in flashback his involvement with Keaton and Keyser Söze. At the End we realize we have indeed watched one story, but that it is a different one than we thought. That perception comes with a shock of insight, dazzling and conclusive. A film like *The Godfather* provides a straight, linear story, like *High Noon,* while *The Godfather 2* is equally effective, even though there are two stories. But they play off each other ironically, as we watch Don Vito's rise and Michael's struggle with Roth: they do not try to occupy the same linear *story time*, although they inhabit the same linear running time of our attending as an audience. *Sleepless in Seattle* is a good example of one story with two story lines that slowly converge, ironically playing off a third, the evoked world of the earlier film *An Affair to Remember.*

It is the handling of time in the story that is crucial: our time sense is sufficiently fluid to encompass enormous variety *so long as the stories in story time do not overtly conflict* in dramatic and running time. That means we experience one plot, however many subplots may supplement it.

Yet although this may be true, it does not take us far enough.

There is a limit to what we will tolerate that is rooted in our makeup, and of which the feeling of slowness in storytelling gives us a glimpse. For screenplay and dramatic structure are not abstractions, not a series of arbitrary rules, but are rooted in the structure of our minds.

Each screenplay, each drama, as we saw, creates an expectation in the Beginning of *how* it works, *when* it takes place, *where* its action is, *who* is involved, and *in what direction* they *must go to solve their problems* in the Middle. We expect to go there with the characters, in the reality defined by the screenplay, and for that journey to finish: we cannot defy this expectation without creating a sense of failure. Certainly, we can be surprised by the originality of a story, by writers' insights into human nature, or by the direction they develop their themes, but they must remain consistent with the story world created in the Beginning: that world cannot become some other world and mix different stories without a causal relation. If we feel multiple stories within a screenplay are disparate we rebel, because that defies our ability to comprehend: hence the insistence on *consistency,* which is fundamental and applies to the entire enterprise of a screenplay, not just to characterization.

Thus many things may indeed be possible at once within our experience, but we cannot deal with multiple story experiences at once; *Hamlet* cannot also be *Much Ado about Nothing, Unbearable Lightness,* and *High Noon:* a screenplay can't even be a mix in itself, a political drama one moment, a personal, romantic drama another. Why?

Because such a way of handling a story *moves past our a priori structuring of the conscious mind, which is linear, into the realm of the ineffable unconscious* where many and one, near and far, past and future live together. To the knowing mind the many and the one must always be at odds: the many not brought into the one and resolved is experienced as a mess. Time then fractures and grows slow. Running time necessarily requires the experience of one story transpiring in dramatic time: a jumbled story line in dramatic time jumbles our attending in running time, and then time stretches out and we squirm in our seats. The mind, then, may have many senses of time, conscious and unconscious, but it is the burden of the successful screenwriter and dramatist to reconcile these within the conscious flow of the action with its strict structural demands.

In sum, a screenplay with disjointed stories gives us trouble telling what bears on what story; too many in the same space cancel one another, so that finally we feel nothing happens—as if, paradoxically, we have watched a film with too little action. Moreover, such action is felt to be endless. In a successful screenplay we feel our experience is unified, including our sense of the time we are in with the characters, because of the success of the protagonists, who impose their own experience with its meanings on all others and whose success wins the future. Amy and Will in *High Noon* can go off into their New Beginning at the End: their old lives are conclusively finished—all their meanings laid bare, their conflicts over, their past truly behind them—with a *now* of infinite possibility, because all is new opening before them.

We crave that experience in our imperfect lives, and for a time a successful story makes it ours.

CHAPTER 2

The *Heavy* as Opposed to . . .

The *Heavy* vs. the Exhilarating

CALLING a film *heavy* is not a compliment: *heavy* means something emotionally unpleasant, a downer of an experience. We feel too that such an experience offends against the writer's art. What in the handling of the inherent conflict of a screenplay that naturally provokes strong emotions in characters and audience makes a story feel *heavy*, as opposed to weighty or substantial, one worth the emotional effort demanded?

Typically, John Book in *Witness* thinks he's in control of his fate at the start of the story, that his life belongs to himself and his time is present, *now*, and also his own. In his case he is unaware of his false modus vivendi, which is characteristic of heroes and heroines' relation to reality in the Beginning and which we share with them. The murder Samuel witnesses is just another investigation to him: he has suspects to show immediately to the boy and is emotionally comfortable holding Rachel and her son until the murderer is caught.

But the growing difficulty of the case and the unusualness of Samuel and Rachel's Amish behavior starts to throw Book out of his conventional, habitual behavior and emotional comfort with his reality. He is shocked but excited when Samuel identifies the killer as a decorated police officer, because he thinks he now understands what happened to a lost drug seizure *in the past*. He rushes to his "friend" Captain Schaeffer to explain his suspicion of a connection between McFee, the killer police officer, and the lost drugs. Book still thinks he is in control and that his sense of time as his own and *now* are the true state of affairs. But Schaeffer arranges for McFee to try and kill Book, once he is sure Book has told no one else of his suspicions.

Now Book's eyes are open: he is not in control; reality is altogether different from what he thought he understood so well, and time, far from belonging to him, is at once fused with the past and about to run out. He flees, emotionally distraught and physically wounded, with Rachel and Samuel, both to save them and buy time to regain control of events.

Terry, we saw in *On the Waterfront*, is also leading a life based on false assumptions. Time doesn't belong to him and hasn't since he took the dive in the past. But even the narrow space left for him to operate in as one of Johnny Friendly's favored few is undercut when Friendly's thugs kill Joey. Terry's guilt is easily assuaged, as we saw, although that guilt makes him give Joey's father a marker to allow him to work the next day. Unlike Book, Terry has conspired in the surrender of his time and of his life being his own, yet in the end both live in as deep an illusion concerning themselves. It is Edie's plea for help that starkly forces out the price of Terry's surrender and its intolerable nature.

To undo his crippling acquiescence to Johnny Friendly, Terry must reclaim his life as his own, meaning, to live by his own conscience: make his own decisions and dispose of his time as he chooses, *now*. That means he must defy Johnny Friendly and his brother, and finally undo the mistake he made in his past to solve the present conflict.

These are strong conflicts and engender powerful emotions. If we judge such emotions are warranted by their circumstances, and generated through a cause-and-effect development of action that is largely necessary and probable, then we accept them, however painful they may be, without pejoratively calling them *heavy*. If we do not feel such emotions are merited, however, at best they feel melodramatic, in excess of what is justified, at worst overwrought and in danger of becoming ludicrous or seeming improbable, so that we dismiss them and the screenplay. The *heavy* then takes us into new territory: emotion we reject although it is neither melodramatic, ludicrous, nor improbable.

Dwelling a moment on the standard of "necessary and probable," let us see a little further into the problem. That standard is difficult for writers. Many actions can be caused in a drama, but unless they are central for the development and resolution of the major conflict, or at least minimally necessary for character development, we experience them as irrelevant and at best feel they make a story drag, as we saw in *Unbearable Lightness* where different stories with different "necessary and probable" actions succeed one another. Worse, a plot and group of characters can be coherently constructed and developed yet fail because too much is improbable in nature. Certainly, we accept underlying improbable premises for stories, like an action long ago in another galaxy, as in *Star Wars*. But within a given premise we instinctively demand the action and characters be necessary *and* probable, if we are to continue to believe in them.

Stories like *Witness* or *On the Waterfront,* let alone *Hamlet* or *Schindler's List,* are judged without any allowances for the unnecessary or improbable: the more ambitious the writing, the more it claims to deal with our true reality, the deeper demand we make on it in these respects.

Thus we come to the paradox of a film experienced as *heavy,* for that quality can arise even where we don't question the causality, necessity, or probability of an action or the appropriateness of a character's emotions. There can be intense, *warranted* action and emotion that yet feels *heavy* in a way successful dramas like those just mentioned do not, even in the case of *Schindler's List.* It is hard to imagine anything more likely to feel *heavy* than the Holocaust, yet *Schindler's List* is moving and, at the End, exhilarating.

In sum, the *heavy* way of handling story and emotion is deliberately intense, deliberately *raw,* one that throws feeling in our face in a realistic style that is dramatically justified, necessary, probable, and causal. Emotion handled this way is not meant to be distanced. It is not experienced as melodramatic, because earned. Yet it is one we reject.

Breaking the Waves goes far enough down this emotional path to reveal the source of the *heavy* feeling in a story, especially if we contrast it with *Schindler's List.*

Bess in *Breaking the Waves* wears every emotion on her sleeve. She has been in emotional straits in the past but now is getting married to Jan, an offshore oil rig worker in Scotland. The elders of her deeply fundamentalist community are concerned but can't stop the marriage, even when she responds, "Their music" to their question of what she likes about the "outsiders." The elders are so puritanical they have removed the church bell from the steeple and mercilessly consign the dead to hell at their burial if they judge them to have strayed in life from the elders' narrow commandments.

Bess, however, is an innocent, ignorant and a virgin: she entrances Jan. She is so eager for life she has intercourse with Jan in the bathroom at the reception, unwilling to wait for a more suitable time. An idyll of marital bliss follows that is felt with an Edenic purity on Bess's part. "You'd give anything to anyone," her late brother's wife tells her, which includes Bess thanking Jan one night for the sexual pleasure he brings her, at once amusing and touching him.

She is distraught when Jan must leave for his next stint on the rig, and flees the scene in a deeply disturbed way well past hysteria. Jan soothes her with difficulty and leaves. Bess copes by, among other things, talking to God in the kirk by herself, a God who is both a split-off part of herself and a harshly condemnatory superego. Intense as all this is, we are only at the start of the maelstrom: Jan is paralyzed from the neck down in an accident, brought to the town's hospital, and experiences graphic, repeated near-death crises.

All these grievous elements are legitimate story elements and convincingly handled: any wife would be beside herself at the first parting from her husband, if perhaps few as openly and desperately as Bess, whose naked emotionality provokes criticism from others, including her mother. Yet we experience these others as repressed and puritanic members of an isolated community. But now complicating Bess's life even more deeply, the crippled Jan asks her to make love to other men and tell him about her encounters so that he may live. This is startling, but then the opposite of death is not life, as Blanche knows in *A Streetcar Named Desire*, but desire.

Bess's reaction to his request is entirely credible: she is horrified, faints, then tries to fake an experience for Jan. He sees through her and reproaches her. Reluctantly, Bess slides into promiscuity. Others think she is a whore, hardly understanding she gives herself to enable Jan to live vicariously through her. To go on, she imagines her love is being tested by God: if she passes the test, Jan will recover. This is entirely in keeping with her fundamentalist surroundings and her experience of "His" harshness, if given an original turn. The doctor tending Jan falls in love with Bess, though he refuses her sexual advances: when he challenges her behavior, she reproaches him for not knowing what his special talent is: hers is to believe. What's more, she knows she's good at what she is doing from love.

The story is trying and uncomfortable for a viewer by this point. If it is hard to say the emotionality of her behavior has become *heavy,* then it clearly borders that characterization by this point. But we accept with

Bess that her descent and emotionality will be justified if it saves Jan even as we recoil from the action, as when she vomits by the roadside after her first sexual encounter. But there's the rub. Jan has moments of rallying but sinks back as far or further each time, each sinking provoking a more desperate sexual encounter on the part of Bess.

Her sister-in-law and the doctor force Jan to sign papers to have Bess committed, as she once was in the past. She is seized, taken away, and escapes. On her return her mother will not open the door to her, children call her a whore in the street and stone her, the minister leaves her where she falls before the kirk, and Jan is worse. Bess has herself taken to a ship where the men are known sadists, a ship she fled earlier. She believes this extremity of behavior is demanded of her for Jan's sake. But she is so brutalized the medical staff cannot save her at the hospital, nor can they console her that Jan is better: she dies in despair.

There is no doubt we have moved now into the realm of the *heavy*.

Compare this to our experience of Zaillian's *Schindler's List*. Schindler begins by wowing the Nazi brass in Krakow, intending to go into business. He is a Nazi himself, able, magnetic, an attractive if heartless personality who happily moves into a luxurious apartment moments after its affluent Jewish owners are forced to leave for the ghetto. He raises money from Jewish businessmen in the ghetto through one of its members, Stern, offering no money in return, only the pots he intends to make for the army that they can barter for goods. They agree to this awful, exploitative offer because they have no other choice.

Stern, however, has his own agenda as Schindler's accountant. He sees to it intellectual or gifted Jews are hired regardless of their mechanical skills. He saves Jews who would be in immediate danger from the Nazis, like a man with one arm. Schindler turns a blind eye to this as long as he makes money, gets contracts, and can sleep with whom he likes. Life, as far as he is concerned, is sweet. He is profoundly uncomfortable when the one-armed machinist thanks him, however, betraying the first sign of a guilty conscience. Perhaps he is more than a war profiteer and criminal after all. Then his conscience is shocked into full awareness of the moral dimensions of his reality as he watches the ghetto being liquidated at the end of Act 1 by Amon Goeth.

He cuts a deal with Amon who recognizes part of himself in Schindler, with whom we identify, and reclaims "his" Jews from the concentration/

work camp. Thereafter Schindler knowingly abets Stern in saving anyone in immediate danger from Amon, steadily bribing camp officials to
add these Jews to his workforce. He even tries to modify Amon's behavior after an orgiastic night, debating the nature of power with him. Power
is the ability not to do what is expected, he explains to Amon: to forgive,
when death is expected, to forbear, because you can.

Amon tries forbearance for a time, caught by the idea, then tries it on
himself in the mirror. Amon has no conscience he can permit himself to
feel: he kills the boy he has just "forgiven" for failing to clean his bathtub
properly. He cannot be redeemed.

Why isn't this heavy? The film is certainly full of weighty and difficult
experiences, as when the camp inmates are sorted according to "health"
so more can replace those sent off to a death camp. It is horrible when
the children are seized and shipped off, to say nothing of when the bodies of the murdered are exhumed and burned. Why don't we rush from
the theatre in repugnance or call all this pejoratively *heavy* and shrug it
off as an unpleasantness?

Because it isn't just *the Jews'* story: it is Schindler's, and as he saves
one Jew after another, he saves himself. The point is driven home when
Amon's camp is liquidated and Schindler, instead of leaving with trunks
of money, his original goal, spends it to buy "his" Jews from Amon for a
new factory in Czechoslovakia. Goodness has to start with what is at hand,
not with abstractions, as Billy tells Guy in *The Year of Living Dangerously*.
Schindler has changed 180 degrees from where he was at the start of the
story. He even goes to Auschwitz to recover his women and children when
they are shipped there by mistake. The dimension of his and his women
and children's risk is driven home as we live through the shower room
and the sight of others being led to the ovens as a snow of burning flesh
falls. In the new factory Schindler deliberately reproaches Stern for worrying about the quality of the artillery shells they are making: if the factory turns out one that works, he will be disappointed.

Unlike Jan in *Breaking the Waves,* Schindler gets better: unlike Bess, his
feelings deepen as he develops his conscience and sense of responsibility
without resorting to a kind of magical thinking in the hope his actions
may succeed. This is not to reproach Bess for her dream: Bess acts from
love. But it does point out that Schindler, with whom, I repeat, we identify
for better and worse, takes us somewhere else. Where? Schindler is on a

journey: at the end, the Jews forge a gold ring for him from their gold fillings, voluntarily surrendered, unlike the piles of entire, gold-filled teeth we saw captive Jews earlier in the film having to sort and weigh. Engraved on Schindler's ring is "Who saves one life, saves the world."

Schindler reacts in sorrow that he didn't save more, that he enjoyed himself so much, kept a fancy car and a gold Nazi pin. He breaks down as they collectively embrace him. They dress him in concentration camp clothes, give him a letter signed by all exonerating him, and wave him off. The moment is profoundly stirring, not, in some pejorative sense, *heavy*.

Schindler moves through hell to enlightenment in a redemptive end that exhilarates: Bess moves ever deeper into pain she experiences, finally, as pointless.

This is a complex issue. Drama and conflict are synonymous, deeply disturbing emotions inescapable in powerful writing. Agave in Euripides' *The Bacchae* awakes from a Dionysian transport to discover the head she is holding from the "beast" she had torn apart is her son's. Tragic? Yes. *Heavy*? Certainly trying, but the moment is earned, and it has been inflicted by an angry god whose worship the Thebans had spurned: what kind of price did they expect they would have to pay? That head belongs to Pentheus, the primary opponent of the god. Lear dies of a broken heart with Cordelia's body in his arms, in *King Lear,* as does Ichimonji with Saburo in his arms in Kurosawa's take on *King Lear* in *Ran.* Lady Kaede in *Ran* exults over the imminent fall of Ichimonji's house and her second husband, Jiro, and is beheaded by Kurogane. She dies completed, however: vengeance is at last exacted for the killing of her family by Ichimonji years earlier. Stanley howls in despair for his wife in *A Streetcar Named Desire* and drives her sister to madness through a brutal rape. We might call some of this appalling as well as tragic, but not *heavy*: these are all masterpieces, as is Zaillian's *Schindler's List,* and we do not leave the theatre or cinema depressed by them.

Nietzsche, meditating on the choice of myths in Greek tragedy, points out a selection was made from a small number of the myths actually available. Why these? Because they provide stories extreme enough for a dramatist to use to break human nature down so we can see what we are capable of doing and being.[1] The stories at issue here—*King Lear, Ran, Hamlet, A Streetcar Named Desire, Schindler's List, Breaking the Waves,* even *Witness*—do just that too. Yet a paradox attached to tragedy, spoken of as early as Aristotle, who speaks of tragic wonder, is that *it ends in ex-hilaration*—not as a downer, not as *heavy*.[2] The *heavy* lacks exhilaration, lacks the tragic solace: it lacks any solace.

Bess dies in despair in *Breaking the Waves,* as we saw: but at her funeral Jan is standing. Her body is secreted from the elders so they cannot curse it as they lower her coffin into the ground as her sister-in-law breaks into their patriarchal enclave and denounces their right to condemn Bess. At the inquest the doctor raises eyebrows with the implication that Bess died of "goodness": when challenged to make that official, he retracts. At sea, after Bess is interred in the depths, Jan is awakened by his friends to come on deck: bells are ringing overhead, the bells no longer in the kirk steeple. We have slipped into the realm of fable.

It is true that Bess acts for a higher reason, and her post mortem success goes a long way to averting a disastrously *heavy* ending. But *Breaking the Waves* goes far enough down that path for us to sense the *heavy* arises from a conflict when emotion is handled in a way where we begin to feel *pain is indulged in for its own sake.* Bess never knows what she has achieved, and dies debased in her own eyes, while we have seen nothing to justify an expectation of sympathetic magic working earlier in the film, nor have we seen any sign Jan is getting better. His appearance standing at the funeral comes as an uncaused surprise. It simply doesn't convince.

Schindler, on the other hand, transforms his character and becomes a world redeemer, as evidenced by the ring's inscription: he is married to destiny and made whole. All is experienced from his and "his" Jews' perspective: the Holocaust is seen through the prism of a *positive* story, which may be the only way we can bear it.

Yet there is more to the sense of a film being *heavy* than just pain being indulged for its own sake, unpleasant and repellent as that may be. Fortunately, we have a excellent guide into this dark realm.

Freud, Civilization, and the *Heavy*

Freud published *Civilization and Its Discontents* in 1930, examining at length the nature of love (libido) and death (the death instinct), or, famously, Eros vs. Thanatos.[3] It presents his late thinking on the subjects of guilt, ambivalence, and aggression/destruction, as well as on the libido/love, and bears on the question of what in our experience makes experience feel *heavy.* Near the end of his life he published two other crucial papers, *Analysis Terminable and Interminable,* in which he questioned the ability of an individual psychoanalysis to reach a final resting point in treatment, and *Constructions in Analysis,* an even more thoughtful piece.[4] There he concedes the truthfulness of what is remembered in treatment is not a decisive feature of a cure achieved by patient and analyst, even after years of the meticulous reconstruction of past events through dream, memory, and regression in the transference to the source of a patient's neurosis, all to free the patient by thus bringing what was unconscious into consciousness. Instead, if analyst and patient have jointly created a version of reality that is not wholly true yet has the effect of curing the patient's neurosis, then *the construction will do.* In a sense it is true because it works.

Constructions in Analysis is a very brave paper, pushing against the limit of what we can know, and how, at that limit, things are not what they seem. Even more remarkably, with this insight Freud ends his career by positing how an *act of the imagination can cure,* just as in the years between 1896 and 1900 he abandoned the theory that actual incestuous seductions lay at the root of his patients' hysterias, wrote *The Interpretation of Dreams,* and showed how *acts of the imagination,* including imagined acts of incest, *could cause ill health,* specifically neurosis.

What is dramatized in *Breaking the Waves* is an attempt on Bess's part through an act of the imagination to cure Jan: her belief is that her sexual escapades will be creatively curative as they are relived by Jan. She dies feeling she has failed, while we are not convinced by her postmortem success. Yet the power of imagination, whether in Bess's beliefs that God speaks to her or love can cure, is everywhere in *Breaking the Waves* and resonates deeply with our own sense of human nature, as Freud underscores. But in Bess's case hers is a creativity that doesn't create, an exercise in Eros that instead carries her into death.

Schindler, on the other hand, grows in his imaginative powers steadily in *Schindler's List.* In the Beginning he cannot imagine the Jews as people at all: they are just objects to manipulate and exploit. He betrays a profound lack of empathy. Which is first, empathy or imagination, cannot be resolved: it's a bit like a chicken and egg argument. It may be empathy is just one facet of our imagination. But a profound ability to imagine himself in the shoes of others brings Schindler to redemption at the End as he sobs in guilty remorse.

We are in Freud's realm here, because writing structure is rooted in mental structure, because our minds work in some ways and not in others, because any writing in depth about a character's motivation inevitably plumbs human nature. I could say Freud is in our realm here, for the same reason. Harold Bloom credits Shakespeare with having invented modern consciousness.[5] Deep insight into human nature has always been one of the facets of writing that makes us call some dramatists great, and that leads to their often being credited with anticipating modern psychoanalytic insights, like Sophocles for the Oedipus complex, or Shakespeare generally. Our great writers have the ability to intimate realities we are unable to put into scientific language, however controversial. But the constellation of guilt, remorse, aggression, love, and destructiveness so omnipresent in *Breaking the Waves* and *Schindler's List* is Freud's subject in *Civilization and Its Discontents*.

He begins by wondering how to explain the oceanic feeling associated with religion. As a scientist, he wants to find a scientific (read: psychoanalytic) explanation grounded in our real experience. He points out infants are governed by a sense of omniscience typically abetted by mothers, who try to meet their infant's every wish while the infantile ego structure is incapable of distinguishing between "me" and "not me." That early feeling he regards as the prototype for the oceanic religious sense. Does, however, the adult mind retain all the intermediate stages back to the beginning? If not, our early sense of omniscience cannot be the root of that religious feeling. Yes, Freud answers: all is preserved in the mind. But if that oceanic feeling proves to have a mental root, oceanic feeling is not the source of religion, which must arise from a need, not a feeling. That need is the yearning for the father, explored in 1927 in *The Future of an Illusion*.

Worse, this adult oceanic feeling of connectedness with all is not a sufficient consolation for our lives, anyway, *because we cannot avoid suffering*. Try and imagine a screenplay without suffering. We may try and deflect suffering, find substitute satisfactions, or bury ourselves in intoxication, but hedonism, isolation, joining a communal effort as in subduing nature, or diminishing our organic sensibility by drugs or stoicism cannot free us from suffering. Even more galling is the fact that the uninhibited satisfaction of any instinct gives us our greatest pleasure, yet civilization constantly and necessarily inhibits such satisfaction. We are reduced to coping by sublimating the libido, Freud's term for our underlying sexual instinct, speaking very broadly, by feeding it into creativity, the scientific pursuit of truth, or just into "work" for those capable of nothing more.

Love alone engages the world with passion, either sexually or in the worship of beauty. Yet "we are never so defenseless against suffering as when we love."[6] If it were not so, the trials and tribulations of love would not be such a staple of our writing. But passion doesn't last and varies in intensity: happiness is fleeting and subjective. While we seek pleasure through the pleasure principle, the reality principle intervenes to deny our attempts at unalloyed happiness. We must try to be happy, nonetheless, and we must suffer. Some men become "erotic" in their relation to reality, some "narcissistic," some "men of action." The inadequate fly to neurosis, which religion spares us, but at the cost of infantilism and intimidating the intellect.

So nature, our own limitations, and society bar happiness. We resent social barriers to happiness the most because we think them most arbitrary. Often we wish to get rid of civilization out of a long dissatisfaction with the limits it places on our instincts, or from the Christian denigration of the world, the overestimation of the primitive, neurotic disappointment at the frustration of unrealistic ideals, and the failure of material progress to make us happy. But civilization is everything we do to protect ourselves from nature and adjust our relations with each other; we cannot live without it, any more than we can avoid suffering.

What, then, is the nature of civilization? It is characterized by science and technology, which are practical; the demand for beauty, which is not practical but essential, with its associated demands for order and cleanliness; and by the exercise of the higher faculties as shown in science, art, philosophy, and religion. Crucially, civilization brings order into our social relationships by subjecting the individual will to the communal, brute force to justice, *which demands a renunciation of uninhibited instinctual satisfaction.* We are in a continual balancing act of liberty and freedom vs. necessary constraint. Civilization very definitely is not about perfecting but restraining human nature.

A most curious facet of this process for Freud is how the development of civilized order echoes individual psychological or libidinal development. Order and cleanliness can be derived from the anal stage, while inhibiting instinct echoes the sublimation of libido into other pursuits, like creativity. We lose savage satisfaction to gain civilized life, but the more civilized, the more instinct is regulated, the more fundamentally unhappy we must feel.

Such paradoxes have only started. Freud describes how Eros founds civilization by binding one to another and forming the family. Yet Freud imagines the "first family" was founded on the murder of a governing male patriarch who monopolized the women, by his sons. After their action, the sons instituted a taboo against incest to maintain the community and to deny themselves what they had sought, from guilt over their action. The result of this primitive psychohistorical drama was the creation of the rule of law, beginning with the first law: the law against incest. But although sexual love drove men into families, necessity into communities, "aim inhibited love," i.e., sublimated libido or desire is necessary to develop a love for all, or at least all those of a given community.[7] *Eros may lead to civilization, but civilization in turn acts against Eros' direct expression in the name of cementing a broader community, inhibiting the family's preeminence and repressing unvarnished sexuality.* The frozen, life-hating world Bess finds herself a member of in *Breaking the Waves* is a salutary reminder of just how inhibiting our rules can become.

But *why* should civilization treat Eros in this way? Or, where could the commandment "Love thy neighbor as thyself" have come from, when it is so extraordinarily untrue of human nature to do so? It is the commandment most conspicuously absent from *Schindler's List* at the beginning. *Because,* Freud answers, *we are far more profoundly destructive/aggressive than we are erotic.*[8] Eros inhibited or sublimated into broader forms of engagement attempts to counteract that aggressive, destructive nature. But that destructiveness is inherent *and its expression is pleasurable.* Law may inhibit its grosser expressions, but only love can establish a communal barrier. Man is *Homo homini lupus,* a wolf to his fellow men.[9] Our unhappiness with civilization has therefore a second and profounder root: we not only inhibit Eros but our destructiveness as well. That aggressiveness/destructiveness is Thanatos, a destructive instinct toward death.

Freud admits it is hard to accept this dualism, especially since Thanatos always seems alloyed with Eros in its expression. Modern psychoanalysis is of a divided mind on this subject, as we will see when we take up D. W. Winnicott. Yet the opposition of love and death, Eros vs. Thanatos, certainly rings with immediate resonance in our experience, viewed historically. Freud points out there are biological parallels to this opposition of love and death, processes of building up vs. tearing down or decay. Difficult as it is to accept, he holds that Thanatos, our destructive death instinct, is part of our nature.

Thanatos manifests itself outwardly as aggressiveness: inwardly it appears as *self-destructiveness*. This death instinct is the greatest opponent to civilization, which embodies the contest of Eros vs. Thanatos "for life of the human species."[10] But now he points out the rub: Eros is unequal to the task.

How is our destructiveness to be controlled? By *guilt*. Guilt is civilization's all-important tool. Freud has a complicated exposition of guilt: suffice it to say guilt arises from both external causes—from what we do, as well as from what we wish and fear. This is complex, as internally guilt arises from, in Freud's primal fantasy, our ancestral slaying of the actual dangerous patriarchal ur-father and, later in our development, through a series of introjections, as of a vengeful father figure into the superego. Additionally, there are the repressions of our own aggressive urges we fear to release outwardly, like those embodied by our Oedipal hostility to our father.

Taken into ourselves through identification, the "ur" or actual vengeful father of infancy falls into the superego and takes control of our own aggressiveness, turning it against ourselves, for even if our aggression toward others is expressed only in private fantasy, nothing is hidden from the superego, or conscience, nor does it draw differences between "actual" deeds and "imagined." The more aggression we feel and repress, the guiltier we feel, so that we confront the paradox of saints hounded by their conscience who have lived faultless lives. All their aggression has been repressed and so fallen into their superego and turned against themselves, which they experience as a profound sense of guilt. An additional factor gives a snowball effect to guilt: the stronger conscience becomes, the more it represses the aggressive instinct on its own account, deepening our sense of guilt. Clinically that can result in the paradoxical need of an analyst to help a patient *lighten* the burden of conscience.

Following from this is the desire of the superego, of conscience, *to seek punishment in reality, whether for imagined or actual deeds.* Terry, for example, in *On the Waterfront* must suffer both for acting against Johnny Friendly, a father figure, and earlier for acting against himself by taking the dive, i.e., repressing his own aggression which could have let him win the fight. He must expiate *through suffering* to be free of the consequences of his behavior, which gives the deep, psychic underpinning to the beating Terry takes in the End from Johnny Friendly and his thugs. Primitive man, on the contrary, faced with failure, punishes his fetishes, not himself: civilization leads us into these dilemmas.

Ultimately the internal/external derivations of guilt are irrelevant for Freud: we feel guilt from aggression whether rooted in actions in the outside world or actions we imagine within ourselves, for the sad truth is that those nearest us whom we hate—actual or imagined, separate or part of ourselves—we also love. *Ambivalence* is another word for human nature. The objection that we are not always conscious of feeling guilty has no merit: guilt exists continuously in our unconscious and consciously appears as anxiety, a sense of malaise, or the need for punishment.

Thwarting the expression of aggression has a very dissimilar effect to thwarting Eros: thwarted aggression gives rise to guilt, while thwarted Eros leads to neurosis. Thus Eros vs. civilization is manageable, but Thanatos vs. civilization must simply be fought.

The final step in Freud's analysis points out the peculiar similarity between the cultural superego and the individual: they are "always interlocked."[11] How this interlocking happens, or *where* the cultural superego is, are left unspecified. Where in a dualistic worldview of "me" vs. "not me," "I" and "the thing in itself," is culture? If this is left blank, at least Freud can now explain the injunction "Love thy neighbor as thyself."

We must try to love one another no matter how contrary to human nature that is, precisely because of the depth of our destructiveness, or we will turn on one another in a destructive frenzy of which the past hundred years has given so many examples.

The Descent into the *Heavy*

Does the sense of *heavy*, then, result from the sense of the destructive instinct, or Thanatos, coming to predominate in a story?

Can screenwriting issues and dramatic writing generally be so rooted in our essential natures?

Could it be otherwise?

Do we see Bess descend in *Breaking the Waves* into a freeing of Thanatos toward herself? Is it possible to see her behavior as anything else than this when she deliberately insists on being taken back to the ship where she will be fatally brutalized? Freud spoke of the paradoxical alloy of destructiveness with Eros: she knows the men on that ship will indulge in sexual sadism. They destroy her.

When a story begins to make us feel a protagonist is falling into a self-destructive pattern, when we begin to feel that self-destructiveness for its own sake has taken over, *even if motivated, even if causally justifiable, even if necessary and probable in a story—even if!*—we recoil with an all too human intensity from an immersion into something we both fear and dread in ourselves. We have long been civilized: primitive humanity is very far from us, though not as far as we wish when we recall the savagery of the twentieth century or watch the Holocaust through the prism of *Schindler's List.* But the death instinct becomes overt in *Breaking the Waves.*

This descent into destructiveness of self or other for its own sake, into a death that is experienced as pointless, overwhelms any point a story can make. That is why the End of *Breaking the Waves* finds it exceedingly difficult to recover from Bess's descent. Even though Bess is out to save her husband and has found what she is good for and challenges the dead Apollonian order of the kirk, even though her goal is high, we cannot recover from that brush with the *heavy,* that whiff of self-destructive action we feel is expressed for its own sake.

Schindler's List, on the other hand, despite subject matter and Götterdämmerung scenes, is couched within an experience of constantly growing character, deepening acts of salvation, *and defiance by Schindler of the aggressive, destructive behavior all around him.* That defiance, and its ultimate success, is what so exhilarates us at the end. Moreover, we have the sense that we can wake up from *Schindler's List* if we wish: everything about *Breaking the Waves* is designed to take us by the neck and force us to go step by step with Bess. It has the unshakeable power of nightmare. Schindler encounters pain and destructiveness of a higher power than that with Bess in its grip, actually, but he struggles to contain it within his own small world.

Hamlet, Schindler's List, On the Waterfront, King Lear, Ran all thrust us past death into a New Beginning, a new community, whether of Fortinbras because Hamlet's line finally fails, or of the saved Jews who now number in the thousands, whom we see at the end of *Schindler's List,* or of a reformed future where guilt has been expunged and a fresh start made possible, as in *On the Waterfront,* or in *Ran* and *King Lear,* as with *Hamlet,* of a future where seemingly successful lines are destroyed and new lines now take over not subject to the same destructive frenzies. *Breaking the Waves* nods in this direction with its unconvincing end, but Bess goes too far into willed self-destruction, into the freeing of Thanatos, even if—and quintessentially Freudian—she does so in the name of love.

What is most interesting in this encounter with the *heavy,* however, is something that goes beyond Freud. In his realm the enjoyment of the un-inhibited expression of instinct is a paramount pleasure, but in the imag-ined world of film and drama the uninhibited expression of destructive-ness when we sense it is expressed for its own sake, even though that seems the quintessential expression of the instinct, *provokes a profound recoil in our hearts,* even though we are offered the chance to live that in-stinctive release vicariously through the protagonist without direct con-sequence. Perhaps if we gave unhindered expression to our own destruc-tiveness directly we would enjoy it, as Freud and our own experience of self-righteous anger suggest, *but when that uninhibited expression is made an object of creative contemplation, as in a play or screenplay or other work of art, we turn against it.*

There is more to ourselves and civilization, then, than Freud credits. Our self-understanding is, after all, a work in progress. There is some-thing within us of which civilization is the creative realization, and we recoil from the expression of its undoing with a visceral sense of betrayal every bit as instinctive as destructiveness. That is where our experience of the *heavy* finally roots.

CHAPTER 3

Moral Substance and Ambiguity

Morality and Screenplays?

T HE Hollywood tradition is confused and uncomfortable with the subjects of morality and intellect in film. But it is fair to ask what morality has to do with screenwriting: films and plays are primarily public entertainments. We can go to church if we want reflections on morality. "I," a typical screenwriter, might say, "Just want to make money." She or he can't protect a script from producers and directors like a stage dramatist can; many hands may be involved in a film's writing, not all credited. Additional production pressures and the need to repay investment and turn a profit make it hard to see how moral issues can be handled coherently in such an "art" form. "Leave it to the Europeans, leave it to the 'art film'—spare me" is easy to imagine our typical American screenwriter saying.

What, then, should we make of *On the Waterfront*, or *The Godfather*, or *Unforgiven*, or *Chinatown*, or *L.A. Confidential*, or *High Noon*, all American films and regarded among our most outstanding? What about *Rashô-mon*, or *Breaking the Waves*, or *Fanny and Alexander*, or the many outstanding films from other film traditions all deeply immersed in moral questions? Something quite simple, I think: if ambivalence is, speaking broadly, another term for human nature, then there is a consequent division of experience into a sense of good and bad, however the contents of those terms vary across cultures. Any story intending to deal with characters reflecting us in any meaningful way inevitably must deal with this inherent aspect of ourselves. Perhaps what sets us apart from the rest of the animal kingdom has little to do with walking upright or possessing our brain, but in being a *moral animal.*

If we can't escape morality, then a film about our lives cannot escape having something to do with moral substance. Is that simply a fact of life and art we can ignore, like the alphabet our words are composed in? Must we only determine our story convincingly and let its moral element take care of itself by association with the success of the protagonist in the resolution of a particular conflict? What succeeds is "good" and fails is "bad"? The rest we can leave by default to public taste and approval or rejection? Or does the considered use of moral substance and ambiguity make a screenplay more commercial? Can moral substance alone do, without moral ambiguity? Am I talking of moral substance and ambiguity in relation to character, or to situation?

Clear-cut good vs. bad contests are endemic in screenwriting. The villains in the *Lethal Weapon* series are simply bad. Jason in the *Friday the 13th* films may be entertaining, but he is evil. Those opponents of the heroes we meet in Van Damme or Seagal stories or in Eastwood's Dirty Harry films are also bad, pure and simple. Their lack of ambiguity does not compromise the success of the writing. James Bond's foes are wholly bad organizations, men and women, yet the films are no less effective for their being so unambiguous. We even have fun with some of the extremes to which the evil caricatures are taken, because evil can be entertaining. Richard in *Richard III* is fascinating. Tony is a successful character in the baroquely overdone *Scarface*.

We take pleasure in what happens to bad characters because they deserve it, as well as in this case pleasure in the vicarious release of instinct. However these characters rampage through a film, they get their due in the End as good and right are vindicated. So we do not recoil from these characters' destructiveness as we do with Bess in *Breaking the Waves*. Evil is not, in itself, *heavy*.

In contrast, we know the characters Van Damme and Seagal play are presented as *morally good* in their films whatever a given character's background may be at first glance, as is Dirty Harry's character despite his violence. That is in response to bad men and condemned by superiors who can't tell the difference between good and evil or attach the right urgency to confronting it. These are easy films to relate to, whether to dislike for reasons of political correctness or enjoy for their black-and-white simplification of experience. Morality, in other words, is inseparable from their appeal in the guise of the triumph of the hero.

But consider Besson's *The Professional*. It's very clear Stansfield is a villain without any redeeming quality, if richly drawn. But what are we to make of Léon, a professional killer who discovers love through Mathilda and ends by killing Stansfield? Wilson, the gunslinger in *Shane,* is simply bad—but Shane is a gunslinger who discovers he can't avoid his nature by becoming a farmer, even though killing Wilson is a good deed. Barzini in *The Godfather* is simply a conniving, dangerous enemy to the Corleones, but the Corleones are mobsters running a corrupt empire, while Michael must give up the hope of a life free from crime in order to stand by his father and family. He becomes the ultimate mobster, the godfather himself. Darth Vader in *Star Wars* appears as the quintessence of evil, but we discover he is Luke's father, and it is Darth who finally destroys the wholly evil emperor two films later to save Luke, redeeming himself. Bishop Vergerus is a hypocrite and sadist in *Fanny and Alexander,* but also a man scarred by tragedy and desperate over his inability to change himself. *Breaking the Waves* shows Bess prostituting herself out of love, while the heroine in *Rashômon* is an outraged wife, a spurned woman, and willing conquest. Michael Sr. in *Road to Perdition* is a dreaded hit man out to avenge his murdered wife and son. All of these films may be no more or less entertaining or commercial than those with less ambiguous shadings of morality, *but undoubtedly they earn a deeper involvement and a higher estimation on our part because of their greater moral substance that shades into moral ambiguity.*

High Noon lets us bring more clarity into this issue. Marshal Kane pursues good regardless of cost, almost losing his life and wife. He is moral and duty bound. There may be an element of expediency that stems from his knowledge he can't run from Miller on the prairie and stands a better chance against him in town, but that is overwhelmed by the moral sense of obligation he brings to his task and his continuing even after he realizes he is on his own.

Will Kane has great moral substance, then, if not much ambiguity. He would be a monster of morality if the action didn't show him wrestling with fear and a growing certainty of death. He won't support Harvey as marshal after him because he believes him inadequate, even though he is desperate for help, but is willing to let him have his former mistress, Helen. That's their business. Amy, if she won't support him, must be let go so his duty can be carried out.

But what of fighting Miller and his cronies for townspeople who do not wish to be saved? Both the lowlifes in the saloon and the proper families in the church abandon Kane, either because they prefer Miller because evil is fun and remunerative or, according to the mayor, to have blood on the streets would be inexpedient for the town's reputation. That rejection throws a clear light on Kane's situation: he is a man of great moral substance in a morally ambiguous situation.

Any discussion of moral substance and ambiguity must consider whether those qualities apply to just character, or to just situation, or to both.

In *Unforgiven* the protagonist, Munny, was once a ruthless killer who reverts to kind again at the *climax,* but in a good cause to avenge the pointless murder of his friend. He, and others, are attracted to town because whores offer a reward for anyone who will kill the cowboy who slashed one of their faces. Little Joe is an efficient sheriff, a poor carpenter, a brutal sadist, and once was clearly familiar with many a gunslinger. By the time Munny tells the Schofield Kid, "We all have it coming, kid," we are living in a deeply morally ambiguous reality in respect to both character and situation.

In *The Godfather*, Michael starts down the road to evil in the name of helping his father. His father may be good to resist the drug trade but is untroubled by how his family has corrupted judges, politicians, and the police, or by how the family carries out its own extralegal punishments. Clearly, here too both situation and character are morally ambiguous.

Chinatown involves us in an even greater moral ambiguity of character and situation. Jake was once a policeman who worked in Chinatown, where anything can happen. He makes his living as a private investigator exposing unfaithful spouses, a morally shabby activity for himself and the concerned spouses. He becomes involved with Evelyn Mulwray at the same time he suspects she is involved in murder: eventually he discovers she is the incestuous mother of the young woman with whom he first thought her husband was having an affair. Evelyn's father is the young woman's father, and tries to employ Jake too. I could go on: the moral ambiguities steadily deepen as the story progresses.

If moral substance is inevitable in a screenplay, then the seriousness with which we treat the specific issues raised is dependent on the nature and premise of the story, and whether the issues are given a conventional or more probing treatment. But moral ambiguity lifts otherwise effective writing to eminence, and moral ambiguity in *both* character and situation the most. Since the more we aspire to in a story the more demand-

ing we are of causality, necessity, and probability, the more we are forced
into an ever deeper examination of motivation and action so they meet
those criteria, *an essential part of which is the equally ever deeper probing
of the morality of character choice and situation.* An examination of motivation is inseparable from morality, for a moral judgment always lies
in how a screenplay or drama develops and treats a given character: this
one is on the right side, but this one on the wrong.

Yet one discomfort we have with moral ambiguity is our sense that it
gives a dark or film noir feeling to a film. Munny rides off in *Unforgiven*
threatening to kill the families of any who shoot at him; Michael in *The
Godfather* lies to Kay about killing Connie's husband just before the men
enter the office to kiss his hand as godfather. Jake in *Chinatown* watches
helplessly as Evelyn is killed and her daughter taken by her incestuous fa-
ther/grandfather. Michael Sr. dies in *Road to Perdition* in his son's grief-
stricken arms after killing the hit man who has pursued them. Bess dies
of "goodness" in *Breaking the Waves*, as we saw the doctor claim at first,
though actually she dies from a brutal rape. Even such films as *Like Water for Chocolate* or *Chocolat* end with shades of ambiguity: Tita dies with
Pedro in the former, a happy life never to ensue; the Comte collapses into
a chocolate-eating frenzy in the latter, with Lent apparently overturned
for a kind of permanent self and communal indulgence.

Yet the ambiguity in these endings fills us with a sense of their greater
truthfulness to nature and revelatory power for ourselves, who live
through them as one with the protagonists with whom we identify.

Typing and Volition in . . .

Typing weakens characterization, as if to say, "You are your drive; your *volition* is removed," whether you are a villain or typed as the ethnic mother-
in-law, ingénue, or braggart. Motivation here is not explored, nor, consequently, morality: characters do what they do because their nature is
so defined, with a standard moral value attached. Typed characters' responses may vary with their situation, but they are always "in character,"
meaning the same character we first encounter in Scene 1, Act 1, and with
the same given values. They do not grow, nor do they reflect. *Volition* and
typing, then, count heavily in sorting out the impact of characters on one
another and their moral substance and ambiguity.

What makes this an interesting problem is twofold: first, *people* generally have a tendency to type: it takes familiarity not just to breed contempt but nuance as well. Most pertinent to screenwriting is the way protagonists are typed in the Beginning and consequently denied volition, however they may delude themselves to the contrary. The false modus vivendi in the reality in which they are caught perpetuates past errors. That means their moral responses are initially given too, and predictable. The first part of the protagonists' development in a screenplay, then, requires that they free themselves from the typing of their past in order to regain their volition: i.e., *that they (re)gain the ability to act from conscience as moral agents.* Until then they are no better than a character type: the "detective," say, like Book initially in *Witness.*

Consider Terry at the start of *On the Waterfront.* He is one of Johnny Friendly's henchmen and a favorite. Terry obediently calls out Joey, lets his guilt be bought off, and shrugs off the Crime Commission investigators at the docks, complaining to his fellow longshoremen that anyone like them should try to talk to *him:* he's no stool pigeon, even if he is one of Johnny Friendly's pets, like one of the pigeons Terry keeps on the roof. He spies on the meeting of the rebellious longshoremen in the church at Johnny Friendly's bidding. If he saves Edie, that does not challenge his allegiance to Johnny Friendly or his character typing initially. When he falls in love with Edie, he reveals his "every man for himself" attitude to life— self-serving, amoral, and deeply ironic—*for Terry does not act for himself at all.* He is a type, one created by Johnny Friendly *and his own acquiescence,* which Edie correctly characterizes when she calls him a bum.[1] Terry is not the hero of anything. He has surrendered his volition and can save no one, not even himself. As such, he has no desires, only a set character to express one facet or another of on demand. This is the true nature of the false modus vivendi protagonists find themselves in at the start.

This is why his falling in love goes beyond simple romance and is so crucial for much broader issues. Edie combats his typing with her own altruism: aren't we all in this together? Don't we depend on each other and need to stand up for one another? If we don't, what kind of lives are we leading? I can imagine Freud watching this scene and, if he could get past his distaste for things American, reflecting on the phenomenon of guilt Terry clearly suffers from yet won't act on until stirred by Eros, locked in what can only be called neurotic behavior, a living exhibit of why denial cannot forever blind us to the demands of conscience *with-*

out driving us ever deeper into a typing that narrows our humanity as it removes our volition.

Terry, however, wants Edie so badly he challenges his typing and asserts his will by responding to the painful proddings of his conscience. Friendly and Terry's brother, Charley, witness Terry flattening one of Johnny Friendly's thugs as Father Barry speaks over Dugan's body in the ship's hold. Then, after Friendly tells him to stay away from Edie, Terry decisively takes her into his arms. Little motivates us so powerfully as the first flood of love, as Freud and so many others remark. Immediately at the start of Act 2 Terry confesses to Father Barry, then to Edie. Now he has weight as a character: *to claim volition is to claim the right to make moral judgments.* Doing so makes one a much fuller person, but at the cost of losing the comfort conferred by the surrender of will and thought in typing. Thus this moral process isn't easy: Terry's suffering steadily increases until in a rage he demands Edie stop using the word "conscience" when he breaks into her apartment.

By then it is too late to stop: Terry entered the path to herohood by declaring his right to his own moral discriminations. That is the right he argues for decisively with Charley in the taxi, when Charley tries to shut him up with another bribe before they get to River Street where he will otherwise be killed.

No on else goes through this moral evolution in *On the Waterfront* or in any other film *except the heroine or hero,* or through them. Characters becomes heroes and heroines by confronting their nature and the demands of their conscience. If it's easy for them to do so, or without much challenge, as in a Seagal or Van Damme character, or in the Dirty Harry or *Lethal Weapon* films, we may be entertained by the action but not engaged as deeply as we are with Terry or Michael in *The Godfather,* nor do we rate such films on a par with *On the Waterfront* or *The Godfather.*

Michael is typed as strongly as Terry in the beginning of *The Godfather.* He is the war hero, the son going straight. He is secure in that persona: he points out to Kay he's not like the rest of his family. Michael is left out of the planning to strike back as a matter of course after the don is shot. He is not the prospective godfather but peripheral, anything but the hero. We watch, puzzled, anticipatory because *we expect to witness the process of the typed hero of the Beginning regaining his volition in order to assume his destiny.* Michael, like Terry, is moved to act by Eros—here, by love of his father, helpless and exposed in the hospital. By swearing to stand by him, Michael asserts his volition for the first time. He then immediately asserts his right to act for the entire family by compellingly putting forth his plan to kill Sollozzo and the corrupt police officer McCluskey over the initial objections and mockery of Sonny, the presumed heir.

Michael's actions establish him as an active agent, as Terry does for himself in *On the Waterfront*. His actions propel him on a road ever deeper into moral substance and ambiguity, while with Terry the same process toward volition moves him from moral ambiguity to clear-cut moral substance, albeit one shadowed by his compromised past. But then the herohood achieved in *The Godfather*, while the same as Terry's qua herohood, has the opposite moral valuation. Both films, however, are weighty because morally weighty.

Léon in Besson's *The Professional* is deliberately typed in the opening action as the hit man par excellence as he single-handedly and effortlessly wipes out an entire gang. This is a riff on action sequences of a similar nature in other movies and enjoyed by us as an entertainment, not for its insight into character, motivation, or action. We soon see Léon's life is entirely sterile: a bare apartment, an inability to sleep in a bed, a Spartan regimen and diet, leavened only by caring for a single plant. Typing in his case has moved him into virtual inhumanity, which is not a moral but species description for him. Extreme typing denies humanity and creates monsters, i.e., characters we perceive as monstrous *because of their denial of humanity* with its central feature of making moral distinctions.

Mathilda's request for Léon to open his door to save her from Stansfield's thugs puts Léon in a quandary: he must make a choice, and *now*. He almost can't decide to let her in; when he does, he has acted outside of typing for the first time in we don't know how long. It is almost unbearable for him: he nearly shoots Mathilda as she sleeps, then tells her she must leave. He is dumbfounded when she tells him he is *responsible* for her because he saved her life. Moral actions have inescapable consequences. Types have no responsibility: how can they, with neither volition nor, consequently, moral obligations? If Léon stays a type and throws Mathilda out, not only is the story over, but he cannot become the hero of anything. Step by step, instead, he recovers volition and its attendant moral obligations and through these the fullness of his human nature. Climactically, movingly, he tells Mathilda how she has made him care, love, and want life as he makes her climb down the shaft while he stands off their attackers.

The appearance of Eros in these stories begins by motivating personal change and ends by going beyond the now activated moral nature of the self toward broader responsibilities: Michael to lead the family, Terry the longshoremen, Léon existentially to defy Stansfield for the love and hunger for life Mathilda has aroused in him.

But then Léon reverts to type: though we care for him as we could never have had he remained a type, at the end he is again the hit man par excellence. If he dies, it's only after having outfaced what seems to be an army with artillery, though he takes Stansfield with him. That's satisfying but, as in a Seagal film, it's *easy,* and below the level of the development of the relation between him and Mathilda. If typing demeans and losing volition dehumanizes, then *morality in turn becomes typed and inconsequential.* The more of that in a film, the more it turns into an entertainment with little dramatic, let alone lasting, merit.

This is worth pursuing briefly.

Riggs in the first *Lethal Weapon* is a desperate, violent, suicidal character working for the "good guys," the police. He is almost mad with grief from the loss of his wife before the action: in one of his last actions in the film he visits her grave with flowers, reconciled with his loss and relatively at peace with himself. He is, in other words, also typed at the start, acting out of a set characterization, not in control of himself, i.e., without volition. He and his partner, Murtaugh, confronting a consortium of evil men is the easy part of the film and demands nothing from us, but Riggs's growing relation with Murtaugh and his family, which he ultimately saves, generates the real interest, as does Léon's relationship with Mathilda in *The Professional.* As his friendship and love for Murtaugh and his family develop, Riggs regains *the ability to make choices and to change,* and moves from type. Volition contains the crucial element of the possibility of change, and what is more necessary to change than the false modus vivendi the protagonists discover themselves in at the Beginning?

But no one moves from the characterizations established at the end of the first story in the ensuing *Lethal Weapon* films. Instead, the interest shifts to the next set of evil men and secondary characters, and we begin to relate to the films not as dramas but entertainments in dramatic trappings with given moral meanings and characterizations. They are not remotely as effective as examples of screenwriting as the first film, and petered out in audience and commercial interest. Entertainments have their vogue but eventually boredom is inescapable, even if the films turn self-parodying and comedic, entirely abandoning their initial substance, which is the inevitable evolution of this sort of writing. It couldn't be any other way unless once more the typing is broken down and volition regained. That would not result in a sequel, but a new film, one of moral substance.

The *Heavy* and Moral . . .

When does moral ambiguity turn *heavy?* Must we sense a story is moving to a redemptive point, not descending to destructiveness for destructiveness' sake, to avoid the feeling of heaviness, as in *Breaking the Waves* before its epilogue?

Yes.

Contrast how we think and feel about films that turn into entertainments, as with the *Lethal Weapon* sequels or those to *Friday the 13th.* Entertainment, we saw, is experienced as light and weightless because moral substance and moral ambiguity have been leached out. Those are a function of conflict and insight into human nature, the natural "matter" of drama. What was serious becomes a joke in entertainment; characters that frightened us become laughable and types.

Tomas, on the other hand, starts off weightless in *Unbearable Lightness.* He overtly speaks of life as light. Certainly moral considerations don't come into play for him where sex is concerned. A smile and enjoyment without consequence characterize his life with the women who allow such treatment and who are consequently also equally without moral weight. They are characters for a Humean universe, precisely the one we do not inhabit.

But Tomas gains moral weight through Tereza who can't tolerate his behavior. He gains weight too, as we saw, by refusing to recant the views expressed earlier in his article against the Communist regime once he returns from Switzerland. He becomes a more meaningful character and ceases to be light precisely in proportion to the degree that morality becomes important. Moral substance is essential for any meaningful character development.

But with Tereza there is a strong whiff of the *heavy* in her relationship to

Tomas, reaching the point at the end of Act 1 where she demands Tomas let her watch him with other women so she can try to understand how he can be, in effect, so immoral. If the attempt to understand gives a point to her request, the request brings the marriage's destructive impact on her into sharp relief and makes us aware of the extent to which she perseveres self-destructively, if from love, as Bess perseveres in *Breaking the Waves*. It is well to remind ourselves that love can damn as well as redeem.

Tereza underscores this self-destructiveness when she throws herself into the affair we already know she is unsuited to enjoy in the End. She feels shamefully debased and panics when she suspects the man may be a government agent provocateur. There is no redeeming quality to the experience. Her self-destructiveness is apparent and overwhelms surface motivation and *feels as if indulged in for its own sake*. The experience is *heavy*.

If we distinguish between character and situation for Tereza, a morally ambiguous situation with a character of clear moral substance has developed into one in which both are ambiguous, as with Bess in *Breaking the Waves*. If we distinguish for Tomas, a character without moral substance gains both substance and ambiguity through Tereza while in the same ambiguous world of Czechoslovakia.

Road to Perdition throws further light on these issues. Michael Sr. is a good father *and* hit man par excellence who seeks revenge against John Rooney, a boss *and* father figure/mentor, after Rooney shields his son who killed Michael's wife and younger son. Everything is morally ambiguous, as in *Hamlet, Oedipus Rex, The Godfather,* and *Chinatown.* Yet we don't experience this as *heavy* despite its violence. At all times the violence is used for something beyond itself. Michael's family is attacked because Rooney's son fears exposure from Michael Jr., whom he can't kill without removing the rest of the family. As a Corleone might say, there's nothing personal involved, just business. Michael Sr. refuses to let himself or the situation be typed but insists on his moral volition in the form of revenge, while Rooney protects his son, even though he laments that sons were put on this earth to torment their fathers. When Michael Sr. finally kills Rooney he is grief-stricken, but the way to Rooney's son is through the father, and Rooney by elevating family over morality sacrifices his authority over Michael as a moral agent. With Rooney dead, Michael executes the son and then is killed by the mob's hit man at the End.

That too is not *heavy,* if grievous, even as it provokes a telling emotional outburst by Michael Jr. Michael Sr. deserves his death, and that death is perceived as a balancing of the books, not a descent into destructiveness for its own sake.

La Femme Nikita provides another insight, for it is at once typed and *heavy* in the Beginning with its initial vile explosion of destructiveness, including Nikita's murder of a policeman in a drugged haze. But the remainder of the film pulls off something remarkable, for the training to make Nikita a callous assassin for the state paradoxically humanizes her by giving Nikita self-control. Her training returns her volition. The subsequent violence that she encounters as an agent is experienced from her point of view as ever more intolerable until she can no longer bear it, particularly the grim developments that ensue after a "cleaner" is called in. She reacts to these developments with horror, and is climactically allowed to escape by the men who love her.

Several conclusions are inevitable.

Moral substance and ambiguity go hand in hand with writing substantive drama. Their absence in a character like Tomas at first in *Unbearable Lightness* becomes a dramatic issue itself, as Tereza forces us to see, in which the nature and importance of a moral relation to one's experience is dramatized. The typing of the protagonist in the Beginning must be broken down so that moral volition can be regained. Furthermore, moral issues deepen the conflict and have the effect of filling out a film, so that the time it occupies becomes weighty and demands a kind of involvement from us alien to entertainment. If the consequence of the action is deepened, then our experience takes on the characters' sense of weight and time: things do not necessarily move slowly—they can seem quite swift, as in *Schindler's List*—but we attend them with greater concentration. The way we feel time speed by thoughtlessly and without weight in an effective entertainment disappears from a meaningful film.

Time loses its lightness without thereby growing slow within a morally significant realm.

Time turns slow as emotion turns *heavy* and we long for that descent into pain for its own sake to stop.

Morality, then, and the sense of the nature of a film's *nowness* are inseparable.

This moves beyond the experience of swiftness vs. slowness in a screenplay depending on the handling of causal sequences in the conflict in a necessary and probable way, as we saw *Unbearable Lightness* sometimes fails to do, for when more is demanded of us by a story, we make two demands in turn. One is for weight without *heaviness* or bogging down, and the second is for time to move cumulatively forward rather than stopping for a character who descends into destructiveness for its own sake. When that happens a new typing ensues, just as limiting for the protagonists as their initial typing in the Beginning.

But What Are We Morally Ambiguous About?

Hamlet grows ambiguous because he does not act; Munny in *Unforgiven* becomes ambiguous as we learn of his background but even more tellingly as we root for him to kill in the *climax,* which he does so well. In *Ran* a profound misunderstanding of the nature of love leads Ichimonji to disaster; in *Road to Perdition* Michael launches into righteous vengeance out of outraged love. In *Analyze This* Ben's marital happiness is dependent on Paul regaining his ability to aggress: Riggs, in *Lethal Weapon*, is suicidal from loss, in this respect a bit like Hamlet, though Riggs kills effortlessly.

Freud observed love and aggression, Eros and Thanatos, are deeply alloyed.

We, let alone a character, *become morally ambiguous when types decay and the ambivalent essence of human nature emerges as we portray our aggression and love simultaneously.*

We like to idealize our nature, which gives the emergence of a contravening truth—in reality and the imagination—the potential to seem *heavy:* we need all our imaginative tools to avert that feeling in daily *and* dramatic reality. But once we sense destructiveness indulged in for its own sake, whether directed outward or inward, our experience as well as that of dramatic characters turns intensely unpleasant or *heavy.* Then we are repulsed because we feel our humanity is debased.

The most upsetting feature of such behavior is our sense of the loss of volition, even if it is volition, as with Bess in *Breaking the Waves,* that initially leads a character in this direction. We take the fates of our heroines and heroes personally because of identification. We know there is a difference between making a choice and being driven. We know when violence is involved that so long as volition endures, Eros, the life-giving possibilities of love, has not been overwhelmed by Thanatos. We know that until moral ambiguity descends into the *heavy*, death does not have us in hand.

No feeling is worse than sensing that is no longer true.

Drama is so pervasive and resonates in peak works so profoundly because it is steeped in that life vs. death conflict, manifested on whatever level a writer pursues in a given script.

Thus, for dramatic success, potentially *heavy* emotion must be felt in some way to be *transcended*. Even in tragedy, so ripe a ground for a screenplay or a drama feeling *heavy*, the decisive differentiation is that such a story end with a sense of elation, with the tragic consolation and wonder remarked as early as Aristotle.[2]

In *Oedipus Rex* Jocasta hangs herself and Oedipus blinds himself. He is led off to exile by his daughters who are also his incest-born sisters. But that is not where the drama ends, or why Aristotle admired it. The chorus has the last word, the chorus of ordinary Theban citizens, *and their prospects are now good*. The truth has been laid bare, which handled properly is exhilarating, as with *The Usual Suspects*. At the End the future has become possible in a New Beginning without the plague from which Thebes was suffering from because of Oedipus's moral transgressions. The gods' predictions are shown to be unavoidable, their divinity reliable; Oedipus is left to find his own salvation, if possible. *On the Waterfront* turns climactically on Johnny Friendly and Terry arguing over the truth of the past and the true nature of their respective behavior. Terry's victory makes him the man to lead the longshoremen. Again, a New Beginning comes into view.

Michael Sr. may die in *Road to Perdition,* but he frees his son for a New Beginning by killing their pursuer. Sometime later from within that New Beginning, Michael's son narrates the action of the film that set him free, in order to find the truth about his father.

Time is freed up and moves forward again.

These intertwined issues of moral substance and ambiguity and the *heavy* are intimately bound up with dramatic structure and our feeling of a screenwriter or dramatist's *practical* success, for the moral substance and ambiguity we experience as *heavy* is problematic within the fundamental story pattern. The experience of the *heavy,* let alone its triumph in a story, destroys Eros and defies a sense of structure where the protagonists make possible a new life for those dependent on them, whether they fall by the wayside themselves or lead the way to that life in the New Beginning we see open at the End of a successful film.

Michael in *The Godfather* triumphs as he sinks into profound moral ambiguity, but the problems of the action, past and present, are transcended, however grimly, and a New Beginning can now open out for the family. That beginning can certainly look ambiguous to us in terms of the values we attach to it; a resolution doesn't have to end ambiguity, for our ambiguity is the métier of our ambivalent natures. But a resolution does end a given story's particular problems with the meanings engendered in that conflict.

That New Beginning can be as ironical as *Ran's*, where it is the enemies of Ichimonji's family who inherit the future, as does Fortinbras in *Hamlet*, the son of an old foe; or the New Beginning can be more upbeat, as for Terry in *On the Waterfront*. But built into the sense of the New Beginning is the belief life cannot be destroyed. Action turned *heavy*, whatever its initial source, is the opposite in impact and implication.

The oceanic feeling Freud traces to infantile omniscience is experienced in drama as the result of moral action carried to a successful conclusion by a hero or heroine who, through the fundamental story pattern of drama, bring us personally, through identification, to the experience of such a prospective new beginning washed clean of the conflicts of the past.

It's heady stuff, and a primary example of how dramatic structure roots in human nature.

CHAPTER 4

Complexity vs. Fullness

Belief vs. Disbelief: Complexity

To call a film full is a compliment that means we experience a co-hesive story, however multithreaded, with a morally meaning-ful conflict necessarily and probably developed with characters who compel belief. We believe the action in such a film: nothing makes us suspend disbelief in order to go on. The suspension of disbelief is al-ways a secondary phenomenon, a breakdown of the primary belief with which we invest a given story until it begins to fail us.[1] Complexity, how-ever, is felt as a criticism of a film: a dramatic story has not added up, and its pieces lie in our hands like those of a puzzle we can't quite fit together. Many roads lead to a sense of complexity. First, complexity grows out of action that is not felt as causal. Everything in a film in the mere hour and a half to three hours of its running time, in which decades can transpire in the action, is necessarily symbolic of our larger reality, whatever style a story chooses to use, whether realism, magic realism, or styles further afield, like surrealism. All styles are equally symbolic ways of handling dramatic reality, and every writer must marshal the action economically and swiftly within his chosen style, for the simplest truth about drama is that an audience's patience is limited. Every scene must bear on the conflict, ideally: anything that doesn't feel causally connected makes the story feel slower, and sacrifices time that could have been put to better use. When the story picks up again we are teased with a sense of begin-ning again: taken far enough, we begin to hold broken story lines in our hands and time congests, with the results we saw earlier.

Second, unnecessary action, whether judged as causal or not but felt to be unnecessary, also has the effect of both interrupting our concentration and of beginning to break the story line. Such action puts a pause in our sense of a story's development and makes us grow self-conscious about our experience, the beginning of disbelief. "We don't need this action," we think, and begin to rewrite the story instead of losing ourselves in the characters and the emotional development of the conflict. Oddly, it is not a question of probability that is raised here initially, although necessary and probable are usually linked. Probability goes to credibility, necessity to structure. Yet what is structurally unnecessary inevitably starts to feel self-indulgent and potentially improbable. If the handling of a story rouses our self-consciousness enough, we will throw up our hands; at worst, we will leave the theatre. Leaving in such circumstances becomes the unexpected pleasure of the evening.

I can make this plain in, third, the use and abuse of the slice-of-life technique. In themselves, slice-of-life treatments of story structure don't pitch us out of our belief in a story, make us self-conscious, or begin to excite questions about how it all adds up, i.e., make us start to feel the story is complex. If a film defines its initial reality as containing a slice-of-life quality, we will accept that as readily as a science fiction premise. We will accept any reality clearly defined at the start of a film, because our sense of reality is almost infinitely plastic. Any reading in the anthropological literature will drive home how our storytelling plasticity reflects our equally diverse ways of organizing our societies.

Moreover, since the impact of naturalism in the nineteenth century, we have had the prejudice that slice-of-life writing deepens the sense of reality.[2] That prejudice, however, assumes the reality evoked in slice-of-life writing is the one we encounter in our lives, as if we all live in the same culture and share the same metaphysical assumptions. An American slice-of-life is radically dissimilar from a Chinese or Indian or Samoan: each looks, in fact, fantastic to the other.

Once within any cultural frame of reference, if we begin to feel slice-of-life writing is indulged in at the expense of the forward movement and cohesion of the conflict, then we experience it as unnecessary. Once perceived that way, slice-of-life writing, far from representing ultrarealism, instead undercuts it and our attention and belief in the story break down. We end with a sense of complexity instead, for the root cause of the sense of complexity is that story elements do not add up—that, in other words, our experiences in a story fail to cohere meaningfully.

Moreover, despite our prejudice, the sense of properly developed conflict is inherently at odds with slice-of-life writing and makes it always teeter on the edge of the faults reviewed here. Everything, we saw, must bear on a successfully handled conflict if we are to judge a film success-ful. But our sense of dramatic structure is not just at odds with slice-of-life writing, but with life itself. We are often overwhelmed with a sense of complexity in reality that we hunger to simplify so we can live with more purpose, do what is truly necessary, and avoid the merely expected or repetitive. Dramatic conflict through its resolution embodies that urge, and thus, fourth, when the conflict is not carried through cohesively, *that structural failure evokes our underlying sense of complexity from which we ache to be freed* and gives considerable sting to calling a film complex.

That is why, fifth, sequences of action causal in themselves but discon-tinuous with one another are so unsatisfactory, another reason why *Un-bearable Lightness* feels problematic. We don't want to be left in the com-plexity and perplexity we bring with us into the theatre. Yet *Unbearable Lightness* is a likeable film, despite its brushes with incoherence. It is held together by our sympathy for the characters and our willingness to al-low the disjunctions of their experience to be excused by our knowledge the Soviet invasion did happen, exile does override other concerns, and repression does drive individuals into isolation and a concentration on purely private matters, making them amoral in the larger picture, even if caused in part by taking a politically principled, moral stand, as does Tomas.

This tolerance for *Unbearable Lightness'* faults testifies to two things: my unwillingness to immerse us in genuinely bad films in order to score points, and the extreme latitude our will to believe grants any screenwriter. Story elements must be handled appallingly badly to break down our will-ingness to accept imaginary experience as emotionally and intellectually meaningful, for the imagination is a part of our experience of reality it-self. Dramatists have few tools so powerful as our will to believe.

The problems in episodic writing, sixth, bring us further into the nature of the experience of complexity. Sequences in an episodic film need not be connected through cause-and-effect action on the protagonist's part, yet are not felt as complex. Rather, *episodic writing goes directly to our ex-perience of our fate being at the mercy of others.* Indiana Jones in *Raiders of the Lost Ark* has a good and necessary cause to go to Nepal to get the artifact that will let him find the Ark, but he has no way of knowing the Germans will arrive when he does, or that his success will not derail the Nazis' plans. Once in Egypt, he survives an attempt to kill him but loses

Marion. Then, at the archeological site, he finds the Germans already at work; although he finds the Ark he is discovered and entombed. Next he pursues the truck transporting the Ark, triumphs, and arrives in Cairo with both the Ark and Marion, only to have a German submarine take both in the following episode.

What is operative here and explains the film's success is an overall *unity of story purpose:* all bears on gaining the Ark from the Nazis, even if the episodes are linked as much by accident or others' initiatives as by the protagonist's perspective. In each episode Indiana does what he must to attain his overriding goal and cause-and-effect writing reigns supreme; between episodes his fate is in the hands of others. By way of contrast, Terry in *On the Waterfront* and Book in *Witness* have a much more thorough sense in Acts 2 and 3 of what kind of difficulties their actions lead them toward: they are the architects of their own development.

If the overall unity of story purpose in an episodic film is broken, then the episodic handling of the story collapses into its disparate parts and is felt as complex. The problem of continuity in story line as we encounter it *Unbearable Lightness* but don't in *Raiders of the Lost Ark* turns on our sense of this unity of story purpose. In its absence, the failure of a story's structure to add up evokes our underlying fear that life itself does not add up and we are at the mercy of imponderables. That angers and frustrates the same desire for clarity and resolution we bring to our experience of the conflict.

We will experience complexity in all of these instances even if we sense a story is substantive and fully engaged with issues of Eros vs. Thanatos. Beyond this, whether we experience elements of an action or an entire film as *heavy* or as lacking in moral weight, and so weightless and without meaning, are separate issues; yet while both the *heavy* and moral lightness can appear in a film we experience as complex, *neither appears in a film we feel is full.*

Fullness

The experience of a film as full, then, can bear a paradoxical complexity of storytelling elements, for when the overall unity of story purpose along with the usual unity of conflict is maintained, a film is felt to be clear and cohesive.

In *Rear Window* there are multiple subplots concerning the neighbors on view beyond Jeff's apartment: the newlyweds, the woman they characterize as "Miss Lonelyheart," the musician, the young dancer, and so on. All have their own story, but all bear on Jeff and Lisa's story, whether ironically through the newlyweds or the dancer fighting off the wolves, or directly, as with the salesman's ill wife Jeff decides is murdered and whom Lisa's courage in investigating goes a long way in convincing Jeff that she is the right woman for him.

Rashômon is equally revealing. Five stories are linked: the ongoing story of those temporarily trapped at the ruined temple during a storm, Tajomaru's story, the wife's story, the husband's story through a medium, and the woodcutter's story. Tajomaru portrays himself as daring and resourceful, taking what he wants and toying with the husband in their duel before killing him. In the wife's story, she sees the contempt in her husband's eyes for her after she has been raped and kills him herself, consumed by guilt and shame, although she implies his death happens as she falls forward with the knife, fainting, as much as to say she is blinded by passion and represses memory. But in the "husband's" story the wife wants to leave with Tajomaru, who is shocked by her request for him kill her husband. He rejects her and asks the husband instead what he should do. The wife flees and Tajomaru frees the husband, who kills himself because of his dishonor. The woodcutter recounts a version in which the husband, freed after his wife's rape, won't fight for her, while Tajomaru has lost interest. The wife taunts them by saying a woman can only love a *real* man, implicitly neither of them. Stung by her contempt, both men now fight at once fearfully and fiercely. Finally, at the ruined temple, they wrestle with their inability to add these stories up until the priest's belief in humanity is steadied when the woodcutter takes the abandoned baby found at the temple for his own, in a concluding act of compassion.

Each story is convincing, yet none is definitive. The potential for a sense of complexity is great; instead, we end with a sense of fullness. Each story transpires within the same context of the men at the temple trying to understand what happened, and each story is a candidate to be *the* story of the same event. We are not left with incoherence or the sense of multiple stories in dramatic time trying to occupy one running time when none proves final, but the sense that however far we go in our attempt to understand ourselves and our actions, we finally reach the point of acknowledging the ultimate unknowability of the truth and one another. It would be a perfect embodiment of the perils of our root Kantian view of the world if it were not for the fact that *the audience is put in the position of entirely knowing a film.*[3]

That uncertainty in *Rashômon* may be disconcerting, and certainly complicates our reflections on character, motivation, and behavior, but *Rashômon*'s end has a transcendent quality, like the *climax* of *The Usual Suspects*. Neither ends irresolute and complex.

This leads to another key ingredient of the experience of fullness touched on earlier: the sense that the fundamental story pattern is fulfilled, that past and present problems are resolved even if that resolution involves a sense of ambivalence or ambiguity in the nature of reality, however defined by a given film. A New Beginning becomes possible and the time of the film's action becomes "set," as we saw thinking through issues of time, as a future opens free of the preceding conflicts. In *Rashômon*, just as in the wholly different *Fanny and Alexander*, we end with infants who symbolize a future filled with possibility in the hands of adults, implicitly in *Rashômon*, explicitly in *Fanny and Alexander*. In the latter, Gustav Adolf wonders if little Aurora or Victoria may not turn out to be a world redeemer.

As these examples also highlight, fullness in drama involves an engagement with issues of Eros and Thanatos, which indicates a real engagement with ambivalent human nature. Fullness is irrelevant to the sense of triviality a film generates even if otherwise successful, as with some of the sequels looked at earlier that turn into entertainments.

Typing, Volition, and Fullness

When we meet Edie in *On the Waterfront* at Joey's death, she is all fire and purpose. She reproaches Father Barry for hiding in the church, energizing him to become more directly involved with the longshoremen. She won't accept cautions from her father, Pop, appearing at the church meeting Father Barry calls. She does not immediately lose her head and heart over Terry when he saves her from Johnny Friendly's thugs as they break up the meeting: she's half-attracted, half-offended by him. She stays to find Joey's killer, although her father wants her to go back to the church school upstate. She won't play deaf and dumb even within the family, as Pop does. When she does fall for Terry, she challenges Terry's false modus vivendi with himself and Johnny Friendly by asking for his help in finding her brother's killer and insisting on a generous approach to life.

Edie, then, is anything but a type: she is full of volition and acts from the dictates of her conscience. But she reverts to a type after Terry confesses to Father Barry and her, breaks into her apartment, sweeps her off her feet and makes her admit she loves him. Thereafter she is just a woman in love afraid for her man's survival and wants to flee the scene of danger even if that means abandoning her attempt to get justice for Joey. Eros in Freud's sense has overwhelmed her: she is not concerned with issues of "civilization" like cleaning up the docks but wants instead the perpetuation of the loving pair "Terry-Edie."

It's an interesting story development, entirely believable and revealing. Typing works against fullness by narrowing characterization and volition in character. *On the Waterfront* would be in danger from Edie's narrowing if Father Barry did not take over her role of awakening and guiding Terry until he becomes fully volitional with the assertion of his conscience and breaks his earlier typing as a bum. Edie can revert to a type and still enrich the action, but now by upping the difficulties Terry faces.

Bud in *L.A. Confidential* is heavily typed as one of the boys in the Beginning. He may thrash an abusive husband but refuses to speak against his fellow officers after the Christmas brawl he participates in at the police station. Dudley protects him and recruits him for his muscle.

Then Bud falls for Lynn, a call girl echo of Veronica Lake. She reciprocates and encourages his unease over the Night Owl case. She insists he's smart and should pursue his investigation, challenging and energizing him as Edie does Terry in *On the Waterfront*. Bud begins a course of action that ultimately allies him with the initially hostile Exley, even after Dudley arranges for Bud to find pictures of Exley and Lynn together. Despite his rage over Lynn, Bud *chooses* to listen to Exley's exposure of Dudley and join forces with him. Bud has become a moral agent, gaining volition as he leaves typing behind, asserting control of himself. When he and Exley triumph, however morally ambiguously, we are pleased and experience the film as full.

Thus drama imitates a pattern of living we almost never encounter, some rare part of our lives with a discernible shape organized around some clear purpose in response to some problem we wrestle with in a state of crisis, suffer through, and resolve so that we can put that part of our lives behind us and move on. Drama does not imitate what we usually mean by reality at all, but, as Aristotle carefully says,[4] *an action,* which is a highly unique, rarely encountered moment of reality in which conflict is joined and resolved in a defining and illuminating manner. Typing prevents the exploration of self/character in conflicted moments of life and drama that we need to reach a resolution of conflict. In life and drama we or a character must find fresh resources to resolve conflict definitively: we must grow. Types do not grow.

Endings

So far I have looked at the End of a screenplay within terms of the fundamental story pattern as that moment in a dramatic story when its action is resolved and we see, without entering it, a New Beginning free of old concerns. I have looked at the sense of fullness we gain through successful storytelling and emphasized the relation of the structural need for the New Beginning to the experience of an action in reality that a screenplay "imitates" or embodies, that root hunger in ourselves for the sense our lives add up and are meaningful as we surmount conflict and the past. An ending needn't be clear, I said, in the sense that it can involve ambiguity and ambivalence, but it must be an *ending.* Earlier I reviewed the lack of *transcendence* in the *heavy,* and of how that sense of transcendence is part of what we include in a sense of the New Beginning. More is involved.

Happy romantic endings are the simplest examples of this structural completion. The hero gets the heroine, or the heroine the hero, whether in a romantic comedy, farces like *Analyze This* or *Married to the Mob,* or serious dramas like *On the Waterfront.* The failure to "get the girl" in *Witness* forces a critical evaluation in us of the societies that make their union impossible, because such an ending gives a resolution that paradoxically defies our sense of resolution. In *Blue* Julie ends up with Olivier, reaffirming a commitment to life and creativity and confirming our own sense of her transcendence of her family's death. In these cases, the idea is that the heroine and hero will live happily *ever* after, conflict free. Time, in a certain sense, is imagined as over because it will always contain the same experience. This is a dream, of course, but one we like to dream and, contrary to conventional critical reactions, anything but superficial. Suffering and life go hand in hand, as Freud so effortlessly shows in *Civilization and Its Discontents,* something we understand very well through our own experience, one from which we seek repeated redemption.

However, when we deal with substantive films like *Ran, Rashômon,* or *Schindler's List,* the New Beginning is not a simple "happily ever after." Ambiguity and ambivalence enter: evil can even triumph as in *The Usual Suspects,* or the truth escape us as in *Rashômon.* Exley may be exonerated in *L.A. Confidential,* but Bud is left to join another police force. Though he "gets the girl," she has been a hooker. The past may be defeated yet linger enough to warn about the future, as Johnny Friendly does in *On the Waterfront.* A killer turned too human to kill may be allowed to escape, like Nikita in *La Femme Nikita;* a hero may even die, as in *Ran* or *Hamlet;* and the future may belong to former enemies.

In all cases life goes on, and not just as a popular dream. There is a transparent triumph of Eros in the obviously happy, romantic ending, but *Eros triumphs equally through more substantial and even tragic endings.* Screenwriting structure culminates through climax and resolution in that sense of a fresh start in which a personal—or personal and communal, or in the case of tragedy, only communal—continuance is ensured. There is no illusion here that time will be a continuous flow of the same experience: instead, it implies the ability of the hero/heroine or community to develop creatively, free of past mistakes, typing, and error. *Life is affirmed,* and the power of destructiveness, even to the extreme of Thanatos, is ended. Hamlet may die in *Hamlet,* but not before Laertes, so gullible, Gertrude, so culpable, and Claudius, so murderous, are killed too, as Fortinbras discovers as he takes over to initiate a new day. Ichimonji and Saburo may die in *Ran,* but Fujimaki and Ayabe lay claim to the future. Something is felt to be ongoing and indestructible at the end of a successful screenplay, something that we experience as our own through identification with the heroine/hero, something which is at least pleasurable and in its more memorable instances exhilarating. Those more memorable instances verge toward tragedy yet are characteristic of films whose heroes succeed, too, as with Julie in *Blue* or Schindler in *Schindler's List.*

A cumulative sense emerges from dramatic actions we go through of *healings.* The unresolved past is brought into the present and, along with present problems, resolved. Protagonists that were split, which is what typing means in psychological terms, are made whole as they regain their ability to act as moral agents. What was unconscious, unknown, and denied has been brought to consciousness, been realized, and by being accepted, overcome. What was separated, most obviously when dealing with male and female aspects of ourselves as in romantic comedy, or good and bad or smart and dumb sides of our selves like Bud and Exley initially in *L.A. Confidential,* is made whole. The oldest of human splits is undone for a happy moment in the New Beginning, that between our living blindly in nature, entirely typed by instinct and role, and taking the fatal step into humanity by becoming conscious of ourselves and thereby volitional agents. We find that step entirely admirable, of course, but such a step separates us from the broad, unconscious realms of nature, from, in Nietzschean terms, the primal mother.[5]

These paragraphs are written very broadly. The usual screenwriting and media studies have a plethora of narrow, self-reflective concerns, as if so great an art exists and roots in a hall of mirrors that reflect only what those involved in its immediate production or criticism say about one another. They are media studies versions of the Platonic cave. Sometimes we need to remind ourselves of the relation of story structure to human experience and imagination and, inevitably in any great art, to our deepest hungers and our most irreconcilable conflicts. Fullness as an experience lies in the direction of embodying these, while the same elements that structurally impede effective storytelling also impede our gaining an adequate sense of the range of our own possibilities. That is what the New Beginning at the end of a story is meant to make us sense, not an Eden we have been excluded from, but one we are journeying toward.

PART II

The *Cooked* and the *Raw*

CHAPTER 5

The *Cooked* and the *Raw*

THE action of an effective screenplay is immediate and emotional: we reflect on the larger meanings of the action when a film is over because of our emotional involvement with characters for whom we have been made to care. But there is a fundamental, common cleavage in how a writer chooses to handle a character's emotion. The *cooked* refers to emotion experienced through some element of formalization, the *raw* to its direct, unvarnished expression. *Both styles communicate emotion with equal effectiveness,* but each leads to noticeably dissimilar styles in handling characterization.

Cooked Emotion

A *cooked* handling of emotion always involves a restraint, a distancing, and/or an element of stylization.

Look at the climactic confrontation between Michael Sr. and John Rooney in *Road to Perdition*. It is night and raining, as it was the first time in the film when Michael went out with his tommy gun. Rooney is surrounded by bodyguards as he goes to his car as Michael starts shooting. We see the flashes of his gun, flashes from the men's guns as they fall, see and hear the rain falling, and see Rooney standing motionless with his back to Michael, *but we hear no firing.*

Rooney turns to face Michael after the others are dead. "I'm glad it's you," he says to Michael. We see them both: then Michael starts shooting. Now we hear the gun, but *see only Michael:* Rooney is out of the shot, his reaction to the bullets hitting him unseen, all focus on Michael's face.

It's very powerful. First, expectation is defied by the absence of the sound of firing, so that we watch yet another killing sequence with a startled freshness and uniqueness. Then we are forced to concentrate on Michael's grief as he shoots Rooney. The inevitable urge toward stylization involved in the use of the *cooked* is very apparent yet here lets the writer, David Self, communicate emotion with an original force, for the *cooked* isolates a key emotion from the flood of incident and makes it stand out in sudden, intense relief.

A similar use of the *cooked* is seen earlier in the film as Michael and Rooney's son, Connor, confront Finn. They have been sent to talk to Finn, not shoot him, but Connor shoots Finn when he begins revealing information about Connor. We watch the ensuing shoot-out through the eyes of Michael Jr. peering in. We hear the firing without seeing men killed, watching instead a stream of shell casings rain on the floor. Then one of the bloodied men falls dead facing Michael Jr., making him recoil. The distancing and stylization again are clear, *the use of the visual effect* of the bloody face and Michael Jr.'s recoil standing in for a conventionally direct handling of the action.

Road to Perdition shows this use of visual effects in the *cooked* handling of emotion well: *Like Water for Chocolate* shows the use of substituting an emotional effect for emotion instead of its direct expression.

Tita and Pedro are desperately in love in *Like Water for Chocolate,* but Tita as the youngest daughter is doomed to care for her mother, Elena, as long as she lives. Elena refuses Pedro's marriage proposal for Tita but accepts one he offers for her daughter Rosaura. Pedro explains to Tita that this way he will always be able to be close to Tita, but she is not consoled: *she* isn't the one getting married, and she has no intention of betraying her sister, while Elena is vigilant against such a possibility.

Cooking is Tita's specialty, aiding and aided by their ancient cook, Nacha. Tita and Nacha prepare the wedding cake as the wedding day approaches. A few of Tita's tears fall into the cake's batter. She does not weep floods of tears, but then *emotion is not hidden at all in the cooked style,* just handled differently. We do not see Rosaura and Pedro's marriage ceremony, only the reception afterward at the house as the cake with Tita's grief is served.

The guests find it tasty, then are driven to tears. Soon the cake's impact drives all to rush from the table to vomit, Pedro and Rosaura not excepted. The depth of Tita's feelings are more than amply revealed *through the effect of eating the cake.*

Elena attacks Tita but is deflected by the death of Nacha. Tita becomes head cook.

Pedro gives Tita a bouquet of roses to mark her first year as head cook. That evening, Tita makes a special dinner. First, she is scratched by a thorn, i.e., she suffers from the thorn of passion, then she crumbles the rose petals into the sauce. One by one the family taste an exquisite dinner imbued with Tita's passion for Pedro. It makes Rosaura ill. Her other sister, Gertrudis, rushes out to cool herself and sets an outhouse on fire from the heat of her arousal. That draws a rider toward Gertrudis as she runs naked across the countryside to cool herself. He sweeps her up and rides off while she embraces him uninhibitedly.

All dramatic emotion is heightened: it is felt by characters in conflict and crisis. The *cooked*, despite its displacement of direct emotional expression into some effect, heightens even that heightened dramatic emotion. There is an implication for style here too: the reality communicated through *Like Water for Chocolate*'s handling of emotion could not be in a slice-of-life or cinéma vérité style: we recognize it as magic realism. In *Road to Perdition* magic isn't evoked, but events become aesthetic through stylization and consequently stand out in sharp relief because such treatment is so unexpected in a gangster film.

Chocolat gives several excellent examples of *cooked* emotion. The Comte resists Vianne's temptation throughout the film, insisting on tradition and conventional propriety taken to an extreme. We see the depth of *his* rage against Vianne's chocolate challenge to the denial Lent stands for expressed *through Serge* when that desperate man takes a momentary expression of the Comte's feelings literally and sets fire to Roux's flotilla, endangering Vianne and her daughter's lives, along with a good many others. The Comte is appalled at the revelation of *his own* anger/destructiveness when Serge explains he did what he thought the Comte really wanted, much as Henry acts horrified when his knights take him at his word and kill Beckett in *Beckett*. The Comte banishes Serge from the town.

Desperate, wielding a knife, the Comte goes to confront Vianne. He doesn't assault or rant at her but breaks into her shop, sees the offending chocolates, slashes them with his knife, licks its blade, and then devours the chocolates in an oral frenzy expressing all his repressed passion and hunger for life before falling asleep in the window.

Vianne and Josephine understand this perfectly the next morning as they give him milk and help him up. So do we. There is no doubt about his emotions at all or the redemptive value of their release: watching his collapse into an eating frenzy is at once funny and quite touching.

The *cooked*, then, can displace emotion from one object or person to another, or omit a conventional, realistically expected element. Any technique that uses displacement, distance, or stylization *cooks* the presentation of emotion. *Cooked* effects don't affect our identification with the heroine or hero, or our experience of the moral substance or ambiguity of a story. But on the face of it, the *heavy* is virtually ruled out by using *cooked* emotion, for the *cooked* isolates single expressions of feeling for great effect and never involves a continuous flood of direct feeling, let alone unrelieved self-destructiveness of the kind Bess sinks to in *Breaking the Waves.*

The *cooked* can obviously go too far, like anything else in writing. Too far into symbol, image, stylization, or substitute effects and the same approach that serves to communicate feeling powerfully begins to distance emotion and make a film seem obscure or literally weightless because emotionless, which we experience as tedium.

But the *cooked* has wider uses in storytelling, beyond emphasizing emotional expression. It can be used to portray *social* structure, especially in a society where the denial of emotion results in the ossification of that society and the repression of its members.

The elders in *Breaking the Waves* and the church they run, as well as the lifestyle they have imposed on their community, are deeply repressive. The steeple is empty, women subjected to men, dress severe, and masochism the order of the day. At Bess's wedding an elder crushes a glass in his hand in response to one of Jan's friends crushing a beer can. Fall afoul of the elders and they damn you or leave you fallen, like Bess on the path, in the hour of your need. The town is frozen, life ossified, love repressed to the disappearing point, the *cooked* technique taken to an extreme of stylization of existence until life feels stifled.

Dramatically speaking, *we expect* an extremity on the order of the elders to be confronted. We are ready for Bess before we understand who she is, the opposite such an extreme inevitably calls up and releases against itself. We can be neither wholly emotional nor wholly repressed in this variant of *cooked* storytelling: something better must grow out of their clash. That is hinted at when Bess's sister-in-law denounces the elders at Bess's funeral and when the bells ring by the oil rig in the End.

If that shows a dark side but valid structural use of the *cooked,* over-plotting shows a fault. When we begin to feel there are one too many plot turns, we are distanced from the story: "It's too much," we say to ourselves. *No Way Out* gives a good example of this: Costner's character goes through so many turns that the plotting in effect becomes a *cooked* displacement of emotion, so much so that the final plot turn throws us out of any sense of emotional involvement as well as probability, so that we shrug the film off in irritation. Beyond this, the misuse of the *cooked* is apparent whenever we move too far away in the action from the emotionality that is due from the conflict, whether because stylization goes too far or overplotting snaps credulity and affect. In that case *cooked* elements come to stand *between us* and the story.

Yet a deliberate and able accumulation of plot complications in a story can move it toward the comedic. *Prizzi's Honor* shows this common technique well. It's one thing for the family hit man to go off and seek to recover money from a freelancer, but another for him to fall in love with and marry her, then have her retained to hit him after a multitude of intervening complications. We can't help but laugh. The *cooked* here displaces the experience of a serious drama into the comic realm.

The *Raw*

Emotion flung at us directly is *raw.* There is no distancing or displacement of emotion for effect, as in the *cooked,* but instead the direct confrontation with feeling in a given character.

We see Bess lying in bed naked to offer herself to the doctor in *Breaking the Waves.* He rejects her, although he tries to soften his rejection; nonetheless she is humiliated, suddenly not naked but indecently exposed because of his reaction. Nothing stands between us and the direct experience of these emotions and their effects. Terry and Edie confront one another in the bar in *On the Waterfront,* culminating with her request for his help; when he equivocates, she is provoked into calling him a bum. Their emotion is in our face. Even more dramatic and classic, as we saw, is Terry's breaking down Edie's door after his series of confessions to Father Barry and herself. Edie's flailing fists weaken into an ardent embrace as Terry gathers her in his arms and kisses her into submission as he demands she admit her love. Nothing could be more direct or unvarnished.

The *climax*[1] of *On the Waterfront* is just as direct. Terry is refused work, yet the longshoremen wait, watching to see what he will do. They follow him toward the dockside building where Johnny Friendly and his thugs are gathered. Terry calls for Johnny Friendly to come out and then taunts him with his own version of events before the longshoremen. He attacks Friendly physically in response to Friendly's challenge, winning until the thugs overpower him. Everything is direct, powerful, emotional, in our face: *raw.*

Tita is not set free by Elena's death in *Like Water for Chocolate.* Elena periodically haunts her like a Freudian guilty conscience given body, harsh and condemning. She continues to stand between Tita and Pedro. Finally Tita expresses her hatred directly to Elena and drives her mother from her presence. Tita's hatred is powerful, direct, and satisfying in its expression: there is no attempt to displace, stylize, or symbolize it. I could say there is no need: the hatred between mother and daughter needed to speak for itself. But Tita's grief over Pedro's marriage could only be expressed as typical grief if expressed in a *raw* way: displacing that into the effect of the cake on others allows that emotion's fresh experience. I emphasize again that each way of handling emotion used at the right moment is equal in power.

The *raw,* then, involves none of the techniques of the *cooked:* it is real in an obviously "realistic" sense, what we would expect of cinéma vérité or slice-of-life writing or from our conventional idea of what is real. The *raw* has the effect of a direct assault on us: the *cooked* does not make the *raw*'s claim of "Here I am, here are my feelings now, take it or leave it." But the *raw* can degenerate into the unearned emotionality of melodrama or *heavy* earned emotion in the form of destructiveness experienced for its own sake.

Raw emotion wants to sweep us away; the *raw* drives toward the ecstasy and intoxication of complete instinctual release. It can be sweepingly Dionysian in effect, as we saw with Agave in Euripides' *The Bacchae,* who dismembers her son in an emotional transport. But she is horrified as that emotional transport wears off. Nothing could be *rawer.* The *cooked* tries to beguile and seduce and tends toward delight; the *raw* wants to overwhelm and submerge us in a character's emotions and tends toward horror.

The *raw* demands our absolute, undistanced assent to the illusion of a story's reality, while the *cooked* invites a sense of illusion *even while making as absolute a claim for our emotional involvement.* The hint of an Apollonian sense of "illusion" lets a *cooked* approach weave its magic and handle emotionality in other than a *raw* way. Nietzsche, in defining the Apollonian, emphasizes its compelling nature that yet possesses simultaneously a hint of illusion, which gives a dreamlike edge to reality.[2] In that sense, a screenplay is a waking dream we know is a dream at the same time we are caught up in and compelled by its action.

Blending the *Cooked* and the *Raw*

An extended pure encounter with either the *cooked* or the *raw* is unusual: both provoke a need for relief from too exclusive, or narrow, a handling of emotion with its implications for storytelling. Usually we find both elements in a film, however marked a given tendency may be, as we saw with the conflict between Tita and Elena in *Like Water for Chocolate,* or in the handling of the elders' society in *Breaking the Waves.*

High Noon handles emotion violently and physically in the fight between Kane and Harvey and the shoot-out with Miller and his friends. Nonetheless, we are never far from a clock and the time shown to be shrinking between Kane's efforts to find help and the moment when Miller will arrive. Finally we need only glance at a clock in *High Noon:* we know what it means. It is a *cooked* element, a symbol standing for time running out to a violent climax. In its inexorability the clock evokes a sense of an iron fate compounded by the betrayals around Kane.

What in *On the Waterfront* is *cooked*? Everything seems in our face, its characters' emotions directly handled and expressed in a *raw* manner. But after his appearance in court has hurt Friendly but not removed him, Terry must consider what to do next. Edie wants him to leave, fearing for his life: they should go upstate and farm. Terry says nothing as she pleads, playing instead with his longshoreman's hook. That has multiple meanings, like the clock in *High Noon.* It is the longshoreman's tool; being a longshoreman is what Terry is silently debating, with all the implications now of asserting or abandoning that role. Finally he dons Joey's jacket, already a *cooked* element, a symbol that stands for reform, and states his intention. "I'm just going to get my rights," he tells Edie, and walks out.[3] It's a *cooked* sequence in a generally *raw* film.

Rashōmon finds critical moments of displacement and distancing too. We never see the husband being killed, even in the woodcutter's climactic story in which the two men fight desperately. As Tajomaru thrusts his sword home, we focus on the bandit's face distorted by the intensely unpleasant experience of killing another, like we do on Michael's grief at the moment of Rooney's death in *Road to Perdition*. An element of displacement, of the *cooked,* enters right at the climax of a *raw* fight.

Earlier the woodcutter relates how he encounters items of clothing in the forest before he finds the husband, wife, and Tajomaru. These items shouldn't be there and indicate by their presence that something awful is underway or has happened. That too is a *cooked* communication, just as are the frequent shots of the sky with clouds serenely passing, so at odds with the emotional rawness and moral misbehavior of husband, wife, and bandit.

Often the *cooked* and the *raw are blended in the same experience.* Note the purely *raw* confrontation by father and son in the field in *Road to Perdition* as Michael Sr. demands Michael Jr. obey him unquestionably in order for them to survive, or the *raw climax* when Michael Jr. can't shoot McGuire, who has shot his father. Michael Jr.'s hesitation gives Michael Sr. time to kill McGuire himself, after which Michael Jr. breaks down over his father's body in a powerfully *raw* expression of grief. Now revisit Michael Sr.'s *cooked* killing of Rooney. We experience Michael Sr.'s grief in a *raw* way as we concentrate on his face; in this instance, a *cooked* handling of emotion, by isolating a single emotion, amplifies its *rawness.*

Similarly, if we revisit Michael Jr. watching his father gun down Finn's men, a scene handled in a *cooked* manner, the abrupt appearance of the bloody face that horrifies Michael has a *raw* impact the *cooked* handling underscores. Even the murder of Michael's wife and younger son has this blending: as Connor appears in the doorway, gun drawn, Michael's wife sees him and shields her son as they are killed, *which we never see.* The *cooked* handling here isolates the horror of the situation *by removing individual reactions.* When Michael Sr. and Jr. later look at the bodies, we see them look but not what they look at, and so are not distracted from their moment of perception, a moment again blending the *cooked* and *raw.*

The problem with *Road to Perdition* is the conventionality of *our* expectations. The *raw* and gangster film seem synonymous: a gangster film that uses *cooked* techniques, as if such a story could become an aesthetic experience, nonplusses us. Habit, as Hume noted, is dominant, and genre writing is an aesthetic habit. Few of us have read Nietzsche, and fewer think as he does that the horror of reality can only be redeemed by its transformation into an aesthetic experience, to make it an object of pleasure. Freud doesn't speak of "horror" but suffering; yet he means much the same thing and points out how creativity is a sublimation of libido, whose aim is to provide a way to master our suffering. Consider, if you are still in doubt, how the continual effort to make films about the Holocaust shows a tendency to transform an actual horror into an illusion (a film) that can be enjoyed, whether in *Life Is Beautiful, The Pianist,* or *Schindler's List.* The goal of such aestheticizing is not to deny the reality of the experience but to find a way to prevent our turning away from it in historical aversion or personal repression of a memory too harsh to bear. Containing such reality in a work of art keeps it present for experience in a way we can bear.

The *cooked* plays to that tendency, the *raw* to its opposite. An entirely *raw* depiction of an individual's experience in the Holocaust, culminating in our following him or her into the gas chamber and furnace, would be unendurable. When the *cooked* moves a plot toward comedy, it makes us see the expression of the *raw* as an absurdity, as Benigni's character at moments succeeds at doing in the concentration camp in *Life Is Beautiful.* That is quite a feat, and Nietzschean in spirit.

The illusion of art does not deny but redeem, and makes possible, in extreme cases, the *possibility* of the experience of a reality we know yet don't want to know.

Antecedents

The *cooked* and the *raw* are primarily techniques for handling the expression of emotion, with implications affecting plot and story style. These concepts have worthy ancestors. Primary in this regard is Nietzsche's development of Dionysian and Apollonian in *The Birth of Tragedy.* He presents these as formative forces of nature *and* psyche, and is ultimately interested in the way they unite in the *climax* of a Greek tragedy. He was deeply influenced by Schopenhauer, and with him is caught up in the argument we are having with ourselves, contesting the deep dualism stemming from Descartes and given its modern impetus by Kant.

Schopenhauer spoke of a unitary *will,* which has a sublimated modern life as the Freudian *libido.*[4] The will is the very essence of being in its urge to become all it can be, to stop at nothing until fully realized, fully alive. It is ruthless, undeniable, immediate, *and* metaphysical. A sense of it is echoed in a Robinson Jeffers poem, *De Rerum Virtute:*

> . . . And the Galaxy, the firewheel
> On which we are pinned, the whirlwind of stars in which our sun
> is one dust grain, one electron, this giant
> atom of the universe
> Is not blind force, but fulfills its life and intends its courses. . . .[5]

That urge of the dust to be, whether of the immensities of the universe or of the dust beneath our feet, and to live fully, exemplifies the Schopenhauerian will. But if there is only the will and its endless appetite, how do we get to anything else? Again, through the will. Once that will achieves satisfaction, it can cease its relentless striving and regard itself, the reason why Schopenhauer entitled his key work *The World as Will and Idea.* Once the will regards itself it moves into the realm of ideation, of reflection and creativity. Nietzsche splits these two aspects, relentless drive and ideation and imagination (creativity), apart in order to speak about their nature once unified under the pressure of intense dramatic conflict.

The Apollonian formative force elaborates image, form, and structure. It is consequently defining, reflective, and in history embodied by the injunction "Know thyself." Something of the dream experience is integral to the Apollonian experience, because an *elaborated* reality is in that sense illusory and dreamlike, such that we have the perception at the very edge of an Apollonian experience that it is after all "only" an illusion. The epic reflects an Apollonian perspective in poetry; today we would make that claim on the part of the novel, however minimalist or traditionally full, with or without an acknowledged omniscient author. Delight as well as self-knowledge characterize the Apollonian experience, which can move steadily into ever more rationalistic formulations until scientific or so technical it abandons the realm of feeling altogether. As a construct it can ossify, as society has in the world of the elders in *Breaking the Waves* against which Bess struggles so hard, for ossification invites its own destruction.

The Dionysian is that destructive force that is also creative, as we will encounter later in the contemporary psychoanalytic thinking of the seminal D. W. Winnicott.[6] The Dionysian man or woman is a reveler carried away by the god's approach (Dionysos), or more generally, someone swept out of a narrow sense of self by passion into a sense of self at once communal and celebratory. The divisions of the mind into ego, superego, and id vanish: a Dionysian is transported into a state of oneness with nature, like Agave in *The Bacchae,* with the results we have seen. Bess in her rawness has a Dionysian force; she virtually becomes grief itself, and has to be called back into herself and some vestige of Apollonian self-control by Jan before he can leave her to go to work after their initial marital idyll. A Dionysian looks mad to an Apollonian; an Apollonian looks pale and far from life to a Dionysian.

When some Apollonian structure—whether a social or an individual psychic construct—stultifies, a Dionysian release sweeps away the dead wood and by doing so makes possible new growth, like the fires that sweep through forests that leave ruin in their wake yet split open seeds for new growth that cannot otherwise open. The Dionysian drive, then, has a paradoxical nature, at once unquestionably destructive yet potentially creative in consequence.

Greek tragedy fuses these forces together for Nietzsche. The chorus, under the Dionysian influence of music, which echoes the Schopenhauerian will in its endless movement and direct impact on emotion, envisages the action of the play as a way of making manifest some of the meaning of the music. That envisaging is seen by the audience through its *identification with the visionary chorus.* What is envisioned are the Apollonian, *specific scenes with discrete characters and conflict that make up the dramatic action.* But tragedy sweeps away the visionary heroine or hero, thus emphasizing the continuation of the life of the surviving community and world, for the chorus endures. Only the waking dream of the action passes away. Oedipus in *Oedipus Rex* goes into exile, his wife/mother Jocasta dead, but the Theban citizens can now rejoice in their prospects even as they lament Oedipus's fate, for he was the source of the plague afflicting them, which ends with his departure. This cleansing and renewal, as experienced by the audience through the chorus, is felt as joyous and is characteristic of the Dionysian experience; it offers an explanation of the source of the tragic wonder Aristotle noted in tragedy's effect on the audience. The survival of the chorus while the individual is swept away brings us into a state of oneness with something enduring beyond destruction's powers.

There is no dualism, then, for Nietzsche in the crowning moment of the tragic *climax,* but the ultimate experience of a *knowing transport* made possible by the union of the Apollonian as it tries to express the Diony-sian. Such an experience defies the typical limitations of Western thought and language to verbalize without first splitting the experience into differ-ent conceptual categories, then claiming those categories reflect different realities, "me" vs. "not me," for example. Nietzsche is on his own crusade, in his own way, early and late, to undo Descartes and Kant. Implicit in his way of speaking of the union of Apollonian and Dionysian is the view that dualism is an illusionary way of speaking of one reality.

The debt owed to Schopenhauer and Nietzsche by the *cooked* and the *raw* is apparent and acknowledged. But the *cooked* and the *raw* are nei-ther as sweeping as Nietzsche's terms nor loaded with as philosophical a weight, however their blending in our films echoes the blending of Apol-lonian and Dionysian, if seen here as techniques for the effective handling of emotion in screenwriting. That would seem a ridiculous narrowing only if we forget that the matter of effective screenwriting and dramatic writing generally is not media or film studies or other screenplays but the stuff of human nature in conflict. The underlying presumptions of how we view ourselves—the argument that our culture is having with itself—are by that measure necessarily built into our dramas and characters, so-ciety and selves, equally.

A second antecedent for the *cooked,* one also explored by Nietzsche as a precursor to the Apollonian, is the concept of the *naïve.* By that he means a displacement of emotion into an image or effect. He is eager to get past that to the Apollonian, but the naïve is a fruitful idea in itself, go-ing back to the early German idealists and the work of the German dra-matic critic Lessing.[7] Certain stories of Chaucer, for example, are thor-oughly naïve, using sophisticated deflections of emotion into images and effects at key moments, most clearly so in the ending of *The Miller's Tale.*[8] The naïve handling of emotion is, in other words, a recurrent feature of storytelling.

The *cooked,* however, has none of the implications built into a word like "naïve": naïveté, lack of sophistication, simple. It is anything but, just as the *raw* need hardly be celebratory in a Dionysian way. Our history has taught us that the Apollonian in the social realm can become pure repres-sion as dictatorship hardens and forces its removal from without or col-lapses from within, while the Dionysian in the form of a mass movement and hysteria can lead to the Holocaust. The *cooked* and the *raw* are free of these terrible implications, if not the *heavy*. What is salient, however, is the realization that either technique taken to an extreme transforms its opposite into a corrective force that *as audience we expect to appear in the action* out of our fundamental expectation as human beings, profoundly moral at root, that extremes of any kind must be redressed and, in the nature of things, will be, even if by their opposite.

A River Runs Through It gives moving expression to this inevitable dynamism in the scene where Paul lands an immense trout despite being momentarily swept away by the rapids. His older brother, Norm, reflects as Paul stands before him and his father that Paul has reached a state of perfection through his art as an angler, and that if anything is sure in this world, such a state cannot last. So he is not surprised to receive the call to see his brother's dead body one morning soon after. Paul has been beaten to death for gambling debts. The fact that every bone in Paul's right hand is broken is no consolation to Norm or to his father, who keeps pressing Norm for more details. Finally Norm wonders if they ever really knew Paul, to which his father replies they knew one thing for sure: that he was "beautiful."[9]

Nothing, as Freud sees in *Civilization and Its Discontents*, is harder to explain than beauty as a *necessary* feature of civilization. Beauty speaks to our desire for perfection, yet nothing motivates our destructive, contrary urge more powerfully and tragically to tear it down than beauty itself.

CHAPTER 6

The *Smart* and the *Dumb*

Just as there are two fundamental approaches to handling character emotion with strong implications for story development, there are two fundamental approaches to handling character growth: the *smart* and the *dumb*. Neither term is pejorative or flattering: the *smart* and *dumb* handling of growth are equally effective and common in dramatic writing. Both also have implications for story development. A review of the old distinction between flat and round characters and their implication for typing will orient us.

Flat and Round

These terms usually have a literary reference and traditionally sum up the appearance and behavior defining a character. We give fresh life to these terms whenever, in building a character for use in a screenplay, we decide the character's age, appearance, drive(s), ethnicity; clothe him or her and decide on economic status, job, and perhaps dreams; and sort out the love life, decide whether the character is emotional or rational, and so on, as well as whatever the problem is the character will face in the immediate action, along with the problem from the past that haunts him or her.

We don't spend much time on insignificant characters. It's enough for a general to be a general in *Schindler's List:* it's enough for the agents photographing license plates at the start of *The Godfather* to be nameless and no more than "suits" in action. By the same token, Tessio and Clemenza fill out their roles in Don Vito's family as the film develops but hardly add any new behaviors or details ranging from clothing to desire; only at the end with his betrayal does Tessio go toward a deeper shading or rounding out.

They are, in this sense, flat characters. The relation of flat characters to *typing* is clear: a Jewish or Italian mother-in-law is immediately recognizable as a type, and as long as suitable in appearance and behavior to her type is accepted by us without a second thought. Flat characters then, superficially described, left undeveloped or hardly developed in the story, have little potential for change and internal growth or, crucially, for volition. They are not needed in this way: instead, they populate the protagonist's world as essential elements of the milieu in which she or he moves.

A round character bulks more largely in our imagination because the action shows him or her to possess a variety a flat character cannot. This can be done swiftly, as with Don Vito's enforcer par excellence, Luca, at the wedding as *The Godfather* starts. His large and powerful appearance suits him. But, curiously, he's not lurking in the shadows or standing with others, inherently threatening; instead, he sits by himself and awkwardly rehearses a speech as he waits to see Don Vito. He is at once characterized as unable to speak well, a cliché, and as someone showing an unexpected vulnerability. That impression is carried through when he sees Don Vito and gives his halting speech conveying his devotion.

Later we see Luca prepare himself in his bare room to see the Tattaglias after the don asks him to gather information by pretending he wishes to leave the Corleones. Luca agreed without question: all he possesses in this world is his commitment to the don. He is not the bumbler he was at the wedding as he walks into the Tattaglias' bar, but almost suave as he carries out his charade, and full of menace, for he is not overawed by these men. When he hesitates, however, to accept their offer, his hand is nailed to the bar with a knife and he is vividly strangled. Brief though these appearances may be, Luca is a rounded character and more interesting by far than a faceless, clichéd presence who kills effortlessly. But none of these appearances add up to character growth: the action just shows what Luca is.

Johnny is another rounded character seen briefly in *The Godfather,* a Frank Sinatra knockoff who makes girls scream and appears the master of his fate in public, yet who weeps in private with the don over his inability to get a big part in a film, causing Don Vito to slap him and tell him to be a man. We hardly see him again, and then as the "star" who of course agrees to help Michael.

We can change films and think of some of the characters in *A Beautiful Mind*. Nash's "assistants" at MIT, former Princeton classmates, were just companion brilliant students at Princeton. They are consistently more conventional than Nash, followers, not leaders. Nash, not they, laments being included with others on a *Fortune* magazine cover before he strides into class in a T-shirt. They are flat characters, hardly better developed than the students in Nash's classroom, with the exception of the young woman he will marry. The typing is clear, and the way in which a few representative details achieve that result as well.

Rosen, the psychiatrist, is another matter. He doesn't grow or change in the film: important as he is, he is also secondary, always the psychiatrist, always a man with one goal, to do in terms of current practice what is necessary to make Nash well. We see him in different settings, however, primarily at the clinic but also in the Nash home after Nash's appalling electric shock treatment. He endures Nash's irrational outbursts, guides his treatment, and interacts with and counsels his wife: he is well rounded.

Two of Nash's figments are well rounded too. Charles we see as a roommate and friend, someone Nash continues to see off and on at MIT; he is in Rosen's office and witnesses Nash's humiliation, and later tries to deflect Nash from his decision to ignore his figments. Charles does not grow, and change is confined to showing different parts of what he is from the start, as is also true of Parcher. Parcher is always threatening, seductive at first, frightening later as Nash tries to emancipate himself from him also. The girl, however, is always the same, and flat.

One of the things we remark as characteristic of distinguished writing is the prevalence of round over flat characters, characters who are tellingly detailed and freshly imagined, even if they have little or no growth. One of the secrets of Shakespeare's appeal is this richness of characterization in high and low characters, so that even a Borachio in *Much Ado about Nothing* surprises us, after he is captured, as he confesses and shows regret. Lucas and Kasdan in *The Return of the Jedi* show this rounding very simply with the trainer of the monster Luke kills in Jabba's dungeon. The moment moves out of the cliché of the heroic encounter when the monster's trainer approaches the beast's body and weeps, giving the moment an unexpected and deeper emotional resonance. Rounding characters makes the action they are involved in matter more to us.

But Borachio brings out a key element of a round character: unlike one that is flat, a round character gives the sense of a *potential for will*. He or she is not a mere type, an automaton of writing always predictable. Tessio makes this clear at the end of *The Godfather*. Up to that moment he has been essentially flat, even as one of the don's key henchmen, but he is the one ready to betray Michael to Barzini in the End, and who is surprised and taken away for execution by Michael's men instead. We can't say he has grown in the sense of changed: it's still Tessio, still doing what he considers "business," who simply makes a bad decision. Yet by his action he becomes rounded, and in his case that rounding specifically involves a heretofore flat character suddenly displaying volition. But neither flat nor even the most developed round characters change in the sense of growing beyond and transforming our initial sense of them. That is the province of the *smart* and the *dumb*.

Hamlet and the *Dumb*

Change, meaning growth, is a constant in major characters and plot handling. That doesn't mean a character has to change into something new by the End: he may change continually in response to a story's challenges without becoming someone new, remaining a major character who has simply grown. Serial writing in television displays this feature: a series is a hit because of the situations it puts particular characters into that have caught our interest, not because those characters are transformed by the action. But series run into problems and fade because we become too familiar with the main characters while the initial inventiveness of the episodes inevitably falls off. They begin to seem merely rounded, become predictable, and end as types.

This kind of nontransformative but revelatory character growth is true also of much of our writing in film and drama more widely. It is the *dumb* way of handling character development in which growth shows as a continual deepening or revelation of a given character's nature and abilities without a commensurate transformation in kind. The single greatest character in dramatic literature is a good example of just this kind of development: Hamlet.

The point can be easily seen if we reflect on the extent to which Ted in *Kramer vs. Kramer* is transformed by the end of the film, or Nash in *A Beautiful Mind*: Hamlet stands in stark contrast, remarkably consistent throughout the story.

The young Nietzsche in *The Birth of Tragedy* largely gets it right.

... Dionysiac man might be said to resemble Hamlet: both have
looked deeply into the true nature of things, they have *understood*
and are now loath to act. They realize that no action of theirs
can work any change in the eternal condition of things, and they
regard the imputation as ludicrous or debasing that they should
set right the time which is out of joint. Understanding kills action,
for in order to act we require the veil of illusion; such is Hamlet's
doctrine, not to be confused with the cheap wisdom of John-a-
Dreams, who through too much reflection, as it were a surplus of
possibilities, never arrives at action.

and

The truth once seen, man is aware everywhere of the ghastly
absurdity of existence ... nausea invades him.[1]

Hamlet is caught up in grief before the start of the action, so much so
he is chided by Gertrude and Claudius: they've moved on into marriage
and governance. Hamlet can say nothing except that his grief is real, not
a matter of convenience: he is not trying to set himself apart artificially.
Left to himself, he mocks Claudius and reproaches his mother for remar-
rying so soon, but in the first of his famous soliloquies also berates himself, "Oh that this too too solid flesh would melt."[2]

If he literally melted he would be dead. This desire, with much of the
rest of the soliloquy, betrays his revulsion against life. We know what has
caused this revulsion: not so much the death of his *father,* as touched on
earlier, but the encounter with *death* that event involved. Since then, Hamlet gives us to understand with painful clarity, life has looked like a pointless show, like, in Nietzsche's words, a "ghastly absurdity."

That is immediately driven home by his meeting with his father's ghost,
who demands Hamlet exact vengeance on Claudius for killing him. Hamlet vows to do so, but does he rush off to do his father's bidding? No: instead he laments, "The time is out of joint. O cursed spite/that ever I was
born to set it right."[3] Why "cursed spite" if *his volition* has not been stunted
by his insight through death's impact of life's pointlessness? From such a
perspective, action is madness and those demanding it, mad.

Hamlet beguiles himself and baffles others with his famous "madness,"
particularly Polonius, as he defers action by looking for a way to prove

the ghost is right: the ghost might be a deception from hell. The plot does not falter from his indecision but pursues the subplots of Laertes, Ophelia, and Polonius, as well as their relation to Hamlet, and follows Claudius and Gertrude's efforts to use Hamlet's friends Rosencrantz and Guildenstern to spy on him. A key strand of action is sparked by Polonius's belief that Hamlet's problem is one of crazed love for Ophelia, commanded by her father to refuse him. In the midst of these concerns the players arrive, and suddenly Hamlet thinks he may have a way "to catch the conscience of the king," by putting on a play recapitulating his father's death.[4] But Hamlet does not immediately go into an ecstasy of anticipation: he is instead repelled by a player weeping over the merely imaginary woes of Hecuba while he has so much greater cause to act and weep.

That is deeply ironic, for Shakespeare and Freud both know we weep over the imaginary as readily as the real: they are different realms that are equally real in their impact on us.

Hamlet berates himself in another soliloquy, "Oh what a rogue and peasant slave am I,"[5] which brings out these points about his having waited and not acted, and in the next scene gives the great soliloquy "To be, or not to be—that is the question," where he makes clear he will neither remove himself nor act.[6] He destroys the idea he is lovelorn in his brutal confrontation with Ophelia, and then as the court gathers for the players' performance jokes with her how little time, meaning psychic time, has passed since his father's death.

That is how we learn *two months* have passed since the ghost summoned Hamlet to act. Despite the remarkable sense of flowing action in the play, *nothing actually has happened.* Hamlet has still to act, yet cannot given his perspective. If we needed further proof, although he exults over Claudius's guilty reaction to the performance, certain now the ghost is right, when Hamlet finds Claudius praying he does not kill him. Olivier got it wrong with Hamlet: the failure to kill isn't a result of Hamlet's reasoning himself out of the action because paralyzed with too many possibilities. Hamlet never acts at any point from *reason.* Instead, a reason is found to express, not cause, his inability to act. But Hamlet does kill when he sees his mother. He sees a motion behind her arras and thrusts with his sword, killing Polonius as he wonders if it's the king, although he's just left Claudius praying. He strikes in a moment of spontaneous rage before he even knows who is there. This spontaneous outburst is the only way he can act, and revelatory for that reason. Sometimes his confrontation with Ophelia is played as if he discovers they are being spied on, provoking a violent, verbal rage that makes the same point.

Now Hamlet reproaches his mother for *her actions* when, implicitly, *any* would have been wrong. In the midst of this the ghost appears to reproach him for *his* inactivity and counsel forbearance with his mother, driving home the paradoxes of his behavior.

Handling growth in a major character in this *dumb* manner drives a writer ever deeper into insight into the human nature embodied in that character, who must find this depth under the decisive pressure of immediate conflict. But within *dumb* development that character won't change in the sense of transform, only reveal with ever greater profundity the capacity of human nature. When a writer's ambition is smaller, *dumb* development turns into the revelation of an action heroine or hero's resourcefulness.

James Bond is betrayed, fails momentarily, and suffers to an unexpected degree in *Die Another Day,* but he still gets the women, has a telling quip for each turn of the action, and finds a way to succeed at the end. He too is a *dumb* character, as those around him know, certain he will behave in a way true to character whatever the events, only adapting his responses, not his character, to each event. Such a *dumb* character is nonetheless interesting in the better Bond films because of the practical resourcefulness and inventiveness the story demands a writer find for him. When we sense a Bond character more rooted in frailty yet as fully resourceful as ever, we are in for a better Bond film; when that is lacking, and the story less memorable, he is a character going through the motions, largely untouchable by emotion, distant, *cooked* in the problematic sense.

Hamlet's *dumb* growth isn't finished yet. Claudius exiles him with letters ordering his execution in England. As he leaves Hamlet observes Fortinbras leading an army to contest a stretch of land and mocks the illusory nature of military glory. He embarks for England, uses Claudius's letters to cause Rosencrantz and Guildenstern's execution, and returns to Denmark. Does he leap to confront Claudius after the king's attempt to kill him, start a conspiracy, rouse a popular revolt? No: he pauses at a grave to lament overtly the folly of life's shows, and shows a spontaneous if overwrought grief over the dead Ophelia, as if in some sort of contest with her brother, Laertes. Then he returns to Elsinore and waits.

It is Claudius who acts through Laertes, plotting the duel in which

Hamlet is killed by a poisoned blade. Only when the dying Laertes con-fesses, and Hamlet sees his mother die from a poisoned drink, does he act again in a sudden, spontaneous rage like when he killed Polonius. Horatio can tell his tale insofar as he understands it: "The rest is silence."[7] Fortin-bras takes over, his relation to action untouched by a sense of life's point-lessness, while we leave the theatre or cinema having looked into human nature to an unparalleled extent.

A search for "Hamlet" on the Internet brings 1,330,000 references: Gan-dhi, Lincoln, Lenin, Thomas Mann, Mother Theresa, Mao, De Gaulle, FDR, even Romeo (and Juliet) have fewer. Madonna and Superman have more, as do George Washington, Hitler, Marx, Einstein, and Freud (the latter by only a few thousand): yet in my cursory search, Shakespeare had twice as many as any of these, and only trailed Jesus. Not bad for a dra-matist and an imaginary character.

John Nash and the *Smart*

Now we can easily grasp a *smart* handling of character growth entails char-acter transformation rather than an ever deeper revelation of capacity.

John Nash in *A Beautiful Mind* arrives at Princeton brilliant, socially awkward, and inept with women. We meet Charles, never thinking he is a schizophrenic projection, who seems a good deal more "one of the boys" than the hopelessly introverted Nash. Nash's tutor tells him his work is un-distinguished as he moves into the room where a professor is being hon-ored for a Nobel nomination: stung, Nash struggles for an original insight ever more desperately, at one point heaving his desk out the window in frustration. Finally he has a breakthrough that is triggered by an adroit linking of his private and professional life in the bar scene. He modifies Adam Smith's enlightened self-interest as the alpha and omega of human motivation into a more cooperative version of self-interest, whereby all in the bar could "get a girl" by ignoring the one blonde they all desire and going for her companions instead. This is the beginning of his *Governing Dynamics*, which now stuns his professor and wins a coveted prize and position at Wheeler Labs at MIT.

Up to this point Nash's growth has been handled in a *dumb* way: Nash has simply been driven to reveal his existing nature under the pressure of events, like Hamlet existentially or a Bond type of action hero in an ac-tion-adventure film. But when we see Nash five years later as a successful professor called to the Pentagon to break a code, he is well tailored and supremely self-confident, transformed by success from the awkward student at Princeton. He has become a *smart* character. This is only the beginning of the transformations he will go through. He is fascinating now to others: the same line that got him a slap as a student gets him the young woman who marries him. William Parcher recruits him for top-secret government work. We don't know that Parcher or the little girl we have met before are also schizophrenic projections.

But we begin to suspect all is not what it seems as Nash sinks into paranoid fear and withdraws from his wife under the pressure of doing Parcher's work, who turns threatening and won't let him give it up. Nash becomes driven and desperate, another transformation. Worse, *because we experience the action from his perspective, we have become part of his madness* in a way Hamlet never lets us share with him, for Hamlet is not mad. We suspect government agents of some sort pursue Nash as he flees from a lecture, not aides to a psychiatrist.

Suddenly our point of view swings 180 degrees: Nash is not brilliant, not an admired professor and mathematician but a paranoid schizophrenic who finally submits himself to electric shock therapy in an attempt at a cure. It is a major Reverse like the kind Oedipus suffers when he discovers he has not avoided his fate of killing his father and marrying his mother but brought it about with every step he took in flight.

We are not done. Nash is next a recovering figure, living simply with his wife and child, trying to resume work but inhibited by the treatment and medication. He relapses and almost loses his wife after having begged her not to have him taken back to the asylum, protesting he can work this out. He stops her flight in the rain with his realization his figments never change, so they can't be real. It's yet another change in Nash, from a false recovery to the beginning of a true one.

Why the lack of change in Nash's figments is crucial to his understanding their lack of reality is fundamental to understanding him and *storytelling*. The simplest way to get to this is by reminding ourselves of Aristotle's definition of drama as the "imitation of an action." Human beings do not live in set, finished time: life is a process, a becoming, *an activity* that drama lets us bring to a point. Freud points out the folly of hoping happiness will overcome suffering: happiness is an emotion in transit, a reaction to an experience caught up in the flow of time. We cannot remain happy: ecstasy cannot endure unchanged. We move on to some-thing else. Hamlet's tragedy is expressed precisely by his inability to move on from the impact of his father's death which has made him *dumb*. He is frozen in time, which only an active drama of peculiar genius is able to make vivid. Blanche in *A Streetcar Named Desire* struggles to move on to a new life with Mitch: when he and Stanley deny her, tragedy ensues, freezing her in a *dumb* relation to how she has become since the death of her love, fixing her in time.

What is fixed in time is over and, worse than dead, no longer real, for growing out of our most basic sense of ourselves, despite the sensed con-tinuity of our "I," is this sense of change in living through time, and what to make out of change as we age and see life-as-becoming ever more profoundly. Changelessness *is unreality,* like the little girl, Charles, and Parcher of *A Beautiful Mind.* The less volition a character has, the more unchanging, the greater the loss of the sense of his reality to us in writ-ing as well as life. Hamlet does not feel remotely real to himself but is caught in the limbo between desire and fear, revealed in his "To be or not to be" soliloquy. The *dumb* development of growth, at its profound-est, taps into this underlying sensibility in us; the *smart* is always more comfortable. How ironic that on the surface *dumb* characters like Bond are so pleasing.

Finally, Nash goes through his last transformation at Princeton, from an eccentric to a man embedded in the living flow of time now instructing the young, crowned with a Nobel award that is honored in the same pen ceremony we witnessed near the beginning of the film. Noteworthily, it is Eros that Nash lauds in his acceptance speech, the love of his wife that made it possible for him to find himself. Thanatos destroys.

Thanatos makes dumb.

In a sense, a happy ending is *always* a transparent Eros triumph, for it is the procreative urge made manifest in life triumphing and moving forward into the New Beginning of the fundamental story pattern. This, however, is true of all drama, even tragedy, as we saw even there how some community triumphs. Films where Thanatos triumphs are, as we saw in *Breaking the Waves, heavy.*

In sum, *smart* characters *redefine* themselves or grow consistently in the cause and effect, necessary and probable development of dramatic ac-tion. *Dumb* characters only *reveal* their unchanging character ever more deeply. Types are by definition *dumb*; a type who changes becomes *smart* and is no longer a type. *Smart* or *dumb* characters will be rounded: they cannot be flat.

Plot-Handling Implications

Typically, the action of a screenplay begins in a *dumb* fashion. The action we see in the Beginning reveals situation, conflict, and character, but the hero and heroine at that point are locked in misconception and responses that are revelatory, not transformative. In *Witness* Book is predictable until he discovers that Captain Schaeffer is a criminal and realizes he cannot be sure about anything, instead of being certain about everything. He is, too, ultimately a *dumb* character, revealed definitively as such when he replies to Eli's assertion that violence is not the Amish way by insisting it is *his* way as he confronts the tourist smearing ice cream on the others. Up to this point he has flirted with the Amish lifestyle, deeply attracted by Rachel: to fit in would transform him into a *smart* character. His response to Eli reveals him untransformed, if with a depth of self-awareness previously lacking.

The same *dumb* development is apparent with Terry in *On the Waterfront*. All Terry does only shows the nature of his existing relationship to Johnny Friendly *and himself*. He stays that way until he finally responds to Edie's plea for help, first intervening to let Father Barry be heard in the hold as he speaks over Dugan's body, then definitively as he takes Edie into his arms. He has becomes a *smart* character as he confesses to Father Barry and her.

Both *Star Wars* and *Blue* seem to start off with major changes: Princess Leia is captured, and the robots flee; Julie lives through an accident that kills her husband and daughter. But as we follow Julie in the hospital, at first she is handled in a *dumb* way: i.e., she is grief-stricken, suicidal, withdrawn. Although she cannot kill herself, she does the next best thing: withdraw from life. Thereafter the action systematically challenges her, once she explains to the woman with the petition against the prostitute, Lucille, that she does not want to get involved, until Olivier finally forces her to make a choice. She is transformed into a *smart* character as she chooses to live, love, and compose (create), just as Mathilda transforms Léon in *The Professional*.

Luke, in *Star Wars,* is similarly handled in a *dumb* way at first. Neither the robots, the appearance of Leia in a projection from R2-D2, nor
the meeting with Obi-Wan does more than bring out the existing nature
of his character. But once he finds his uncle and aunt charred by stormtroopers and decides to help Obi-Wan, he sets off on a pattern of *smart*
development.

This, I repeat, is not to imply a preference for handling character growth
in either a *smart* or *dumb* way: both, as we have seen, are equally valid,
common, and popular. But it does show that in *plot handling*, in the initial
stage of the action, both the situation and main character(s) are handled
in a *dumb* manner, despite appearances to the contrary. That bespeaks the
reality that far from living with volition, the main characters are caught
up in a false modus vivendi with past problems, preventing the present
from having, paradoxically, any real *nowness*. That present, seeming so
immediate while actually a continuance of the past, is necessarily *dumb*
and cannot change until volition is (re)gained and the failed choices of
the past revealed and rejected.

In Hamlet in *Hamlet* we see how plot and character development diverge in screenplays where the main character is *dumb*. The plot shows
constant change and transformation, as does a *smart* character. But that
same transformative nature of a developing plot drives a *dumb* character to find ever deeper expressions of his nature. Both *smart* and *dumb*
characters show volition too, even if in the profoundest example, as with
Hamlet, that volition is expressed in a refusal to act. In different ways both
kinds of characters bring us to drama's successful *climax* and resolution.

Yet that raises profound questions about the real nature of the dramatic
journey of heroines and heroes and of the experience their action takes
us on, irrespective of the seemingly all-important nature of the specific
story within which we find each. I sometimes wonder if beyond the obvious the specific dramatic story we call "the film" matters at all. But before I take up the ultimate nature of dramatic experience, we need to have
the nature of the comic experience in hand too.

PART III

The Lost Poetics of Comedy

CHAPTER 7

The Lost Poetics of Comedy

The Comic Universe

No one knows what Aristotle's lost chapters on comedy contained, so I am free to imagine what such a basic analysis of the essential nature of comedy might be. It will not be one of the plethora of comedy-writing "how-to's" but instead refer to what comedy is in itself, and how and why its viewpoint is necessarily so at odds with that of tragedy and serious drama generally. Typical comic techniques can be left to a review like *A Poetics for Screenwriters*, where mistaken identity, reductio ad absurdum, physical humor, misuse of language, witty dialogue, and irony all get their due.[1]

The comedic universe is so dissimilar to the serious that writers tend to excel in one or the other. Crossovers happen but are not the commonplace: Shaw could never entirely leave the comic universe behind, if only in his cerebral and witty dialogue in plays like *Saint Joan* and *Heartbreak House*. He never uncorked a tragedy on a par with those of Shakespeare, who, however, is as famous for his comedies as his tragedies which constantly appear in screen adaptations. Laughter is not what springs to mind when we think of Ibsen or Strindberg, any more than of O'Neill, Williams, Miller, or Albee, let alone most of the outstanding modern dramatists of other countries.

Bergman may have written *Smiles of a Summer Night,* but we hardly think of him as amusing, while we don't approach the screenplays Capra or Wilder directed in the same way as Bergman or Antonioni's screenplays. Hitchcock brought a powerful sense of the comic and absurd to the screenplays he directed, yet they are not comedies, however mordant or witty. The divide between the two ways of seeing reality is profound.

Paradoxically, we expect comic elements to exist within serious drama, a taste rooted in the deliberate mix of Elizabethan theatre at the root of our own sense of dramatic reality. That theatre's combination of native romance, popular farce, and university drama embodying the Renaissance attempt to revive tragedy with the nature of the Elizabethan stage and the short temper of the groundlings created the flowing, variegated style re-embodied in screenplays that we take so much for granted. *Witness* may be serious, but Book is forced to pause with his mouth full of food as Rachel and Samuel say grace in a fast food outlet. Later, the Amish clothes Rachel gives Book to wear are too short: the effect is ludicrous. *On the Waterfront* is unusual in its lack of humorous elements, but they are certainly present in *The Godfather,* whether as Luca stumbles over his speech or Sonny makes love upstairs at the marriage party while Hagen listens at the door and smiles at the woman's ecstatic moans.

Umberto Eco in *The Name of the Rose* imagines the rediscovery of Aristotle's lost work on comedy in a medieval monastery wracked by murders. A faction of the monks dreads the release of those chapters into common knowledge and kills to prevent that happening; in an apocalyptic ending, the library is burned down, Aristotle's work on comedy once again lost, the murders resolved, and the murderer incinerated. Why go to such lengths to block the dissemination of a treatise on comedy? The monks dread the subversive character of laughter, *of people being taught to laugh* instead of, say, to worship: of the danger that *laughter will make the serious* absurd, which is, indeed, the essence of the comic angle of vision. That perspective goes a long way toward explaining why crossover writers are so unusual, and so honored when they appear: they are the true masters of reality in all its facets.

Aristotle devotes very little comment to comedy in the existing *Poetics,* the heart of which is:

> Comedy is, as we have said, an imitation of characters of a lower type—the Ludicrous being merely a subdivision of the ugly.
> It consists in some defect or ugliness which is not painful or destructive. To take an obvious example, the comic mask is ugly and distorted, but does not imply pain.[2]

Book in *Witness* in his too-short Amish trousers is an excellent example of a "defect" making a character ludicrous, though there it is a matter of costuming. The defect is certainly not painful or destructive. On the other hand, Book is certainly not a character of a lower type, an object of derision and farce, like Dogberry and his fellow constables in *Much Ado about*

Nothing, so tellingly adapted into film by Branagh, or like Paul's thugs in *Analyze This.* Nor is a defect inherently comic: serious, let alone tragic characters often suffer from a flaw, like Sonny's unmanageable temper in *The Godfather* or Oedipus's in *Oedipus Rex.* It is the *comic angle of vision* where laughter replaces tears that separates the serious from comic writer and determines whether a story is developed in which inevitably flawed characters are funny or not.

That the ludicrous might have a philosophical element, a perception of the absurdity of experience, is also absent from what we have of Aristotle, as well as the perception of the subversive possibility of laughter. *Tootsie* may have farcical elements and be out to make us laugh, yet it also contains an assault on our easy separation of masculine and feminine. Ted is more successful as Tootsie than as a man without any implication that he is not masculine. Political comedy takes this a step farther as Billie in *Born Yesterday* recites the Bill of Rights to the tune of "A Partridge in a Pear Tree."

Finally, we may agree that the comic mask may not imply pain but must ask, *pain for whom*? Certainly comic figures routinely feel all the emotions felt by the noncomedic, whether we consider Charlie in *Roxanne* as he pours out his love in letters credited to another, or the duel in *Smiles of a Summer Night,* or Benedick in *Much Ado about Nothing* who is so deeply wounded by Beatrice's sharp tongue he wants to flee. In *Analyze This* Paul at one point is reduced to deep, near-fatal grief.

But do *we* always feel their pain? Sometimes, we answer; at other times we simply laugh at the characters in proportion to their suffering. These are the two main directions of comic story development, covered below in "The Two Roads": flirting with tragedy, and farce. The *heavy* as an experience for *ourselves* seems ruled out by the nature of comedy: what could be less comedic than a willed descent into the experience of destructiveness for its own sake through a hero or heroine? Freud offers little insight into the comedic world, it seems: nothing in his views contributes to a sense that humor is the order of the day in the psychoanalytic universe. His early work on slips in *The Psychopathology of Everyday Life* is at pains to show how these betray underlying psychic, often neurotic, conflict.

So we must answer the question of what it is that makes suffering funny, if we want to understand the comic angle of vision, remembering we undergo that laughing experience in the realm of the imagination.

Winnicott and Play

The insights of the British psychoanalyst D. W. Winnicott, 1896–1971, provide some invaluable tools for understanding this problem and even more so for the later consideration of the true nature of dramatic action. Winnicott imagined himself Freud's true successor, and the very sweep of his thought has slowed its progress in the psychoanalytic field and beyond. Play and creativity are central to his thinking, together with an entirely original way of considering destructiveness that liberates it from Freud's dichotomy of Eros and Thanatos. Winnicott establishes the idea of a third reality in defiance of the dualistic "me vs. not me" at the center of the argument our culture is having with itself. His work is only starting to come into its own now.

He calls the third reality in the "me vs. not me" universe we think we live in the *transitional space,* and rewrites our dualism into: "me–transitional space–not me." At one point he uses Kantian terminology, talking of the "thing in itself," although he does not consciously elaborate a philosophical position in contrast to Kant's.[3] But that is implicit in his work which offers a fresh way of viewing experience.

Winnicott labors to separate his views from those of Melanie Klein, who bridges the gap between the late Freud and Winnicott.[4] She developed Freud's Thanatos into a clinical death instinct and set in motion a "Kleinian" belief system espoused by Kleinian analysts who often behave with evangelical fervor. For Klein the newborn is immediately subject to primal fantasy without any perception of a reality separate from the self in a state of primary Freudian infantile omniscience. In that state an infant splits good experiences from bad, which are then experienced as persecutory elements. Infantile rage is experienced as attacking and destroying even good objects when desire is thwarted, leading to further splitting, repression, and guilt. I use the term "object(s)" because it is standard psychoanalytic language for whole or part *persons,* remarkably dehumanizing in so human a science.

These terrible infantile transports go on regardless of the environment, of how a mother or father acts: there is only the infantile realm, the infantile self, the infant's imagination, in Klein's view. Klein moves beyond the Freudian perception that the power of guilt results from the repression of aggressiveness from within or without and ultimately from our inherent ambivalence. In Klein the *external is guiltless*. It's an odd view for a woman to develop who experienced a markedly unhappy childhood. In fact, this view of a guiltless environment in which all faults stem from infantile fantasy, a kind a psychoanalytic version of original sin, provoked her daughter, also an analyst, to denounce Klein in a public psychoanalytic meeting for attempting to put these ideas into her as an invasive, inhibiting act that evaded self-responsibility.

All this accumulating destructiveness for which the infant is wholly responsible happens in the first six months and is given a suitably Kleinian name: the paranoid-schizoid position. For the next year and a half an infant enters the depressive position, marked by reparative efforts to one's objects. The imaginary nature of the infant's destructiveness does nothing to diminish its impact: as we have seen, psychoanalysis has known from its start that the imaginary can make us ill, just as at his end Freud saw in *Constructions in Analysis* it can make us well.

It's worth pausing here to remind ourselves again *the imagined isn't unreal: it is just a different order of reality.* Just as a play may not be real in a way a car is, or our own immediate anger or laughter, a play *is real* in a way that a car *is not.*

For Klein the infant's primal rage demonstrates the presence of a death instinct. That is manifested in self-destructiveness as well as the destruction of the infant's objects. This divorce of the death instinct from environmental features amounts to a view of extreme solipsism, one that is always a peril for psychoanalytic theory, let alone psychology more generally, both of which reflect our underlying conception of reality: there is a knowable "me" at the center of "my" experience, but an ultimately unknowable "you," a "not me" that equals the environment, beyond. It is a culturally and personally unhealthy view.

This brings us to the radical nature of Winnicott's thought, which redefines our way of thinking about the nature of experience itself and so encounters the considerable resistance in understanding and acceptance such ideas generate. The power of Hume's vision of the role of habit in human affairs is not diminished by time or limited to trivia, but applies to the intellect and its fashions as well: however uncomfortable we may be with our way of viewing things, it is our way and changing it is more of a wrench than many can bear.

Winnicott reacts against Klein's extreme rethinking of psychoanalysis and statement of dualism decisively by insisting that the environment is as important as the psyche in development and becomes part of internal structure. An infant doesn't have enough of a self to pursue the organized mayhem, destructive and schizoid, imagined by Klein. Primal fantasy is a feature of human beings, and primal rage, and the Freudian state of infantile omniscience, but there is also usually a "good enough mother," who at first conspires to maintain an infant's omniscience by meeting its every need, as she must at the start of life, and then progressively begins to fail that omniscience in order to wean the infant as mental structures slowly make their appearance. At the moment that the weaning process begins, the infant starts to establish external object relations, and often makes use of a "transitional object" whose use is not challenged or questioned—like a blanket, a special toy, or a pacifier—to ease its transition.

The transitional object is at once imagined by the infant and supported by the mother: it stands in Winnicott's view as a substitute for the mother who is progressively withdrawing herself to facilitate the infant's adaptation to external reality. *The transitional object reflects a loss of omniscience and denies that loss at the same time.* It is at once the first symbol and first external object that is also not wholly external because of its meaning. Here Winnicott takes a decisive plunge: the transitional object is in another sense a doorway into a *third area of experiencing,* being at once the unseparated mother *and* her absence.

Thus the Winnicottian facilitating environment of the mother at first abets her infant's omniscience out of a sense of its need, then progressively thwarts that omniscience through weaning so external reality can be reached as mental capacity develops. That opens the way to the development of a "transitional space" which continues to have this simultaneous quality of being and not being what it is, of being "me" *and* "not me" simultaneously.

The transitional object and the transitional space it opens experience to bring us to play, for the transitional object is clearly a play object too.

Play arises from the infant being able to use a transitional object in the mother's absence, trusting she will return; in other words, to play with her in her absence, which then grows into being able to play with the mother in her presence now perceived as a fact of external reality. From there, as we mature, play *grows into the world of shared experience.* That world of experience is not mysterious but where we live most of the time, whether seeing a film or working with others in a scientific laboratory, whether we are involved in a game of golf, playing with our children, or enacting a role that others in an audience identify with and enjoy. It is not *all* of experience: there is still the world of just "me" and the world that is only yours, "not me," *also.*

Play and creativity are inseparable: play is the primary form of creativity. Winnicott spoke of the need for psychoanalysis to familiarize itself with Jungian thought, in which, among other things, creativity is treated as a "complex" on a par with any other basic mental complex, like the Freudian libido, and not reducible to something else. Winnicott has found a scientific, psychoanalytic language for this primary importance of creativity.

As we mature more specialized areas begin to emerge in our creative play. In the Winnicottian view *creativity is the fundamental characteristic of a healthy person,* whether in arranging a bouquet, setting a table, or writing a poem. It is not some special preserve of artists but characterizes a key, common component of our psyches. Such a healthy person is able to engage with internal and external reality in a fluid, progressive way, for reality for Winnicott, as for Aristotle, is an experience of flow, of *becoming.* It is not set. Moreover, it is through play that we experience our whole personality and find ourself, for the behavior of the environment in which we live is part of our development and sense of self, and we experience the environment and ourself simultaneously in the transitional space.

In fact, at the mature level the transitional space finally makes sense out of the difficulties Freud runs into when he speaks of the cultural superego. How the private and cultural could echo one another, encounter one another, and in what medium, is answered by Winnicott. That encounter is in the transitional space, which is the space of our *and others' experience,* where we join together in activity, which as adults we call culture. For Winnicott we live in a cultural space, where the "me" and "not me" join as elements of one another. Freud lacked the language and, implicitly, the philosophical ground that would have allowed him to see this.[5]

If, however, we are compliant with *others'* expectations in this realm of experience, then we exhibit a false self: if we express our true self, which can only be expressed in creative interaction in this third area, the area of experience, then we are in a state of health. The self, however, is not simply this interactive reality: the true self, in itself, is secretive and not shared. We can only be in accord with it through our experience, or act against it by complying entirely with others' expectations in the realm of experience, the "third area" in which we primarily live, Winnicott's transitional space.

When we treat a character as flat, let alone as a type, and when we first encounter the protagonist in a *dumb* relation to his or her experience, then we are not in a state of ill health but one of *limited humanity.* If it endures, then ill health is the right way to label such experience because, among other things, it indicates a compliance with others' views of our nature instead of expressing our true self. Terry is in a bad way *because* he conforms to Johnny Friendly and Charley's expectations: Edie arouses in him a painful desire to act in accordance with his true self. But that can only be found through exploring in concert with others the choices open to him, a Winnicottian form of play, meaning experience, in which Terry begins to react creatively to his circumstances rather than being bound by them. In drama we don't dismiss "types" as neurotic, but neither do we accord them the fullness of our response: we do not feel ourselves fully echoed there. Identity in all its forms bespeaks a sense of consonance of ourselves to another: we may recognize types as representing human possibility, but only in the sense of being reduced to one of its aspects.

Psychoanalytic experience itself, however scientific its aims and researches, is in this sense an example of play for Winnicott, as would be any other *shared,* defined activity. And when we play, we play, if you will, one game at a time: play is defining, though we are capable of playing in many ways. If patient and analyst, we are not consumer and producer, teacher and student, doctor and nurse, or cowboy and Indian, regardless of what aspects of these other ways of playing may spill over. When, in *Unbearable Lightness,* we move abruptly from a personal, romantic conflict to political, we are disjointed because the nature of the reality we have been relating to and "playing along with" as audience has changed. We can no more substitute one kind of playing in the midst of another than the conscious mind can tolerate two stories being told *simultaneously*; however, we may realize later the story we have watched is not the one we thought it was, as in *The Usual Suspects.* This is just another instance of the profound way dramatic structure is rooted in psychic structure.

Even more interesting than these aspects of Winnicott is his work on destructiveness. Play in its creative variety is not a sublimation of the libido, as Freud would have it, or of the destructive impulse; in fact, to the extent libido, or aggression, desire, or destructiveness, erupts into our creative activity, it destroys play. To play presumes instinct is controlled and does not overwhelm our creative response to experience. Yet what are we to make of the destructiveness the late Freud and then Klein elevated into Thanatos and an instinct toward death? Both Klein and Freud, in his *Civilization and Its Discontents,* speak to the terrible force of our destructive impulses, as if the lamentable sagas of our history are not sufficient to remind us in themselves. If such destructiveness is a fact of life, then what role does it play in a view where the creative response to experience is synonymous with health?

Winnicott understands the paradox so rampant in Nietzsche's view of the Dionysian in *The Birth of Tragedy.* There as the Dionysian impulse sweeps away, which means destroys, some stultifying Apollonian, rational, ordered response to reality, it simultaneously makes possible a renewed, fresh reaction to experience and thereby restores creative possibility to living. Is it, then, destructive?

For Winnicott, destructiveness creates reality.

Destructiveness is an unquestioned feature of primal fantasy and adult nature. Psychoanalysis is at one within its warring sects on this, and goes on to point out that primal destructiveness continues unabated in the unconscious after we have matured, quite aside from its endless manifestations in behavior. If, indeed, our destructiveness *was as effective as we fantasize or imagine,* the human race would not now exist. It's hard to see how such a passion for destructiveness could have developed as a feature of successful evolution. But our *destructive urge is not effective,* particularly as infants, usually as adults, for all the strength with which we may feel or vent our destructive urges. It is the ability of our "objects" *to survive our destructive impulses* that separates them from ourselves and which creates a "me vs. not me" universe and which simultaneously *makes them available for our use:* that use creates a "me–transitional/cultural/experiential–not me" universe. Is destructiveness, then, destructiveness or creativity? It's hard to see how we can ever answer, *apart from its actual results,* and those often have a paradoxical meaning. If this somehow lightens the implications of destructiveness, then it darkens the implications of creativity.

This dual nature of destructiveness is one of those insights at once so strange and so familiar we can't help but say, Aha! How odd—but of course! That dual nature of destructiveness is an omnipresent feature of screen and dramatic writing generally.

Consider Kieslowski and Piesiewicz's *Blue.* Julie loses her family, as we have seen, and proves unable to commit suicide. Instead, once out of the hospital, she puts her home up for sale and moves into the city. There she attempts to live withdrawn from involvement with others. *Now* Antoine, the boy who witnessed the initial accident, shows up with her daughter's cross. Life isn't going to ignore Julie. She makes an attempt to destroy her husband's manuscripts, but even a flautist on the street plays one of his tunes. A mouse shows up with a litter of young: Julie must borrow a cat. Olivier, the lover she thought she had put behind her, tracks her down. She becomes involved with Lucille, one night even answering her call for help, where she accidentally discovers Olivier is going to finish a key composition of her husband's by witnessing an interview on television at Lucille's dive. Olivier deliberately shows pictures in the interview as if they are of Julie but which are actually of a mistress Julie knew nothing about. When she confronts Olivier in a rage and asserts he has no right to pursue her or her husband's music, he is unrepentant: he will do whatever it takes to force Julie fully back to life.

In other words, the direction of action taken at the end of the Beginning by the heroine to solve the problems that have emerged *repeatedly suffers a destructive assault* in Act 2, failing or approaching failure in the *crisis.* That resolve, then, undergoes a climactic reformulation into *a solution that can succeed,* the true resolution of the conflict.

We see a profound twist given this process in *Schindler's List,* where Schindler's effort to war-profiteer at the expense of Jews turns steadily into an effort to save Jews until, at the *crisis,* he discovers he is willing to use his ill-gotten money to save lives. His initial effort to solve the problem caused by Amon Goeth's liquidation of the ghetto at the end of Act 1 *for himself* collapses under testing, to be replaced by a profounder goal/effort *that does succeed.* Schindler saves *his* Jews.

This testing by attempting to destroy continues in Act 3, notably as Terry in *On the Waterfront* fails to unseat Friendly by testifying in court. He is ostracized, and Edie wants to flee. But Terry goes down to the docks to get his rights and finally overcomes Johnny Friendly. Those attempts to solve his problems that were inadequate *succumb to destruction:* only his final action is right, because that is the one that *survives destruction,* hard as Friendly tries to win climactically.

In comedy, this process of testing is funny: in serious drama, the reverse. Nothing, for example, is more typical of romantic comedy than for the romantic relationship to be subjected to increasing pressure until reaching the *crisis,* meaning a way must be found to put the romance on an enduring footing or *it will not survive but be destroyed.* It will fade from reality. What survives such testing, however, is real, created as an ongoing fact of experience by that "testing." The ritualized labors given Ferdinand in *The Tempest* are a reflection of this process: if he fails them, gaining Miranda will become far more difficult; their purpose is to prove his love, and *he must not fail*—i.e., his resolve must not be destroyed—if that love is to be shown as *real.* Reality and survival are synonyms in drama and reached through the creative process of storytelling.

The Two Roads

Now we can move closer to understanding comedy.

I start with the simple question: Is the denunciation of Hero by Claudio in *Much Ado about Nothing,* so vividly filmed in Branagh's adaptation, to be taken seriously? We know the truth already, which has been found out in the subplot: Hero is innocent of Claudio's charges. Claudio and the others have been set up by Don John. *But they do not know this.*

Except for that we could see the outburst as ludicrous, or as overwrought as Laertes and Hamlet contesting their grief in Ophelia's grave, or as Paul's various sobbing fits in *Analyze This.* All such outbursts are inherently overwrought: worse, derangement and jealousy border on the *heavy,* which we get more than a whiff of as Claudio pours it on the innocent Hero and Leonato considers taking his daughter's life. For if Hero's infidelity is true, which as far as Claudio and the others know is the case, then Claudio's emotion is dramatically justified.

Tragedies can turn on accident, like *Romeo and Juliet,* and mistaken judgments, like *Ran;* what is to prevent something of a similar kind happening here? Suddenly we are outside the comedic realm that seemed to govern the story to this point and have a tantalizing sense of the awfulness that can characterize reality, *so absent from the preceding action.* Tragedy denies the comic vision altogether.

Crucially, as audience, we feel at this moment, as we always do in a comedy of this kind, that we don't want or expect the denial of the comic vision to succeed. First, and not least, and deeply rooted in the nature of "play," we want the story—literally, the "*play*" or "screen*play*"—to stay consistent. If a writer hasn't prepared us for a drama turning serious as part of the reality a screenplay defines from the start, abruptly changing gears from comic to serious destroys credibility. A reality which we expect to turn serious, however, will not involve us in the comic angle of vision. In *Much Ado about Nothing* we know we're within the comic realm and neither want nor expect what we take to be reality with its dreadful possibilities to become the reality of the screenplay, and that's the point.

That irruption of the possibility of tragedy into the comic action makes us feel *our wish to deny reality.* Reality is, in fact, undeniable outside the realm of a given comic screenplay. That wish, of course, is not just unrealistic but *illogical:* the comic, the *cooked* may exist, but so does the *raw,* and it cannot be gainsaid.

That flirting with the tragic in *Much Ado about Nothing* brings us to the realization that the preceding comic action has been *absurd,* not lower than average as Aristotle would have it, but *ludicrous* in relation to the *serious nature of true reality.*

Swiftly the comedy returns in *Much Ado about Nothing.* Don John is exposed and Hero's innocence established. Claudio, as penance for a Hero he is told died of grief, marries another girl of Leonato's choosing, only to discover this is his Hero. Beatrice and Benedick, having been tricked into becoming lovers, decide to get married, nonetheless, when they discover each has been trying to write love poetry for the other, if not very well. Before the ceremonies are carried out, they all break into a celebratory dance that spreads over Leonato's estate, driving home just how illusory is such a line of happy, funny development.

Playing as dancing literally engulfs their behavior in *Much Ado about Nothing.* At the same time, by pursuing this vein of comedy with its *flirtation with tragedy,* we have a pure *cooked* handling of emotion that in this case is also Apollonian: the drama is experienced as a *known dream, perceived as illusion,* and all the more convincing thereby. What makes the action feel *cooked* here? The displacement of tragic passion into comic absurdity.

Yet this flirtation with tragedy brings about our simultaneous self-awareness of its possibility and an intense pleasure in its denial, however illusory. For we are caught up in our *will to believe,* laid bare by the fact that we will believe an act of the imagination like a screenplay only so long as it is consistent with and develops coherently from its initial establishment of dramatic reality, its rules of play for the imagination. Allied to the will to believe, then, is our sense of story elaboration, the *mythopoetic instinct* that organizes experience into coherent, consistent wholes for their fun and/or ability to illumine and make it possible for us to grasp our experience. The mythopoetic instinct grows from and expresses our ability to play. We do not, after all, even as infants once the experience of the environment as a "me vs. not me" fact begins, ever play without an attempt to make experience coherent. But we elaborate only one story at a time.

This flirting with tragedy is a kind of comedy capable of great and revealing poignancy; when it succeeds it brings us to a wise but humorous and tolerant view of our limits, as Benedick does at the end when he speaks of man as a "giddy" thing.

Farce, however, develops the comic story in a different manner and brings us far closer to realizing the radical nature of the comic vision.

Farce, too, contains apparently tragic elements; sometimes these provide needed pacing between bouts of laughter as a fillip of sobriety so we can catch our breath, or appear in the moment of the *crisis,* which is always predicated on the notion of failure and consequently flirts with a more serious reality, even with the *raw* and *heavy.*

Consider the *crisis* in *Analyze This.* Paul is convinced Ben must be killed, fearing rightly that he is working for the feds. But Ben begins to discover key elements about the past he has been trying to help Paul recover from as they meet in the restaurant where Paul's father was killed years ago, and goes to the bathroom to remove the wires letting the feds overhear them. When Paul rips Ben's shirt open, he is clean: nonetheless Paul takes him to the river and threatens to shoot him.

Ben asks him a "last question" which leads to Paul recalling the memory, so far repressed, of his father's death. We discover Paul saw his father's assassins and realized what was going to happen, but did nothing. "I should've said something," he admits to Ben now, beginning to sob: "I let him die." The remorse that had been repressed and has been progressively disabling him is out at last. "I'm sorry," he says, and breaks down into helpless sobbing.

Taken out of context, we could be in the midst of a very serious film at an equally serious moment. Yet we know several things: Paul has been tracked to the river by enemies. The feds, in a detail of pure farce, listening to repeated toilets flushing, finally sent someone into the men's room and discovered Ben's discarded wires. We are not in a tragic frame of reference, nor do we experience this moment in *Analyze This* as we do Claudio's denunciation of Hero in *Much Ado about Nothing*. We never believe Ben is going to be shot, and Paul Vitti's grief seems ludicrous *to us*, however tragic to *him*. We're waiting instead for a comic topper, which follows immediately on Paul's breakdown.

The pursuing enemies arrive and begin shooting. Ben gets Paul to cover, and implores him to shoot: he's released his repressed memory, he's cured, it's time to blow away some thugs. When Paul can't stop sobbing, which is even more ludicrous now, Ben grabs his gun and begins shooting in his stead. The thugs are killed. Ben discovers he didn't hit anyone, but shot the refrigerator.

A topper has been found, tragedy has not irrupted into the story at all but been made absurd in context, and the will to believe and mythopoetic instinct been satisfied by fully realizing the improbability of the moment, *which is what is necessary and probable here.*

Or take *The Importance of Being Earnest* in its recent film version. Jack Worthing is leading a double life, a responsible country gentleman with his attractive ward, Cecily, in the country and a life in the city as a playboy named Ernest. He explains his departures for the city as a need to see his brother, Ernest, who of course is him. However, as the action begins he decides to put his affairs in order, get rid of "Ernest," and propose to Gwendolyn. She accepts him but informs him she is destined to love a man called Ernest: someone called Jack would be unacceptable. Jack's quandary has only started. Lady Bracknell, Gwendolyn's mother, interviews and rejects him as unsuitable because he does not know who his parents were: Jack/Ernest was found in a satchel. He is criticized for his carelessness in misplacing them and advised to find some relations.

One turn follows another until the climactic confrontation between Jack, who is prepared to change his name to Ernest, Lady Bracknell, Gwendolyn, Cecily, and Algy, his friend and nephew of Lady Bracknell who has pretended to be Jack's "brother," Ernest, to win Cecily. A past has been found for Jack which makes Algy a relation, an older brother; all turns on how Jack was actually christened. On review of the military records of his father, Jack exclaims he was named "Ernest," which makes him acceptable to Gwendolyn and is accepted by Lady Bracknell, resolving the threat posed by her against a happy ending and a double marriage.

It is the height of illogic and improbability, and necessary and probable here if the story is to complete itself consistently, if its kind of playing is to be carried through. Moreover, the consciousness of the illusory quality of such action isn't derived by risking tragedy, but by the sheer magnitude of the improbability and denial of any version of reality we would regard, actually, as likely. That denial, which we accept as consistent with the nature of the story, doesn't destroy the story's impact on us—it never asked to be taken "seriously." Yet it is the very scope of such a story's denial of reality that makes us aware that no, of course this isn't how the world works.

Hero's pain may be ours in *Much Ado about Nothing*; Paul's in *Analyze This* is not, although we recognize its nature and recognize his suffering. But we find that suffering ludicrous. Nonetheless, farce arrives at the same place flirting with tragedy brings us. The experience we fear may become real in flirting with tragedy is denied with such extravagance in farce that, as we laugh, we know this isn't the nature of reality at all. We laugh for that reason. Both directions of comic plotting bring us to a perception of the truth through its denial. To minds that have lost their ability to respond to experience creatively, like the monks in *The Name of the Rose*, such behavior must seem outrageous, disrespectful, and subversive, rather than a road to the truth. But such a frame of mind as theirs has strayed from that road so far they have elevated their straying into the truth and cannot bear anything that reminds them of their falseness.

Comedy does so as it lets us have our cake and eat it simultaneously.

The Bones of the Comic Angle of Vision:
The Impulse to Illogic and Perseverance of Style

We demand an absolute persuasiveness in serious drama, let alone tragedy, insisting the action follow a cause-and-effect sequence and strike us as necessary and probable. We demand the same in comedy. How then can I speak of the necessary and probable, as I have just done, insisting on the necessity of improbability?

All screenplays establish their particular reality in the Beginning. In *The Importance of Being Earnest* we meet the improvident Algy fleeing from his creditors and are immediately transported to a comic realm. We meet the sober Jack with his charming ward, Cecily, in the country, where he is responsibly raising her. In the city, however, Jack is friends with the improvident Algy, and as a matter of style as "Ernest" refuses to pay bills at the Savoy or anywhere else. If Jack has an imaginary brother and alter ego, Algy has an imaginary friend, Bumburry, that lets him escape periodically from social engagements with his formidable Aunt Augusta, Lady Bracknell.

Jack, we know, comes to town to propose to Gwendolyn, a simple cause-and-effect sequence of action that puts him in the situation of satisfying Lady Bracknell's illogical demand. What is necessary has become action that accords with that illogical, improbable line of development. A style once established perseveres wherever it takes a writer, just as in the other arts a style once established is pursued until it reaches exaggeration, as in the increasingly irrelevant flourishes on medieval Romanesque capitals, or is exhausted, like expressionism or surrealism, or finally perceived as passé, like abstract expressionism.[6] These are all forms of play, of specific creative responses to our shared cultural experience, and each drives to its logical conclusion if not abandoned due to its inanity. Thus the infinite variations of reality created and defined at the start of every specific screenplay define a style of playing that must be carried through—if it threatens to alter, as it does in flirting with tragedy in comedy, we balk, insistent the defined reality be maintained—or it will cease to be what it is and collapse.

Cause-and-effect conflict is not affected by differences in dramatic reality: cause-and-effect conflict is how *any* dramatic action proceeds. But our perception of what is necessary and probable in comedy is neither in serious drama. Consider *Analyze This*. We begin by a comic reliving of the 1957 mob meeting and its breakup by federal agents. A new meeting has been called because of a contemporary killing, but Paul Vitti finds he can't bludgeon someone to find out who was behind the killing. Shortly thereafter he can't breathe and ends up at a hospital, where he is told to his disgust he is suffering from an anxiety attack. His henchman, Jelly, has Ben's card from an earlier accident when Jelly was so concerned about Ben seeing the body in his trunk his only concern was to shoo the solicitous Ben away, assuring him there would be no insurance problems.

Now he guides Paul to see Ben. Paul hides his dilemma behind a transparent "friend." Ben seems brilliant to Paul when he pierces this charade and helps him. Ben goes off to Miami to get married, only to be roused out of bed by Jelly because Paul is also visiting Miami and needs more help: Paul is suffering from impotence with his mistress. When Ben doesn't want anything to do with Paul, Paul breaks down and weeps, swaying Ben to help him. Again he is seen as a genius and promises to treat Paul in New York after his wedding. But the wedding doesn't happen, interrupted as the body of a man trying to assassinate Paul is thrown out the window and lands on a table full of hor d'oeuvres next to the wedding party.

Again, all is seen from the comic angle of vision. Paul needs help to become, again, a thug. Ben is drawn in step by causal step. By serious standards, it is all deeply illogical and improbable, anything but possessing that sense of gravitas usually associated with action conventionally seeming necessary to us. By the time we are at the *crisis*, as Paul sobs through the shootout, the reality of the absurd world of *Analyze This* has moved even further from what we take conventionally as reality, and *convincingly* so.

Central to the comic angle of vision and the movement of comic action which the perseverance and culmination of style underscores is the *impulse to and naturalness of illogic*.

The *climax* of *The Importance of Being Earnest* underscores this further. Lady Bracknell recognizes Cecily's tutor, Miss Prism, and corners her after a ridiculous pursuit. The truth comes out: years ago Miss Prism disappeared with Lady Bracknell's brother's child. Miss Prism is a would-be Victorian novelist. She had her multivolumed effort in a satchel and young Jack in a pram, and in a comic series of mishaps ended with Jack in the satchel and the books in the pram. She lost the satchel: when she discovered only her novel in the pram, she fled. When she identifies the satchel Jack was found in—which Jack has kept all these years—as hers, all realize *he* is the missing baby.

What makes this convincing is both the satisfaction of our expectation that the style of farce creates for action ever more absurd and the pleasing satisfaction of our expectation of the *illogical and improbable* treatment of reality that underlies such a comic endeavor. As we have seen, the ex-

tent of this illogicality makes us all too aware of the nature of the denial
here, yet it is that illogicality and denial which makes it possible for this
form of playing to culminate and for the underlying, contrary reality paradoxically to be intuited.

It is our sense of the need for dramatic action to be *necessary* that brings
us here: in the comic angle of vision it is the illogical that becomes necessary, the improbable, probable. That sense of necessity is rooted in human
nature, in our sense of what the necessarily defined coherence of play itself and the mythopoetic instinct require to proceed.

To say, then, as Aristotle might in an attempt to define comedy, that it
imitates an action in which the subject is the absurd or ludicrous doesn't
bring us very far. The nature of the action "imitated" is *necessarily illogical:* that is where the essential ludicrousness of the comic angle of vision resides.

The action imitated is the flight from reality.

That flight can only be ludicrous, for the real, except in madness, is
where we live. But because comedic flight with its accompanying veil of
laughter is transparent, comedy becomes another way in which we perceive the actual state of affairs.

Cause-and-effect writing simply connects the action sequentially, but
that vision which ends by standing reality on its head is not one of a defect of character or a lower type of character or story, but a perception in
which reality is inherently absurd. What is so striking about comic reality is the extent to which it is prepared to go to reverse our valuations:
the noncomedic, tragic substance of our lives becomes absurd while the
comic realm becomes real. That is its true absurdity.

Comedy attempts to say, like Hume, that things just aren't as serious
as they seem, but we know that to be false in our heart. Alas that our history makes comedy so very necessary.

The *Cooked* and Comedy

Comedy itself displaces our sense of the seriousness of reality and so is
inherently a cooked medium emotionally, while the raw can never do
more than threaten within its realm, as happens in those comedies that
flirt with tragedy. However, in farce, the raw readily appears, although
never experienced as such by us: it is only experienced by the characters,

whose experience is an object of laughter to us. Farce laughs at the raw; flirting with tragedy evokes the raw to deny it.

This is true, but broad. The *cooked* shows up continuously in comedy as its primary modus operandi and works in a way noticeably different than in serious drama. There we saw there is an element of stylization to it, as in Michael's shooting of Rooney and his guards in *Road to Perdition*, as well as a displacement of effect, as when the wedding guests weep from the impact of Tita's tears in the wedding cake in *Like Water for Chocolate*, or the Comte in *Chocolat* assaults Vianne's chocolate display.

In *Analyze This* Paul is guided by Ben to try and be more open. He calls his competitor in New York, Primo, wanting some sort of "closure," using Ben's word, for the confusion and violence going on, most recently the attempt to assassinate Paul. Primo, on his end, can't figure out what Paul means by "closure." It's not mob lingo: we are amused as they struggle over language, a very *cooked* effect here, inasmuch as they aren't throttling one another instead. Paul has trouble keeping calm; he finally empties his gun into a pillow, after which he feels good. The shooting is in character, the pillow ludicrous, however; *the object of displacement for a cooked emotion in comedy is always absurd.* We saw Ben shoot a refrigerator in the shoot-out in the *crisis* just as absurdly. In *The Importance of Being Earnest* we see, literally, Cecily's fantasy of being saved by a knight in shining armor. Once Algy is on the scene, she fantasizes him in armor astride the white steed. Given what we know of Algy, that too is absurd.

Involved in this use of the *cooked* in comic writing is the technique of reductio ad absurdum. The *cooked* in serious drama is never merely an example of reductio ad absurdum—never, by definition, something wholly laughable—but the contrary. Thus the reduction of the Comte in *Chocolat* to an attack on the chocolates instead of Vianne may turn a serious moment comic, yet because we are empathetic with the Comte's feelings there is an overlay of poignancy to his absurd, belated release.

The displacement of emotion involved in the *cooked* in comedy is always from the immediate, serious-to-tragic implication of the action into something laughable, yet that substitute action/symbol is always *transparent* enough for us to see through to the noncomic, serious original that has been displaced and transformed: Paul shooting a pillow instead of Primo, and so on. There is no poignancy involved or any other emotion to work against a sense of comedy. Farce takes this transparent substitution to an extreme: we no longer judge a displacement against the underlying reality implied, but against one *cooked* displacement of emotion leading to and *exceeding* the next. It's harder to write a great farce because of this than an effective comedy that flirts with the tragic: few writers have the sheer inventiveness to pull it off.

The Importance of Being Earnest manages to do so built around the revelations concerning the satchel, the pram, and the novel by Miss Prism: *Analyze This* doesn't succeed as well, even with the fountain and Vic Damone singing at the end: both are farcical but have the quality of being dreamed up in a story conference and feel stretched, while the absurdity of Miss Prism's revelations grow out of character and resolve conflict. They feel organic and developmental to the story: those at the end of *Analyze This* do not.

The New Beginning in Comedy

Something very curious happens at the end of comedy. Jack and Gwendolyn, Algy and Cecily succeed in their attempt to get married; Ben and Laura dance as Vic Damone sings and the fountain burbles away in *Analyze This;* Hero, Claudio, Benedick and Beatrice all end up together at the end of *Much Ado about Nothing.* On the face of it, this seems in keeping with the point made in the fundamental story pattern that the end of conflict offers a glimpse into a new future where the issues the characters have just struggled over are definitively at an end, the time of those issues is now set, past, and lives can move on.

The farmers in *Shane* will no longer have to contend with the gunslinger Wilson or the men who hired him; Shane has killed them. Julie in *Blue* will no longer try to avoid life but accepts Olivier and love, and presumably is now going to compose in her own right. The Jewish nightmare is over at the end of *Schindler's List,* and Schindler himself, though fleeing, is going to end up being perceived as one of the righteous. Munny in *Unforgiven* avenges both the slashed whore and his friend's murder and gains the necessary money to start fresh in San Francisco, where we are told he thrives, while the action has shown the effort to deny his true nature was futile. Billy will stay with Ted in *Kramer vs. Kramer* because Joanna recognizes the rightness of that solution.

All of these endings represent what we demand from a successful piece of drama, and nothing implied by the future for the various heroines and heroes flies in the face of expectation or the dramatic realities in which they have been involved. Terry in *On the Waterfront* will lead the longshoremen but remain a longshoreman. Munny will no longer be a gunslinger, but then he won't try and persevere as a farmer either. Bess in *Breaking the Waves* and Maximus in *Gladiator* die—but Rome will apparently see Marcus Aurelius's dream carried out, and the elders in Bess's village find themselves denounced by her sister-in-law, while bells ring for Bess at Jan's oil rig. There is no essential change in the *nature of reality* itself in the New Beginning in serious drama, only a completion of conflict and a moving on of the lives of those involved.

The same is not true in comedy, which is one of its essential differences from serious writing. The comic angle of vision, the impulse to illogic, and the flight from reality these support, with the latter's paradoxical affirmation of reality through denial and laughter, all come to an end in the New Beginning for comedy. We are led to believe Paul is a changed man in *Analyze This* and has withdrawn from the mob; the implication is of a new life free of crime once he's released. *Analyze That* shows all that can go wrong when writing a comic sequel: *the repetition of the same flight* strains credulity past the breaking point. Why? The New Beginning implied in comedy *is a return to reality.* We don't expect it to be followed by further comedy.

The comedic New Beginning may be in the form of "And they lived happily ever after," as happens for serious drama's New Beginnings too, yet the implication in comedy is "like everyone else." Presumably Ben and Laura are now going to settle down to normal married life. He will be a better psychiatrist for his experience, his son will grow up, maybe he and Laura will have a new family—who knows? But there is nothing to betray a comic angle of vision.

Jack and Gwendolyn and Algy and Cecily will be married, we assume at the end of *The Importance of Being Earnest*, and will "settle down to reality." Jack will have a formidable mother-in-law, and Cecily will have to come to terms with the fact Algy is not a knight in shining armor. There is nothing unusual here: they are embarked on the pursuit of normal reality at once predictable and familiar. Comedy has gone from their lives as a governing principle. The tyranny of the real has been reasserted. Comedy simply makes the reassertion of reality a relief, a reassertion to be desired after its laughing flight.

Perhaps this is the true reason for the need the Greeks felt to append one satyr play to three tragedies. It would have been a unique audience indeed that was content to leave the theatre after a daylong immersion in the *raw*, inescapable mandates of character, tragic conflict, suffering, and destiny. Nor would the bawdiness of some of the satyr plays have been out of place in proportion to the grievousness of the preceding actions. After so strong a dose *of the inescapable suffering of our lives,* despite the sense of wonder and exhilaration at the end of true tragedy, nothing could be more pointed than a flight that at once affirms reality through denial yet makes us laugh even as we know the laughter is illusory.

Here we need to take note again of Aristotle remarking that the "comic mask is ugly and distorted but does not imply pain."[7] A frequently remarked difficulty in reality is making the distinction between extreme grief and joy: tears of joy are distinctly not tears of pain, yet they are tears. If we wanted to ask ourselves, what in reality is most likely to distort a face and make it ugly? the answer would have to be: the impact of death. Freud's insight into our insistence on beauty being a crucial part of our requirements for civilization takes on an unexpected life when put in the same sentence where ugliness does not imply pain.[8] Beauty, the very embodiment of desire, is the denial of death. Comedy denies death *by denying the painfulness of the pain-distorted face.* That is the deepest level to which we can take our understanding of comedy's flight from reality, and it lends a powerful shading to the implication of "happily ever after" in both comic and serious writing.

We do not live by bread alone, nor by fact, or even by a profound attempt to grapple imaginatively but seriously with reality and experience, but by deliberate, *knowing* illusion too, by our imagination's dream that reality doesn't matter and if it does, it is a deathless delight. That we can take a stand free of reality's imperatives, however briefly, is a remarkable facet of our nature.

The *Smart* and *Dumb* in Comedy

These categories of character growth apply in the same way to comedy as to serious drama, just as does the need for cause-and-effect development of the dramatic action.

Paul in *Analyze This* is a *smart* character, as is Ben; Laura is *dumb*. Being either doesn't make either funnier or more serious. Jelly is *dumb,* a type, and amusingly so; Primo is also *dumb,* a straight man, a type, if you will, what Paul was but is no longer by the end. Types in comedy tend to become the butts of jokes; in serious drama they are just part people.

Jack is a *dumb* character in *The Importance of Being Earnest:* he has already decided on his course of action in pursuing Gwendolyn and settling down; the impact of Lady Bracknell forces a revelation of resourcefulness but does not alter his initial nature or goals. Algy, on the other hand, is a *smart* character, his growth one of considerable change through his involvement with Cecily. Gwendolyn and Cecily prove resourceful and show a clear pattern of growth by discovering their abilities, but do not alter and become *smart* in the sense of transformed, like Schindler in *Schindler's List* or Julie in *Blue.*

As we have seen with Hamlet, a character need not be developed in a *smart* manner to be effective, moving, or, in comedy, funny. What we do see in both serious drama and comedy in developing a character in a *smart* manner is a story in which *growth as transformation* is necessary for the resolution of conflict, not growth as in deepening capacity being developed in a character in a *dumb* manner, whether for action-adventure type heroes like James Bond or Indiana Jones, or for a tragic character like Hamlet.

What is more decisive is the nature of the New Beginning and the return to reality in comedy, or the "happy" reality "*ever* after" in serious drama. That a *dumb* development can be every bit as effective in serious or comedic writing rubs against us a bit: we like to think of growth as transformation, and wonder how always transformative dramatic action can have a hero or heroine who deepens but does not otherwise alter. This is not a problem for comedy then, but for drama, and turns on the nature of the journey the protagonist takes us on, and the meaning of dramatic action.

PART IV

The Nature of Dramatic Action

CHAPTER 8

The Weight of the Past

What Is the Past?

ALL knowledge rises from experience, but often on reflection our noonday certainties give way to unexpected doubts and the suspicion arises that whatever reality may be, it is not what we experience immediately. That suspicion deepens as we discover experience can now seem *this* but then *that*. That suspicion hardens to certainty when we add to it our sense of the relativity of time, where time may feel swift to me but slow to you as we go through the same events.

That suspicion underlies a film like *The Matrix*, where experience turns out to be a virtual reality program fed into us while we sleep our lives away in vast assemblages of nutritive pods where we are bred and stored for use as "batteries" by living machines. This sense that reality exists beyond the illusion of the moment underlies Plato's great image in *The Republic* of the man in the cave who must turn around and leave the cave to find the realities casting shadows on its walls.

That is even harder than meets the eye, as change instantly puts us into conflict with what we are used to. It is no wonder Nietzsche singled out change itself as a profound challenge, realizing the implication of our Humean dependence on habit. Modern psychology lets us understand that part of the problem is the way in which we identify, not just with others, as we might with a heroine or hero in a film, but with an entire lifestyle with its implicit set of values, as Freud intimates with his point concerning the similarity between private and cultural superegos and Winnicott shows a way to understand through his shared, transitional area of experience.

The truth is that the man or woman who stands up to find reality lives in a social reality where others resist any change with all the power of their habitual identifications and comfort with the familiar, even in the face of a shared need to the contrary. Thus it is almost impossible to imagine a private conflict without social ramifications. Terry in *On the Waterfront* may wrestle privately with Edie over his decision to go down to the docks to "get his rights," but acting to get them precipitates the final confrontation with Johnny Friendly, while inaction would leave the longshoremen in Friendly's power. Nothing the hero or heroine does has only private consequences.

These issues are part of the warp and woof of every story a screenwriter/dramatist develops, however lightly or seriously. They are daily commonplaces with individuals in all walks of life who issue their criticism and call for change, always inevitably causing turmoil, whether whistle-blowers of corporate malfeasance or social reformers or prophets. With each call those affected suddenly face the possibility that those whom we trusted cannot be trusted, social habits that seemed fixed are malleable, and beliefs that claimed immutability are time-bound, evanescent, and replaceable. We have and will shed oceans of blood in the name of what we believe, believe threatened, or believe others should believe.

Even the counterview concerning reality, so well expressed by thinkers like Aristotle, that our experience *is* real never goes all the way to saying: it *is* exactly what it seems. Experience for such thinkers is, instead, shaped by formative forces that may be immanent in it yet which require reflection to find or, in modern science, hypothesis followed by testing to confirm or reject. There is always in fact an asterisk to experience* the moment we seek to explain and understand ourselves. As we saw from Kant, Schopenhauer, Nietzsche, Freud, and Winnicott, experience* comes to consciousness on the basis of a good many shaping physiological and mental structures, including accumulated responses to formative experiences* in infancy and youth. We stand in a constant creative relationship to our experience* even in the dullest of lives where opinion and lifestyle appear ready-made. Governing opinions and lifestyles are simply the congealed responses of others to experience* we call tradition.

Drama cannot avoid so fundamental a part of our lives or so deep a root of conflict. In fact, *dramatic structure re-creates and attempts to move forward from exactly this conflicted experience of awakening to the deceptiveness of experience,* whether serious or comedic.

In so doing, the immediate action of drama collides headlong with the "past" with very curious results. The past, we think, as we saw in earlier chapters, is what has happened but is finished: its time is set, its conflicts are over. The truth is radically different. The past holds everything that is received and that we have done: our unthought-through relations with others and ourselves; tradition; and all that has created our super-ego/conscience, meaning the culturally shaded values we have integrated into our senses of self and social reality. It is so much a part of our lives, which we experience* deceptively in a constant *now*, that we forget the past is in fact the reality we live in, interact with, and bring our responses to and from. The past is what governs us. That whose time is truly set is on the order of Greek or Roman or medieval history, though, if we look closely, we are startled to see how much of those are still in fact active in our lives. If we go back to the first protohuman who discovered the use of fire, or earlier to the first who stood altruistically beside another in danger, even to the first who looked in a pool of water and thought, *I am*, we find the past is not over. It *is* the experience in which we are constantly physically and mentally mutating. The present is the mutational, transitory moment of such experience.

This is not how we usually think or the characters whom we create. They believe, as we do, the past is past and they are living in their immediate *now*. Time, we saw, has this quality of *nowness* in our experience. Screenwriters give lip service to the "past" by working out what they call the backstory, but that is always a small part of the treatment they develop whose emphasis is on the immediate, structured action. The backstory is rarely worked out in any detail. It is sufficient, for example, to say of *Hamlet* that Hamlet's father is dead; his assassin uncle, king; his mother newly married to his uncle; and Hamlet grieving. Only when we try to grapple with the nature of that grieving under the pressure of *a demand or event that involves rethinking the past*—in Hamlet's case the Ghost's request for vengeance—does the importance of past events come into view: we see how Hamlet *continues to react* now *as he did* then.

Terry in *On the Waterfront* shows the same characteristics. Hamlet can't act because of his insight into the pointlessness of life sparked by the impact of his father's death; Terry takes *another* moral dive as he lets Johnny Friendly buy him off after Joey's murder. *The present action in the Beginning repeats the* continuing *past.* The only thing new, or "present," is the variation of the repetition.

Schindler in *Schindler's List* makes this point very apparent when explaining his success in Krakow to his wife. What was missing in his life of previous failure wasn't some essential capacity: it was *war*. Circumstances have changed but not him—what he was and continues to be now thrives because of special circumstances. Only when circumstances lead him to act mercifully, at first without thought, then deliberately, do we move into something new in him, something not already in his past.

Thus, when we establish character and conflict in the Beginning of the fundamental story pattern, including the milieu of the action, the nature of its reality, and the problem(s) generating the forward motion of the story with their cause-and-effect nature, handled in a more or less necessary and probable way as defined by the story's reality, we dramatize a shared illusion: our and our characters' belief that what we see is present, while the past is past. That is the false modus vivendi of the hero at the start of the action, and it exactly echoes our own condition in life. We may never come to terms with that unless forced to live dramatically, while dramatic characters have no choice in doing so. What ensues in the Beginning is an action that bares this illusion *and* the necessity for moving past it. That action betrays the fact our *now* consists of reliving the past.

This is always a revelation for ourselves and our characters. This situation also shows in what sense character *and* situation are *dumb* in essence at the start: the initial action can only reveal the nature of its past-bound reality in which change is illusory. This is so even in the case of characters who know something important is problematic in their past, classically like Oedipus in *Oedipus Rex*, who governs his life by flight from the prophecy he will murder his father and marry his mother, or contemporaneously in a character like Sonja in the Australian film *Lantana,* who craves passion and has sought therapy before the action starts. In a film like *Wild Strawberries*, old Isak Borg must come to terms with his entire life as he realizes neither he nor it is what he thought.

For the problem with this continuing "past" that drama makes its characters aware of is that, continue though experience may in the present moment, experience is "frozen" in the sense that the characters—and ourselves through them—have lost or surrendered volition. They, and ourselves through them, are under the control of others or of previous responses to conflict we merely continue in fresh guises. The heart of the problem is this: the creative flow of our lives has stopped.

That is the weight of the past that dramatic action strives to lift.

High Noon

Usually a film ends with "boy gets girl" or the reverse in a "happily ever after": *High Noon* starts off that way with Will and Amy's marriage. It is an inventive beginning: they and the townspeople are expecting the "happily ever after" to ensue as Will embarks on married life and gives up being the town's enforcer. It is like putting the New Beginning of the fundamental story pattern first.

The unlikelihood of that succeeding, once stated, leaps off the page. Yet at first even the news of Miller's imminent return is no more than a passing cloud for the married couple: not until Will has had time to think does he realize he can't go and that the New Beginning must be deferred. When he turns back we understand immediately two elements are going to be subjected to testing: Amy's love for Will and his convictions about the townspeople.

This is Winnicottian, i.e., the action attempts to destroy their love and his convictions *to establish their reality,* which is their *survival quality.* But, returning to the Beginning, Will and ourselves as audience realize several other things as he turns back. The past that seemed set is not. That was an illusion. Amy's love is in question, meaning their modus vivendi is revealed as false. That falseness expands as Will discovers the unreliability of the townspeople: everything Will does *he has done before,* whether turn to the judge, try to raise deputies, or expect Harvey to stand by him. None of this is shown finally to have survival value.

Now Kane realizes the past and so the present are not what they seem, which means *reality is not what it seems.* This comes as a bitter surprise to him because of the *moral* values he ascribed to those around him, which he discovers are false. The illusion he lived in is apparent, and the extent to which he had surrendered volition; since Miller's imprisonment Kane has behaved habitually in this false modus vivendi. That discovery isolates his exercise of volition *now* and subjects it to a harsh examination, for it engenders profound conflict with those around him who do not wish to see themselves through Kane's eyes, most obviously when Harvey physically tries to force him to leave town from his own guilt. Change provokes conflict; dramatic conflict enforces change.

Now the usefulness of misplacing the New Beginning is apparent. It couldn't yet happen: the past wasn't "past." *For when drama ends con-*

flict in the New Beginning, it does something that does not happen in our lives; we saw what a profound mutational sequence of experience we are in fact caught up in. Time is "set" only by convention in our experience, but not in fact: we always live to some extent in illusion, but *illusion ends in drama*. Moreover, the fresh start achieved in drama and so hungered for in life can't just be private. The initial New Beginning in *High Noon* was for Will and Amy and, in effect, *selfish*. The town was hoping to go on as it had, unaffected by their departure. That, of course, was the illusion of the townspeople.

But once Will and Amy kill Miller and his friends, a true New Beginning can ensue. It is a New Beginning for everyone, because the past, embodied by Miller, is indeed past. That is what his death signifies. How to evaluate Amy's love and the townspeople is now seen truly too; all have been subjected to a destructive assault and what has survived is crystal clear. Leaving town is now definitive: the town and all it stands for is not a place for a true, awakened hero and heroine to live, literally or metaphorically. The hero is a hero by virtue of finding the solution for everyone involved in his story's dilemmas, however bitter a pill to swallow that may be for other characters in that story.

Lantana

We begin with what we will discover is Val's body waiting for discovery in the brush. We move back in time.

Leon is a detective having an affair while incapable of dancing with feeling with his wife, Sonja. He is savage in a police break-in, behavior that has become rote we discover through his partner. Sonja is seeing Val in therapy, where she bares her hunger for passion. Val, in a public speech occasioned by the publication of her book on her murdered daughter, speaks of her confusion of what to feel and believe when struck by tragedy. So we understand there are two troubled marriages on hand, Leon and Sonja's with a loss of passion, and John and Val's marred by a daughter's murder. If Leon can't respond to Sonja as she wants, John can't grieve as Val does, and certainly not publicly. Leon suffers from sudden breathlessness and pain, like Paul Vitti in *Analyze This;* that also interrupts his making love with his mistress. Val and John have given up lovemaking and cannot carry through on one occasion when they try. When Leon's mistress, Jane, tells him she thinks there should be more between them, Leon tells her he still loves his wife to end the affair, which was only another passionless activity for Leon.

This is all immediately active, as drama must be to gain and hold our attention and move the action forward. But what is shown are lives in stasis. John and Valerie are trapped in grief, suffering from the burden of the dead daughter, as frozen in response to life as Hamlet in *Hamlet* by the death of his father. The death of a child is the death of the future. Yet to continue living this way is anguishing. John retreats from Val's emotions in proportion to her breaking down from the pressure of loss. Sonja and Leon repeatedly display the stasis of their failed marriage: Sonja may want passion, but Leon feels "numb."

Val's disappearance brings John and Leon together in Act 2, the Middle. Leon approaches John in the same rote, habitually numb way in which he has been acting so far, believing that, as the husband, John must of course be the murderer. Since we know John is innocent, Leon's persistence in error becomes the focus of the action. We understand now that *Leon has been persisting in error from the first moment of the screenplay*; there is nothing present in his action at all. He has no creative response to experience: the weight of the past is stifling him and those dependent on him, just as we so often feel we are in danger of being stifled in our lives and act out or turn to others for help, as Sonja does with Val. Val and John's relationship while Val is still alive is equally revealing: Eros has been stifled in their lives, and Thanatos is tearing them down.

Thus Leon's rote behavior is tested in the Middle: if it succeeds, Thanatos triumphs. He lies to John about his own infidelity, shocked by John's revelation of how guilt and remorse can hold a loveless relationship together, a description perilously close to home for Leon. He is surprised when John isn't found at a suspect's home in a homosexual relationship; Leon assumed the man an aggressive patient of Val's—Patrick—hides "of course" was John, and that Val as a consequence had been the victim of a homosexual plot. Then Leon confesses his affair to Sonja because he has taken one of Val's tapes and heard Sonja say that being lied to is what she would find unforgivable. Naturally, his admission revolts Sonja because it is so unexpected and lacking in any real feeling. Real, fresh, creative responses to experience are what Leon cannot make. Finally Nick, Jane's neighbor, is arrested when it is discovered Nick was the one to give Val the ride the night of her disappearance. We see in the *crisis* that Leon has been on a completely wrong tack.

Does he learn yet? No. He resists. There is still Nick to misjudge. Leon now assumes that Nick is of course the murderer. But the truth comes out irresistibly as Nick tells his story and helps them find Val's body. He innocently gave Val a ride the night she disappeared. There was no murder. Val, we see in Nick's flashback, panics as he turns into a shortcut, *afraid the same thing is happening to her that happened to her daughter.* She throws herself out, runs into the woods and takes a fatal fall. Now the falseness of all Leon's rote, repetitive behavior is laid bare. No one is guilty. Leon finally listens all the way through the tape taken from Val's office and hears Sonja say after a very long pause that she still loves him. He breaks down and weeps.

Crying is a form of atonement, and more than anything else that is what Leon needs to do if he is going to be able to live: atone for persistently misusing his volition to affirm illusion. He must admit the profundity of his erroneousness and surrender his habitual reaction to experience.

We see the issue of volition in a new, darker light with Leon. The problem for the heroine or hero goes beyond the loss of volition in the false modus vivendi that characterizes their lives in the Beginning. It is true they have surrendered and lost volition. It is also true they *assent* to that loss. To admit that assent to falseness is difficult indeed: Schindler must acknowledge evil-doing, Kane finally must thrust fear aside and walk down an empty street to meet his destiny, Terry must suffer Edie's rebuke that he is a bum.

There is another, revealing way to see Leon and the hero and heroine's behavior up to the moment they assume responsibility for their volition and past errors. Until Leon weeps he has been in compliance with a frozen version of himself, *a false self,* just like John and Val, who at least share tragedy as a causative experience. But most lives in the modern industrial and postindustrial elite nations are not rooted in tragedy; most are like Leon and Sonja's. Time moves imperceptibly for such, so that we hardly know how one day we arrive at such deep dissatisfaction. Leon has not just been in compliance with a false self but aggressively so, fighting to maintain error. Change can only be traumatic.

Val, however, is most revelatory. So powerful is the weight of the past in her case that she is fixated on its one salient feature and conceives her own experience wholly in the light of another's tragedy. She has surrendered her own life. Her death makes visible the extent of that surrender. Action, in drama, is revelatory as a matter of course.

Wild Strawberries

In the Beginning Isak Borg readily admits he's "difficult" to get along with. He is a model of self-centeredness, widowed, callow, superficially polite and courteous yet ruthless. He embarks on a journey to receive an award, a symbolic journey quest, if you will, accompanied by his son's wife, Marianne. On the trip he is assaulted by memories of his childhood home and his young love, Sara, who finds Isak's cousin Sigfrid so much more interesting in Isak's flashbacks and eventually marries him. They pick up a young, hip Sara with two companions who both are in love with her, and briefly an older couple enmeshed in a venomous relationship whom Marianne throws out for the "children's" sake. Isak admits the older couple's relationship echoes his and his dead wife's. Sara's two lovers argue over faith vs. materialism at a lunch stop, and, surprisingly, Isak knows the words to a poem that celebrates God's love everywhere. Love is in short demand, however. Isak, we now sense, is caught in a false modus vivendi on which his self-esteem is built.

Isak's memories deepen in the Middle as he relives a scene of his wife's infidelity and her summation of how cruelly understanding he will be later. Apparently he was. In a memory that turns into a dream, he is taken into a room and examined. He is a doctor, but suddenly cannot understand or do anything. He is incompetent, not a man going to get an award for distinguished service. He has forgotten a person's first duty: to ask for forgiveness. The presaged awakening at the end of the Beginning has now been made overt.

But Marianne is uninterested in Isak's dreams and memories: to her, he's just like his son, Evald. She doesn't believe there's any change going on in him at all. What is Evald like? He is a man who, like Hamlet in *Hamlet*, can only perceive the horror of life, and is appalled Marianne wants a child. Marianne is pregnant and went to visit Isak to have some time alone to decide what to do, for Evald wants an abortion. Marianne has decided to keep the child. Isak is horrified at this vision of his son; between his own memories and this revelation he is motivated to do something wholly out of character: to help. He will even, in a symbolically huge step for him, tell Evald to forget repaying an outstanding loan, revealing how dry—like a ledger book—has been this father and son relationship.

He receives his award in the End, after they reach Evald's, and tries unsuccessfully to talk to his son, who misunderstands him to be asking for reassurance the loan will be repaid. Isak is unable to sort this out before Evald leaves for an evening with Marianne; nonetheless, Isak has tried to ask for forgiveness in his way. He tries to move to a first name basis with his old housekeeper and in effect companion, but she refuses; change, as always, is an issue, and from her point of view, this one is too late. In fact, Isak is about to fail, achieving no change between him and Evald. But later that night Evald comes to see him and confesses he cannot live without Marianne and will accept the child, to Isak's great relief.

It is a deceptively simple story, with the key change out of the hero's hands and reported after the fact. Yet Isak himself has changed through what happens to him on the journey, and can fall asleep and die sure there will be a New Beginning. The child and future that Val and John lose Evald and Marianne gain, and so too does Isak through them, even at the end of life.

A film without a New Beginning cannot end.

The weight of the past is even more obvious in *Wild Strawberries* than in *Lantana* or *High Noon*. All through the first act, the Beginning, the action drives at revealing Isak to himself: the man who has forgotten to ask for forgiveness, as he is specifically told in Act 2, the Middle. We live that directly through him and through the great contrast of the old, embittered couple and Sara and her young lovers. Active as the journey is, the burden of its action is the way Isak is trapped in an uncaring, habitual response to experience, which has poisoned his son and so endangers Marianne and the future. Isak and Evald's creative response to life is frozen: they are trying to impose that symbolically on Marianne with Evald's demand for an abortion. Thanatos *hates* Eros. Marianne is quintessential, a life force in her pregnancy, a loving, living manifestation of Eros's drive toward love and family. But the testing all three are subjected to leaves only Eros standing at the end. If we imagine, for a moment, that Evald and Isak triumphed in the demand for an abortion in the End, the consequences would have been as devastating for Marianne and for all the others as is Val's end in *Lantana* for John—and would have moved us deeply into an experience of the *heavy*.

All three films show the power of love through its survival of destructiveness. Love as a transcendent value is *created* by the failure of destructiveness.

Love may not be as powerful in reality as destructiveness, as Freud shows, but it is nonetheless a power and triumphs with Marianne, as it does with Sonja in *Lantana* and Amy in *High Noon*.

Lifting Weights

Drama, if we think of it in Aristotelian terms, is said to be an imitation of an action. We could ask what action is being imitated at the beginning of a screenplay, then, and begin to answer by saying: it is *the act of living in the past* to an intolerable point. That is certainly a major part of the reality from which comedy is in flight. In drama, however, a specific, intolerable moment is dramatized, with the result the heroine and hero are aroused and energized to regain their creative response to experience and find their true selves through the conflict and their climactic response to the *crisis,* which makes possible the New Beginning. The prevalence of "the happily ever after" ending bespeaks Eros's triumph over Thanatos and the renewal of life through death's defeat. If that is an illusion, then it is one *necessary* for life. The absence of an Eros triumph results in tragedy for the heroine or hero, but not, as we saw, the absence of a New Beginning and an Eros triumph *for others*.

But this only takes us so far. A dramatic imitation is not one that says "this," the screenplay, is like "that," reality. Reality, we have seen repeatedly, is rarely like a drama. Instead, drama claims to be an imitation of an action, a form of reality that we have seen is rare. But this too is wrong: there is nothing rare about drama or what it imitates, particularly in its cinema variant; it is the daily fare of countless millions of people worldwide. It caters to *common experience*. Defining drama as an imitation of a rare reality, an action, is wide of the mark, even if we suffer from the hunger for such defining experience. A screenplay, a drama, is a metaphor that makes the claim that the reality of dramatic action is, *through our identification with the drama through its characters, our reality*. The imagination *is real* in its own way. But the claim is not that the screenplay is an act of the imagination, which is obvious, but that the action which is imagined is real as "real," i.e., is reality.

This has an echo in Winnicott's review of the first transitional object, which the infant is allowed to think it created, even if given it by the mother; its use and meaning are potent while it is not challenged. The infant's play is encouraged. The reality of a work of drama is potent so long as it too is not challenged, i.e., nothing in its handling undermines the will to believe we bring to a story until something goes wrong. What matters here is not the "object" per se, be it a screenplay or film, but its use, for however much we may study texts in academic settings, they live only in the use we put them to in our imagination through our experience as part of the audience. Self-consciousness about play destroys play, not because it denies the reality of a work of the imagination, but as a result of the fact that self-consciousness belongs to our private, "me" world, not the world of shared experience.

Aristotle approached this perception in reviewing metaphor in *The Poetics,* then shied away as he realized metaphor was a function of genius, not practice, which he was at pains to illustrate. He never thought through the implication of action being a metaphor, although he understood the nature of metaphor quite well.[1] Yet a mind as astute as Aristotle's would neither have lied nor avoided an obvious difficulty: what possessed him, then, to drag in the word "imitate"?

To answer that question we need to remember screenplays are just that: *plays.* A dramatist is a *play*wright. Playing, if we follow Winnicott, is what creativity arises from in its ever greater sophistication. But if we said when children play a game of, say, doctor and nurse, that they are imitating the reality of being a doctor and nurse, we would immediately be struck by how bad a description that is of what they are doing. Those involved in the game *are* doctor and nurse. Drama is a very sophisticated kind of playing indeed, one in which the identification of an audience is involved with the characters playing the game, who certainly are enacted as real in the given story. We take their reality for our own while playing their game vicariously through them.

A mature, successful play leaves us with a sense of fullness, not complexity or the triumph of the *heavy.* Leon at the end of *Lantana* can dance with feeling. Isak is consumed with the desire to be helpful in *Wild Strawberries.* Amy is able to kill, to be destructive, at the End of *High Noon* in the name of love, for creative purposes, while Kane is confirmed in his rectitude.

Julie in *Blue* is able to cry at the End, love, and contemplate life and creativity overtly as a composer. Michael becomes the godfather in *The Godfather*; Schindler in *Schindler's List* is given a marriage ring and, if for a profounder reason, weeps as Leon does in *Lantana*. The "playing" that these characters go through is one in which they play themselves to wholeness, to volition, to selfhood, wherever that takes them, which can be satisfying *and* dark, as with characters like Munny in *Unforgiven* or Michael in *The Godfather*. Whatever vicissitudes Winnicott's way of thinking may go through in psychoanalytic circles, it provides a useful language for summing up what is at the center of a screenplay for a hero's development, a playing into the fullness of the self that was smothered by compliance with the dead hand of the past at the start of the screenplay. Italicize "is" in the preceding sentences: a screenplay makes the claim that its characters' reality *is* our reality.

One dramatic consequence of the failure of the hero to break through in this manner, and for ourselves through identification, is seen in the inability of the other characters around them to escape to the future. Their movement is dependent on the movement of the hero. In *On the Waterfront* Father Barry realizes that he cannot undo Johnny Friendly: someone else must, and it turns out to be Terry. If Terry succeeds, then the dead, corrupting hand of the past that Johnny Friendly embodies can be overcome and a New Beginning follow. The longshoremen will be freed from Friendly; Terry will have overcome his past, regained volition with his conscience, and have a personal future *free of the past* with Edie. But if he fails, all will be trapped in how things have been. The "past" then will *be* and its weight not lifted. We would find such a story unendurably *heavy* in effect.

Dave comedically flirts with the triumph of the past as Dave learns the accusations made against the actual president, who is in a coma, are true and threaten his own ability to continue impersonating the president. Dave fakes a heart attack after first setting the record straight, and escapes back into his private life, where he goes into politics and is tracked down romantically by the ex-president's wife. *If* the past triumphs, there cannot be a New Beginning: the New Beginning is the restoration of that mutational, evolutionary moment we think we live in.

There are no screenplays where the past triumphs definitively. They may, as in *Hamlet* and *Ran*, lead to tragedy, but there are successor characters who take over for the failed hero or heroine. We are not left with a total failure. Characters can certainly fail, and when they do, those characters are necessarily handled in a *dumb* way: Hamlet can reveal himself, or, more interestingly in this light, Blanche in *A Streetcar Named Desire* can struggle to change in a *smart* way, but when that is blocked by Mitch and Stanley, tragedy ensues: tragedy by death, tragedy by incarceration, tragedy by insanity, and tragedy by the hopeless repetition of the past, its conflicts, its compliance to false solutions and false selves.

This doesn't help us with Aristotle directly, but it may let us sense perhaps what he intuited in using "imitation." The action "imitated" by drama is that of fantasy: our dream of a reality cleansed of the unrelenting past where something new and with the innocence of the new becomes possible and can be entered by ourselves as whole personalities.

Lifting the weight of the past is the burden of drama.

Its claim to be *our reality* is true for the running time of a drama.

CHAPTER 9

The Weight of the Wrong Decision

T HE weight of the past with which the protagonist struggles is often made up by life experiences that have steadily gone wrong, as in *Kramer vs. Kramer* or *Lantana* or *A Beautiful Mind* or *Wild Strawberries*. Sometimes an event thought past, like his father's death for Hamlet in *Hamlet* or the missing drugs for Book in *Witness*, are found to be vividly alive as the ghost haunts Hamlet and Book is almost killed after he links McFee to the drugs. Sometimes there are past events of which the heroine or hero had no knowledge, as with Julie in *Blue*, who knew nothing of her husband's infidelity, or Oedipus in *Oedipus Rex*, who thinks he has fled from his true parents. Sometimes there are known elements of the past mistakenly thought settled. These, with their variants, are all part of the general weight of the past that turns out to be the characters' repetitive present which the action strives to make known and lift. But in some films the weight of the past takes on particular focus because of a key wrong decision taken then that thereafter goes on impacting the protagonist's life wholly negatively. A critical variant of such a wrong decision in the past is a similar wrong decision taken in the immediate action of the Beginning. The weight of the past is decisive there too, if in unexpected ways.

The Wrong Decision in the Past

The past remains definitive until the wrong decision that determines the hero or heroine's loss of volition and creates a false modus vivendi is redecided. A writer knowing what the key wrong decision in the past is for the protagonist should know to develop the immediate action of the screenplay to a climactic recontest of that decision to let the protagonist remake it with the right outcome, barring tragedy. The hero's failure to challenge the wrong decision in the past empowers the past and makes any notion of a genuine present *nowness* an illusion. A *smart* handling of character growth results if the protagonist succeeds in remaking that decision: otherwise he or she must ultimately be seen as *dumb,* for those characters caught in the past can only reveal a continuing, unchanged or trapped response to experience, as happens with Blanche in *A Streetcar Named Desire.* Their creativity is frozen into a repetitive mold they cannot break, and tragedy ensues.

Characters trapped in such a continuing past deny others what they deny to themselves: think of Terry in *On the Waterfront* as he resists Edie's request for help and her altruistic, moral vision of behavior. He wants her to see that his "every man for himself" way which binds him to Johnny Friendly is right. So he refuses to help her and Glover from the Crime Commission, when he meets the latter on his roof, on the docks, and in the bar where he is served a subpoena. In Terry's case this all expresses the self-denying, frozen nature of his response to experience, since he made the wrong decision in the past.

The wrong decision in the past is definitive and focused in a way the general weight of the past is not. We see the Comte's dilemma in *Chocolat* without any sense of its proceeding from a specific wrong decision in the past; it is character-driven instead. *The Godfather* and *On the Waterfront* let us see the unique characteristics of the wrong decision in the past clearly.

The Godfather certainly comes with a general weight of the past: all of Don Vito's career, the Mafia, the war that made Michael a hero, and the recent past where drugs have become a hot issue. Don Vito doesn't know of Barzini's machinations, of the way the Tattaglias are fronting for Barzini, or of Sollozzo's real patrons when that individual asks for the Don's help in moving drugs. But outweighing all of this is the past decision that Michael will stand aside from the family and go legitimate.

Although Michael occupies the position of an outsider at Connie's marriage reception, he is necessary nonetheless—the don won't take a family photo until Michael is included, even though the rest of the family gathers for the photographer. By singling him out this way, the story underscores his unique importance, for *he* is the hero the others think they can do without. Kay's appearance underscores this in another way, for she is not Italian but as blonde and "Anglo" as possible.

The consequences of removing heroes or heroines from their destiny are inescapable *for everyone.* Terry missed his chance to be a contender, and his ensuing bumhood preserves Friendly's rule, meaning it preserves a false hero. Sonny in *The Godfather* may be colorful, dominating, high-spirited, and hot-tempered and act as if he is the hero when the don is shot—isn't he the eldest? Fated to take over? The answers may be yes, but he isn't the hero, just a particularly well-rounded type whose "typed" temper leads to his death. The decision to let Michael stand aside empowers the wrong character, just as Terry at first empowers Johnny Friendly. Sonny endangers the entire family and hasn't a clue concerning the true nature of his opponents.

This wrong decision in the past ensures the continuance of the same error and the entrapment of the present in that "past," which we see as the preexisting Sollozzo-Tattaglia-Barzini conspiracy is revealed progressively. The action, by singling out Michael and simultaneously allowing the wrong decision about him to stand, almost writes its own developmental prescription: that decision must be challenged and undone if those for whom Michael is the hero are to triumph. Sonny must be shown, not just inept, *but be removed,* no less than Johnny Friendly must be overcome in *On the Waterfront.*

The process starts when Michael is moved by love for his fallen father and saves him at the hospital, promising to stand by him now. That doesn't make him head of the family, and his plan to kill Sollozzo and McCluskey is laughed at initially, but Michael won't be thwarted. Michael carries his plan through too, but still isn't head of the family. He must flee to Sicily until the clamor dies down.

The consequences from the wrong decision in the past continue fatally and disastrously as Sonny continues in control.

Michael's Sicilian journey is essential, however. This is the place of family origins, the root of all he was going to stand aside from, the source of the Corleone "seed power" where Michael begins to find himself. He does so by choosing to become Sicilian in the sense of marrying Apollonia *and the past he thought to stand aside from,* but makes a crucial error like Will and Amy in the Beginning of *High Noon.* He and Apollonia cannot have a New Beginning that *is just their own* in the Middle. Michael pays a price for this error with Apollonia's death; he no sooner seems to have lost the deep bruise from McCluskey's blow than the explosion from the car knocks him flat.

Protagonists who have made the wrong decision, you see, have to pay, i.e., *they have to suffer grievously in proportion to the error committed.* There is an Old Testament sense of proportion in screenwriting and drama: do *this,* and *that must* happen. In Winnicottian terms, Michael has to be tested by being subjected to potentially destructive experiences to see if he has survival quality, i.e., to see if he possesses the reality of a hero, for the hero is the one who survives, except in tragedy, which transcends his loss.

Contrasted with Sonny, whose passions govern him, Michael is a man of self-control. On his return from Sicily he is vaulted into the leadership by the don, who has finally discovered what the true nature of affairs is concerning Barzini and the others. Since Michael can control himself, he can control others: he displays *self*-mastery. He is so patient he waits to strike until the don is dead and he becomes a godfather. At the End, with all his opponents dead, we see the others acknowledge him as the godfather as Kay watches, absorbed now into Michael's world, no longer a symbol of his standing aside.

Michael is a *smart* character because he succeeds in remaking the wrong decision he made in the past. His success, like Terry's in *On the Waterfront,* means a New Beginning is now possible for the family, given concrete form in the move to Las Vegas. Michael, of course, is a deeply ironic hero; his is, if you will, the dark side of heroism, for his success is a sinking into evil. He murders his rivals as he renounces Satan and his works at the christening. But we experience his success as exhilarating, in part because only the family and other mob families are involved in the story, and fundamentally because his success completes the dramatic drive to lift the weight of the past, establish the true self of the hero, and regain a creative response to reality. The price Michael pays for this success is morally ambiguous but not structurally inconclusive.

If the whole personality is found through playing, as Winnicott holds, the results needn't always be admirable, as is true of Michael, Munny in *Unforgiven,* and Verbal in *The Usual Suspects.* Human nature is not a pretty thing. What we see in the success of these stories, however, is the structural predominance of regaining volition and creativity, of finding his true self on the part of the hero and so for ourselves through our identifications. The Dionysian is lauded by Nietzsche, but Nazi torchlit parades were Dionysian events, as are drug-filled rock concerts. We may conventionally laud a particular set of values and denigrate another, but in drama we experience ourselves freely; a dramatist of ability reveals the scope of our nature.

There is a curious echo to Freud here. He is at pains to underscore the negative impact of human destructiveness, its greater strength than love, and the need for guilt and almost inhuman ethical admonitions like "Love thy neighbor as thyself" to contain our destructiveness. Yet there is one instance when not Eros but Thanatos binds people together instead of destroying them: when one group confirms its own sense of cohesion and identity by attacking another. In *The Godfather*, the binding power of destructiveness gets a rare outing we approve of in the context of Michael fighting other mob families who want to introduce drugs into society. It's hard not to cheer for the Corleones. But in *On the Waterfront* it is undoing such criminal behavior centered on Johnny Friendly and maintained by violence that is the central thrust of the story.

If I turn to *On the Waterfront* and pull together my earlier remarks, then we see a story that shows a more positive and typical result of undoing the wrong decision from the past. That wrong decision in the past is both determinative and clear, as we see in the immediate action through Terry's behavior who is locked in compliance with a narrow, self-defeating version of himself, complying with a false self at every turn in the action, whereas Michael's goal of going straight in *The Godfather* does not seem a self-betrayal.

We see how *the present* for Terry is a repetitious past, however much *nowness* there seems to be in the immediate action. Just as clearly, everyone else is bound up in his self-betrayal, while competing "hero" figures are tested and disposed of, first Joey and then Dugan, by having a load of liquor dropped on him. Johnny Friendly's grip on the past, and so the "present," is unbroken; Edie can't break it herself, nor can Father Barry. The Crime Commission is essentially helpless. *All* are betrayed in Terry's self-betrayal.

Here Freud's vision and our own experience of the power of love in its first flood bear on our experience of the action. Freud describes love as a way with which we deal with suffering that moves differently than withdrawal, restraint, or intoxication: love leads to engagement with experience. Yet we never suffer so greatly as when in love, while one of our great sadnesses is the fact love's first flood fades. Yet love's first tide can make a Montague love a Capulet and dream of peace, its denial drive Ophelia to madness, and its paradoxically *enduring* quality in John Nash's wife provide the environment and ultimate motivation to control his phantoms in *A Beautiful Mind.* In *Witness,* the failure of passion to bind Book and Rachel intentionally angers us against the societies that make their union impossible.

As we saw, Edie's impact on Terry exemplifies this power in a deeply moral form, for Edie is motivated by altruism as well as revenge. That means *Terry can't have Edie without a moral reform.* The terrible fact is that however uneasy the hero is in complying with a false self at the start of the action, he is not so unhappy that he has to act. Something must happen to make him act. Not just, say, falling in love per se, but in the demands love makes on him as defined in a particular story. Those demands always challenge his ability to maintain a false self. If love is not involved, then a critical emergence into reality of the full meaning of his actions challenges the hero to alter himself, as happens to Schindler as he watches Amon Goeth liquidate the ghetto in *Schindler's List.*

This is the nature of the *inciting event,* structurally. It sets a screenplay on that path where "past" and "present" are seen for what they are and culminate together as they are resolved in the *climax.* The inciting event makes intolerable the continuing solutions based on the weight of the past in general or on the wrong decision in the past in particular. Change, we saw, is painful: moral transformation is agonizing, the very demand Edie makes on Terry as a prerequisite to any satisfaction of passion. The burden of the wrong decision, and the more general elements that go into the weight of the past, are the *immoral* consequences of those errors.

Consider a story where this wouldn't seem to be the primary focus, as in the maritally centered *Kramer vs. Kramer.* Joanna has simply lost touch with herself in her marriage, and Ted lost touch with her in his pursuit of career success. If we think about the implications of that commonplace behavior, however, they are immoral. Ted colludes in the repression of another human being, while that human being, for the best of reasons, acts against her own nature until she hardly knows who she is or what to do, except that the extent of self-loss has become intolerable and she leaves Ted and abandons her child. Book does not keep Rachel for moral reasons at the end of *Witness*; his is the way of violence, and hers is not. A specifically moral turn is given events in *Chocolat,* as the priest in his final sermon celebrates a life marked by generosity and inclusion as opposed to the Comte's former self denying exclusiveness. In *Like Water for Chocolate*, Tita remains at home to prevent her niece being used by Rosaura as her mother used her. Tita is on a moral quest: to mistreat another is not just anguishing but *immoral.*

Love as a primal force combines with guilt for Terry in *On the Waterfront.* It plunges him into suffering; i.e., he is tested. Friendly wants him to stop seeing Edie: he sees Edie. Father Barry wants to speak over the body of Dugan: Terry keeps one of the thugs from silencing him. Christ is here in the hold, Father Barry tells the men. He is everywhere—love is everywhere, as the poem asserts that Isak Borg surprisingly knows, despite the lovelessness of his life in *Wild Strawberries.*

Edie is horrified by Terry's subsequent confession, while he is beside himself from desire and in a fury over that word "conscience." He is stunned when Charley pulls a gun on him after he *now* refuses to be bought off and reminds Charley it was he who betrayed him in the past, just as he is betraying Terry again *right now* by trying to buy him off. Past and present have a way of wholly coinciding in our best writing in decisive moments because they are the same in drama, which strives to awaken the protagonist to this reality so she or he can move beyond it. Charley lets Terry go as he takes in Terry's point, the key complaint of which is that Charley should have behaved altruistically with Terry. Terry's reproach to Charley is in essence Edie's to him earlier in the bar. But Terry isn't done suffering yet. He has a lot to pay for, including murder.

So Charley is killed, then Terry is ostracized. When he finally confronts Friendly, they debate directly the nature of the past: does Friendly have it right, or Terry, who now presents the past as a continuous sellout of all of them by Friendly? When they fight Terry does so with renewed vigor. "That kid fights like he useta," a longshoreman observes.[1] Terry relives and remakes the wrong decision from his past. Although he is beaten by the thugs, he still gets to his feet, something the longshoremen *had to see together with the beating* for Terry to be free of his association with Friendly. Now he can lead the longshoremen to work. He is the winner, the hero to whom the past belongs, and so the future. The destructiveness aimed at him has failed, and that failure made him the man to follow. *His* view of reality prevails. Terry, in short, is profoundly *smart* in the nature of his transformative growth.

So we can say everyone is trapped in the specific nature of the wrong decision in the past that affects a protagonist, who is the only one that matters. He or she is the agent of change, and that wrong decision removes him or her from effecting the change necessary. Instead, confusion reigns, and/or a numbing stasis, suffering, continuance of the past, and the constant paying for the wrong decision in repeated consequences flowing from it whether violently, as with killing Joey and Dugan in *On the Waterfront,* or ethically, as in *Wild Strawberries.* But the inciting event in the present action draws in that fatefully wrong decision from the past and makes possible its being decided differently. If the hero typically succeeds, the decision is reversed and the hero becomes a kind of Moses who leads his flock from captivity into a New Beginning, however defined by a particular story. The *nowness* of experience ceases to be an illusion, but actual, and a creative response to reality ensues. It's always hard to imagine specifically what that means, although easy to imagine generally: sequels fail on that reef alone. If the hero fails and tragedy ensues, a New Beginning still follows but without the hero or those intimately involved with him. A different community inherits the "happily ever after," as we see in *Ran* and *Hamlet.*

The Wrong Decision in the Present

The wrong decision in the past leads to a story where present actions repeat its consequences in new guises. The inciting act in the immediate action forces this repetitive, ongoing past into consciousness and drives the heroine or hero into an action where that decision can be relived and altered as necessary for the resolution of the conflict.

The wrong decision in the present does not alter the balance between past and present: both must still be recognized and resolved together for the immediate conflict to reach an end and a New Beginning to emerge. But the wrong decision in the present is itself the inciting event, *and it too empowers the past* but in this case to a degree it would not have been, on the face of it, otherwise.

The great lord Ichimonji in *Ran* divides his kingdom among his sons. He will keep the trappings but not the substance of power. Each son receives one of the three key castles; Taro, the eldest, First Castle. Ichimonji has his sons easily break a single arrow, then hands them three to break at once, which Taro and Jiro fail to do. Stand together and you cannot be overthrown.

Ichimonji goes through this performance before Ayabe and Fujimaki, both old foes Ichimonji has overcome who now represent subject states assembled to witness an orderly transfer of power.

Ichimonji seems wise on the face of it. Instead of clinging to power over impatient youth, he voluntarily hands it to his sons. It shows his certainty of his sons' fidelity and that they can be relied on to maintain him with appropriate dignity while they rule. He seems the opposite of Johnny Friendly who fights to keep his power; Ichimonji gracefully adjusts to age instead while ensuring the continued obedience of Ayabe and Fujimaki.

His behavior is wrong, however. His youngest son, Saburo, directly challenges Ichimonji, wondering if he has lost his mind. Saburo is bold, not deferential, and apparently ungrateful, inconsiderate, and false compared to Taro and Jiro who overflow with honeyed gratitude. But Saburo tells the truth to the egotistically blind Ichimonji. He demonstrates his father's folly by taking the three arrows and breaking them over his knee. Taro and Jiro act shocked: Ichimonji is beside himself and, as Saburo persists, banishes him. It is a disastrous decision.

Taro and Jiro are left in control, but neither is any more the true hero than Sonny is in *The Godfather*. Nothing more positive can be expected with Saburo out of the picture than with Michael standing aside in *The Godfather*. Worse, Taro is married to Lady Kaede, seductive, powerful, and—unknown to them—driven by the desire for vengeance for her family, whom Ichimonji killed on his ascent to power. The First Castle Taro is given at first was her family's. Had Ichimonji realized the truth and made Saburo head of the family, Kaede would simply have been a secretly venomous figure with only a small arena in which to act. As a result of Ichimonji's decision, she is empowered: she is "first lady," far stronger in character than Taro or Jiro, and with a lethal agenda.

The consequences from Ichimonji's decision flow swiftly. Taro is easily manipulated by Lady Kaede into a confrontation with his father, who leaves in a rage. She has Taro forewarn Jiro that Ichimonji is coming to him, vengeful and clinging to the trappings of power. Sadly, if a person wishes to give up power it must all go, trappings included, for power is a kind of Schopenhauerian will. Its appetite for more is insatiable. Thus Jiro refuses to let Ichimonji into Second Castle with his entourage. His father leaves Jiro too, his eyes now opened to his folly. They must open wider.

He takes refuge in Third Castle, which was to be Saburo's. There Jiro and Taro attack him. In the ensuing battle Taro is assassinated by Jiro's retainer Kurogane. Ichimonji walks off into the wilderness, aided only by the fool and the faithful Tango, swordless, distraught at the death of his wives and retainers, now realizing the depth of his sons' treachery and of his own misjudgment.

The old hero, who banished the young hero, has a long road of suffering to explore. The weight of his misdeeds from the past is enormous, while the grief he has caused himself in the present drives him mad. I said there is an Old Testament sense of proportion in screenwriting and drama: do much evil, suffer much evil. That is Ichimonji's fate. He refuses to appeal to Saburo from guilt and wounded pride; these too must be burned out.

Lady Kaede's ascent is now clear. She immediately half-seduces, half-frightens Jiro into taking her as his wife, swiftly establishing her power over him to the disgust of Kurogane. Saburo reenters the action at the head of his small army to confront Jiro and rescue his father from the wilderness, while Fujimaki, who aids him in his banishment, appears in moral support on a hill's crest. Jiro, under Lady Kaede's urging, can't allow Saburo to have Ichimonji. Too much legitimacy would be conferred on Saburo, too dark a light cast on Kaede and Jiro. A plot is hatched to let Saburo get Ichimonji but ambush them on the way back to the army.

Lady Kaede wins if the plot succeeds; if it fails, she loses nothing that she has and will have further reason to rule Jiro through his incompetence. The plot succeeds, and Saburo is shot after a joyous reunion with his father, *who now is in touch with the truth and sees things clearly and accepts Saburo's aid, begging his forgiveness: he recognizes the true heir, the true hero.* His heart breaks at Saburo's death.

Now Ichimonji, Taro, and Saburo are gone. There is just Jiro who leaves the battlefield in haste as he discovers Ayabe, who also appeared on a hill's crest to encourage Saburo, had feinted and instead marched on First Castle. Jiro returns in disorder from the battle with Saburo's army and can only prepare to die. Lady Kaede reveals her satisfaction that at last her family is to be avenged. Kurogane beheads her, but it is too late: all of Ichimonji's house will be swept away.

The past triumphs through Lady Kaede. Ichimonji's entire lifetime and predominance are shown to have been built on quicksand. He may have been the author of his own rise, but so too was he the author of his own demise. Ayabe and Fujimaki finally triumph, just as Fortinbras does in

Hamlet: the future doesn't stop but moves away from those unable to inherit it. Thus the wrong decision in the present, if not undone, leads inevitably to the reassertion of what appeared to be past and overcome as the now newly triumphant future. The New Beginning then belongs to others than the protagonists or their followers. They seemed to be primary but turn out to have been an unhappy interlude in others' lives.

One consequence the triumph of the wrong decision in the present drives home is that what the characters in conflict fight over in a screenplay is *to whom the story belongs.* Does it belong to Ichimonji and his heirs or to Lady Kaede? Is it Johnny Friendly's or Terry's? Is it Captain Schaefer's and the other corrupt officers in *Witness,* or Rachel and Book's? We hope for a particular outcome, but that outcome is not guaranteed any more than the desired outcome can happen easily and satisfy, for that thwarts the harsh sense of proportion and consequence in dramatic writing. In *Ran,* the story passes to those from whom the old hero Ichimonji took it. The testing power of the action destroys his clan: the future belongs to the community of the survivors, who have been found and made fitter by surviving.

An action is a conflict to own the story: to own the reality the story represents, the lives within it, and, by extension and identification, to own us so that we sense reality adding up as the hero or heroine adds it up. For not all wrong decisions in the present result in tragedy. A brief consideration of *Blue* helps bring into light the nature of the protagonist's more typical success in undoing the wrong decision in the present.

Julie, we saw in *Blue,* moves to the city after her losses and refuses to be involved with anyone, choosing the Freudian choice of stoicism and withdrawal to cope with suffering and avoid fresh pain. God knows Julie has a right to choose so, given the depth of her loss, yet it is impossible to withdraw completely and claim one is still alive. Julie tries to make any growth in herself *dumb:* there is to be no transformation from the state the accident left her in, as there is none for Hamlet from the impact death has on his perception of reality in *Hamlet.*

But she is progressively involved and provoked despite herself. Periodically she goes to visit her mother in a retirement home who doesn't remember who Julie is and who has truly withdrawn from life, spending her days before a television set, unable to remember the past. Without the past we are no more than a shadow watching shadows. Thus the metaphor of the Platonic cave points beyond the absence of the perception of the truth to the absence in any meaningful sense of life itself.

Dumbfounded by Olivier's challenge to live, and his resolve to do whatever he can to make that happen, Julie realizes in the *crisis* that her effort to be uninvolved as a solution to suffering is impossible. She meets her late husband's mistress, who is pregnant with her husband's child. She gives her the family home, and, assured Olivier loves her, goes to him. In the final sequence, we see her both make love and weep as she rejoins the suffering that is life. Freud's variety of methods to cope with suffering cannot hide the fact that suffering endures; the implication is that to live fully, one must embrace that suffering. It's like C. S. Lewis with his wife in the film *Shadowlands* as she makes clear to him one day that the happiness they share *now* while she is in a state of remission from cancer *is part of the pain then,* when the remission ends. Pain and pleasure are as inextricably bound, as we saw, as are creativity and destructiveness in Nietzsche and Winnicott: they are contained in each other.

The action in *Blue* also makes it clear that far from being a muse, Julie was the compositional force behind her husband. In the End it is clear she will create as a woman and an artist in her own right. She has found herself, and in the act of finding herself makes the New Beginning her own. It is Julie's story that will continue, not another's: Olivier and the others in her life are caught up in her choices.

This positive outcome is the more usual direction the action necessarily follows in response to the heroine or hero making the wrong decision in the present. The action of such a story necessarily focuses on what, then, is the *right* decision, which can mean as much or as little as a screenwriter has the ability and vision to create.

Both the wrong decisions in the past and in the present bring us to the same end down different roads, one through discovery of a repetitive past that is challenged, one through challenge to the wrong decision taken in the Beginning of the action. Both lead to a moment when the wrong decision can be relived and undone. Tragedy grows from a failure both to relive and to change that decision, serious drama from a successful effort. A screenplay/drama with either form of the wrong decision gives screenwriters and dramatists a very practical idea of how they must develop the story. This is as true of comedy too, where those decisions and their consequences may be laughed at as absurdities, yet an end is reached where continuance into normal reality becomes possible and the past is laid to rest. Either the past is overcome, as in *Analyze This,* or turns into the present, as with *The Importance of Being Earnest,* where "Ernest" succeeds by recovering his past and making it the present in the form of his name, which allows the marriages to go forward.

True Heroines and Heroes and False

Heroines and heroes are a varied lot. We can identify and triumph with them, as we saw, from good to bad. They may begin as weaklings and become admirable and strong at the end, like Terry in *On the Waterfront.* Bess may take us into a descent into the *heavy* in *Breaking the Waves,* or Tomas and Tereza into a moment of earthly paradise certain to be brief in *Unbearable Lightness.* John Nash takes us through madness to a sanity rooted in love in *A Beautiful Mind,* while Ichimonji in *Ran* takes us into tragedy by misjudging his unloving older sons.

Comic heroes and heroines are caught up in the comic angle of vision where what might be tragic turns absurd. They take us on a flight from reality either by their flirting with tragedy or taking denial to the extreme of farce, with us all the while conditioned by our underlying awareness reality cannot be escaped. But comic protagonists move just as much within realities conditioned by the weight of the past and whatever wrong decisions are made there or in the present. They too arrive at the promise of a New Beginning where reality is reestablished and normalcy will prevail. In doing so, comic heroines and heroes complete themselves too, whether Paul Vitti resigning from the mob in *Analyze This,* or Jack becoming Ernest and winning his wife and life with a past in *The Importance of Being Earnest,* or the denizens of *Much Ado about Nothing* dancing riotously around the estate before a double marriage is held.

There is so much variety in stories, so much similarity in storytelling pattern. That Julie, Ichimonji, Terry, Edie, Jack/Ernest, Algy, Gwendolyn, Paul Vitti, and Michael Corleone are all heroes and heroines drives home to us the peculiarity of dramatic structure, as reflected in the fundamental story pattern that encompasses so many wines in one bottle.

Similarly, we have encountered equally diverse false heroes—Taro and Jiro in *Ran,* Sonny in *The Godfather*—and failed heroines and heroes like

Val and John in *Lantana*. Their similarities are revealing. Val is no more in control of her emotions than Sonny; Taro and Jiro are manipulated as easily as Terry before Edie electrifies him in *On the Waterfront*. It is hard to say how true heroes and heroines differ from false and failed in the Beginning, although we are immediately able to spot the difference because we are pointed to it by the story. But Taro, Jiro, Sonny, Val, and John are all *dumb* in handling—not that all *dumb* characters are false heroines and heroes, like Hamlet. The failure of a true hero or heroine leads to tragedy, while the failure of a false one may be sad or dramatic but not decisive in consequence in the way characteristic of a true hero's failure. Nonetheless, a *dumb* development seems typical of the false hero, at best. All too often the false hero turns out to be a well-rounded type, like Sonny. What we are sure of with a false hero is that he cannot complete the journey of the action and bring it to a New Beginning except in the case where he is swept away with all around him, as with Jiro in *Ran*, so that the possession of the story moves to others.

The possession of the story is the key. That possession may be contested, but the story belongs to the true hero to take control over: he will go through whatever growth is necessary to do so. *Hamlet* is paradoxical in this as in so many other ways. Hamlet indeed grows in the *dumb* mode, yet to possess the story must act in a way his growth makes impossible for him. So we constantly see him in the story not acting at the very moment he should, as in his return to Elsinore from England knowing Claudius has tried to kill him. He slides by us, his inactivity disguised by the activity of those around him, until his final, lethal and spontaneous outburst at the climactic duel. Yet just as with the false hero, Hamlet loses ownership of the ongoing story, thereby giving the future to Fortinbras.

We go with the hero through his struggles sometimes with gritted teeth because of his moral nature, but by the end his triumph is ours and his failure moves the triumph we share to others. His wholeness, so typical a feature of the hero or heroine in the moment of success, is ours too. The wealth of his character laid bare in tragic defeat is also ours, for the true hero does not go down easily. But understanding the journey the hero takes us on is served only so far by observing the workings of the fundamental story pattern in a given screenplay or drama or by tracing the impact of the weight of the past or key wrong decision taken then or in the

Beginning. The structural pattern of dramatic action may contain the hero's journey, but that journey presents a second pattern embedded within the greater. We need to look at the nature of the journey these figures take us on within the action that contains their variety without stultifying the imagination or making the immediate action predictable.

CHAPTER 10

The Nature of the Hero's Journey

ALL the preceding essays lead toward contemplating the nature of the journey on which our endlessly varied heroes go. That journey is rooted in the psychic realities described by Freud and Winnicott and embedded in the argument we are having with ourselves beginning with Descartes' extreme dualism, a model that Freud accepted along with the materialist, reductive nature of nineteenth-century science. Nietzsche rebelled against that model, and Winnicott developed an alternative to dualism in the language of contemporary psychoanalysis. Drama comes down firmly against a dualistic view of reality and experience; the necessity for spelling out how that occurs and both what that means and what its relevance is to screenwriting has arrived. Exploring the dramatic alternative to dualism goes a long way in answering the question in the preface I sometimes pose to writers concerning why we shouldn't get rid of the world of film and drama in the name of some altruistic endeavor.

First we need to review Joseph Campbell's work, which sums up the pattern and role of the hero in human behavior as reflected broadly in mythology, just as we saw Freud in effect give a primer on the roots of conflict in *Civilization and Its Discontents,* Nietzsche wrestle with how opposing, formative forces can reach a point of union, and Winnicott reflect on the relation of destructiveness to creativity and the point of playing in relation to finding the true self.

Campbell's Hero

The Campbellian hero quintessentially goes on a journey at the end of which, if successful, he returns to society with a great gift, an elixir of life: "The boon that he brings restores the world."[1] That has an uncanny echo to the sentiments at the end of *Schindler's List* as Stern gives Schindler the ring the Jews have made with its inscription "Who saves one life, saves the world."

The mythological hero is lured, carried away, or voluntarily proceeds to adventure. At the threshold of adventure he encounters a guardian which he must defeat or conciliate, although mythologically winning or losing comes to the same. Win, and the hero goes on alive; lose, he falls into the underworld and has his adventure there. The hero finds himself in a strange land once across the threshold and is tested severely. At the nadir of his fortunes, the hero obtains the greatest gift, the ultimate award which the ordeal carries as its prize. That can appear as a sacred marriage, meaning union with the mother goddess or one of her avatars, or as recognition from the father-creator. The hero may even become divine himself. If the powers that be are still in opposition, then the marriage appears as a bride theft, recognition by the father as fire theft; both marriage by theft and father recognition/fire theft represent a maximum expansion of being involving "illumination, transfiguration, freedom."[2] The hero returns as the powers' emissary, or in flight. At the edge of the strange land the hero must overcome any obstacles in his way and leave behind any supernatural, transcendental figures before returning to familiar ground. The "elixir" he returns with is, as we saw, restorative.

Campbell gives a circular diagram of the stages of the hero's journey: the "Call to Adventure," appearance of a "Helper" (or opponent), the "Threshold of Adventure," "tests," more helpers or opponents; and (1) "Sacred Marriage" or (2) "Father Atonement" and/or (3) "Apotheosis" and (4) "Elixir Theft." This is followed by "Flight" and return to the threshold, as a "Return" or "Resurrection" or "Rescue."[3] These latter involve a climactic struggle to cross from the world of adventure into that of everyday reality, where the community endures from which the hero departed on his adventure. The hero then bestows the elixir on his community to renew its life force.

Curiously, a three-part journey is revealed if one straightens Campbell's circular diagram. We begin with the "Call to Adventure" and end with the hero's successful return and giving of the elixir. In the Beginning, which is up to crossing the threshold, a problem appears which the hero feels impelled to deal with; in the Middle, across the threshold, the hero is tested but deals with that problem; and in the End he must struggle across the threshold again back to the reality he left behind with whatever he has gained to renew the life of his community. It is not identical to the Past, Beginning, Middle and End (Acts 1, 2, 3), and New Beginning of drama's fundamental story pattern, but the family likeness is striking. The Past is implicit in the life the hero is leading up to the point he is called to action. The third part of Campbell's schema combines the End with the New Beginning. The *crisis* and climactic return are placed together by Campbell, the flight and the threshold struggle that enable the hero to return to his community. In drama the *crisis* ends the Middle, Act 2, and propels us into the climactic action of the End, Act 3. There is both a transparent consonance between dramatic structure and the overall mythological pattern of the hero's quest and, just as importantly, a difference manifested in how much more tightly defined and causally structured drama is. At the same time, dramatic stories are rarely myths, although carried out by heroes and heroines. Thus the most curious thing about the consonance between Campbell and drama is the *structural* nature of that resemblance.

This is a critical point. Campbell points out myths rarely tell the entire hero story, concentrating often enough on some aspect of it. But the fundamental story pattern is always the same, while simultaneously infinitely varied in actual story content. It is the *underlying pattern of dramatic structure* that echoes Campbell's full hero's quest, which every screenplay thus carries through *structurally:* we could say, *drama is the story with a thousand faces.*

It is more intriguing than this. Heroes start off on a "primordial" level in mythology cycles, moving from primal, timeless creative figures to extraordinary but created ones. Those give way to purely human heroes involved in the hero's quest for the elixir that renews the world. It is the hero's burden to restore the creative flow of a world that has lost its way and become frozen, so that the present is an illusion and the past wholly, and repetitiously, dominant. The Winnicottian implication is striking, given his position that a creative response to experience is the sign of health in an individual. In *Breaking the Waves* we witness the frozen society represented by the elders with which Bess's emotionality is at such odds. To think of that society as an Apollonian order that has rigidified is interesting and true; to think of it as an unhealthy perpetuation of the past into the present is more revealing.

The Campbellian divine or semidivine hero becomes a culture hero, once heroes move from the fabulous into human history. Huang Ti, in

Chinese mythology, may talk at the age of seventy days and be emperor by the age of eleven, which indicates the continuing strain of the miraculous in him, but his key characteristics are his ability to control passion, explore the arts, and elaborate culture and the state.[4] This ability to control and use passion is a central feature, for the culture hero, the father-founder of a society, is one who is not a plaything of either Eros or Thanatos, any more than Michael is on his return from Sicily in *The Godfather* or Kane is in *High Noon*. It is Book's failure to control his violence that betrays him in *Witness* and leads to his inability to "keep the girl." Schindler, from the start, lacks self-control where greed and sex are concerned; by the end of *Schindler's List*, he has recalled his wife and spent his money to save lives. A heroine like Julie in *Blue* tries to withdraw from passion, with the result the action tests her withdrawal and forces her to discover what she needs in order to live: love and creativity.

The hero either descends in his adventure or ascends; in either case the deeds he must accomplish are proportionate to the depth with which the myth is treated. In drama, a hero can be a James Bond or Indiana Jones, their deeds bound to the familiar world, displaying only the extraordinary depth of their capacity, or the hero may be involved in profound moral transformation like Schindler in *Schindler's List*. The hero's power may be treated as predestined, in which case he is someone to be contemplated, or he may manifest his powers through action, in which case he is to be imitated. Both roads for Campbell lead to the revelation of the omnipotent self that is in all of us. If the hero takes off from a historical figure, culture soon invents deeds suitably mythological in nature for him from childhood. It's worth mentioning Emerson's view, so sadly lost as we trace American thought from him through Thoreau to a figure like William James, that the more deeply we are in touch with our true selves, the more we are in touch with the true self of everyone else.[5]

For Campbell the hero's life goes through distinct, recognizable stages. Since the hero even as a child has the burden of restoring the creative power of the universe to his community, he usually has special powers from birth. Often the hero as child or youth goes through a period of exile: Abraham is hidden from Nimrod in a cave, and as a child discovers the angels and nature of God. Heracles "only" strangles serpents in his crib. Often the young hero is despised or abused. "In sum: the child of destiny has to face a long period of obscurity."[6] Terry has been a bum for years in *On the Waterfront;* Schindler has been a failure in everything he has undertaken before he comes to Krakow. In *Shane* or *Pale Rider* or *Unforgiven*, the hero has a past he is trying to escape and goes through a period of disguises as a hired farm helper, a minister, and a pig farmer. In *Blue* Julie subordinates self and creativity to her husband in a false view of the world before the accident; in *Wild Strawberries* Isak Borg discovers a lifetime of supposed achievement has been lived in a moral wilderness and he must, even at the end, try and set things right.

It is during this period of obscurity that the mythological hero learns the lessons of the "seed powers," those primeval forces governing the universe. This is less true in drama, where the period of "obscurity" often amounts to an avoidance of self and responsibility that must finally be overcome. Once the mythological hero returns from this period of obscurity, he wins recognition by provoking a crisis through the assertion of his heroic nature. In *On the Waterfront* this is echoed in Terry as he begins to assert his own conscience, which threatens all those who had taken him for granted. Schindler must steer a careful course among his Nazi cronies after his conscience is stirred into action with the liquidation of the ghetto in *Schindler's List*; nonetheless, at one point he ends in jail, and at another the "joke" of watering Jews in broiling train cars grows thin as Schindler mercifully perseveres after the others stop. The western hero shedding his clerical collar or farm clothes is instantly a figure of menace to the bad guys. Why is the hero such a danger? *Because his "return," or assertion of his hero nature, threatens to break apart the patterns of experience prevailing to that point.*

The hero as warrior is easy to grasp. The upshot of his action may be to "pour creative power into the world," but that is because he is the champion of things *becoming*.[7] He is the killer of the status quo, specifically of "Holdfast, the keeper of the past."[8] No clearer examples exist in dramatic literature of holdfast characters than the ghost in *Hamlet* or Johnny Friendly in *On the Waterfront*. Edvard Vergerus is such a figure in *Fanny and Alexander;* Alexander specifically runs into trouble with him by using his imagination *to reveal Edvard's nature:* a man who at least spiritually caused the death of his last family and who is well on the way to doing the same with his new.

The warrior version of the hero myth lets a salient feature arise: there is always a villain, the evil one who holds and abuses power and forces time to stop, so experience only repeats the forms of his control. He mistakes, it may be, shadow for substance, like the man watching shadows in the Platonic cave, but he is nonetheless powerful. His power increases in proportion to that given the hero in a particular tale. Time cannot be stopped, the past holds on forever: the tyrant, the holdfast, is a tyrant of fact, a visionless man and doomed. The hero is his doom and will sweep him away, whether the hero encounters him as a beast, man, or god.

The hero appears too as a lover. Romantic comedy and romantic drama in general draw freely on this aspect. Here woman symbolizes the life energy the hero has to win from his opponent and restore to the world. It doesn't matter whether it is Ferdinand seeking Miranda in *The Tempest*, or the struggling father in *Sleepless in Seattle*: "getting the girl" is getting *life*. The heroine here is the "other portion" of the hero himself.[9] She is exactly what Book cannot keep in *Witness* because he cannot control his violence; he fails a key test of being the hero. Johnny Friendly in *On the Waterfront* doesn't think of Edie as a "life force," but he is the tyrant, the holdfast of that story who does recognize the threat she poses through her influence on Terry.

In drama the action of the romantic hero story becomes the hero overcoming whatever the resistance is to his "having the girl." If that resistance has taken the form of being tested by a holdfast, then the hero must finally overthrow him. Typically in film, however, the holdfast is either another rival or the testing resulting *from the heroine striving to be sure he is the destined hero*, as Cecily imagines Algy to be as she fantasizes him as a knight in shining armor. Nonetheless, Cecily, as Gwendolyn does with Jack, puts Algy through a largely symbolic testing to make sure he's the right one. There are further variants: the rescue of the threatened virgin and the "damsel in distress." This principle, however, is maintained: the hero's romance tests his suitability, and he must pass the tests whether of rivalry, prohibition, or doubt to "get the girl." Underlying "and they live happily ever after," however, is our sense of the Campbellian union of sundered halves, volition joined to life-giving capacity.

Plato gives an amusing variant of this in *The Symposium*. Aristophanes conjectures that the romantic problem facing men and women arose from jealousy on the part of the gods. Once man and woman were not separate but a single supremely satisfied, *potent* being. The gods were not just envious but worried by the apparition of such a complete being, and split it into male and female parts. Ever since, men and women have been run-ning around desperately to find their other half.

The hero can be supreme, not just a warrior or lover. Such a hero makes us aware of the universal, creative source itself, not just through a symbolic marriage or the provision of a life-renewing elixir to a community. Char-acteristic of this aspect of the myth is "a going to the father," for "the father is the invisible unknown."[10] The supreme hero's adventures consequently fall into religious forms. If he finds and is blessed by the father, the hero returns from his adventure as a Moses, or as a cultural, founding father, a Huang Ti. He is, if you will, a representative center of the universe. But if the hero confuses the power of the universe with his own, *he becomes the tyrant, the holdfast:* he becomes a Johnny Friendly or Edvard Vergerus.

For the true villain the hero must face is *a fallen hero,* one who fell by selfishly confusing the creative power of the world/universe with his own. Lucas was friends with Campbell, but fortunately his ideas for the first *Star Wars* series make dramatic sense as well as owing Campbell a debt. They give a popular screen version of several strands of Campbell's hero myth, especially in the way Darth Vader is a *fallen hero* as well as father who in the end redeems himself by killing the emperor. It's worth not-ing he is motivated, at last, by love for his son, a form of Eros, for what is more powerful than even the first flood of romantic love than the love of a parent for a child?

The hero as world redeemer we have already met in drama in the Schindler of *Schindler's List.* This hero may do all the deeds the hero as warrior does, but only to make evident to the clouded eye what the na-ture of the "truth" is. The supreme hero almost predicts the story he will be involved in: he appears in a time of moral degeneration and destroys the tyrant/villain, the source of the pollution. Yet as we have just seen, even he confronts the danger that he will confuse *himself* with the truth and fall into villainy, and become the very figure a new, unfallen hero must overcome.

Implicit in the myth ultimately for Campbell is an identity between the slayer and the slain, the hero and the villain. In the mundane world we are riven by dualities: we are caught up, if you will, in the Cartesian dilemma. The hero myth points to illusoriness of the dualistic approach to reality.

We can depart from Campbell here and remind ourselves of how fig-ures as diverse as Nietzsche and Winnicott struggle with exactly this issue. Nietzsche's fascination with Greek tragedy grows out of the way in which he is able to show how the Apollonian and Dionysian fuse in its action. In sum, for Nietzsche the Dionysian impulse is one that intoxicates, that takes us out of our narrow selves and makes us mass celebrants to whom the ordering of reality into clear, well-lit structures typical of the Apollonian impulse appears as an absurdity. Music is central to Nietzsche's thinking, because it is an art with a direct impact on emotion which sparks images in the mind as we are carried away. Those images are Apollonian attempts to render the meaning of the Dionysian experience of being carried out of ourselves into a sense of the indestructible flow of nature itself, an experience much greater than any image can evoke. But to an Apollonian a Dionysian reveler seems mad and dangerous, and, if provoked or not controlled, wildly destructive.

In tragedy the Dionysian is evoked by the chorus, the streams of specific imagery sparked by the Dionysian experience appearing as the concrete dramatic scenes between choral interludes that were sung and danced and which reportedly on occasion had electrifying impacts on the audience. The specific dramatic scenes Nietzsche sees as the visions of the chorus *we see through our identification with the chorus.* The definition of character, refinement of dialogue, development of a specific story content, and conflict are Apollonian forms; the chorus, music-driven Dionysian celebrants. In those specific dramatic scenes, the Apollonian characters through their conflict and tragedy finally give voice to Dionysian insights. It is no wonder these plays were semireligious in nature, performed at the great spring festival, the Greater Dionysia, that celebrated the renewal of the creative life force in the world. Nor is it any wonder Greek tragedy atrophied with the death of the chorus and the movement of religious observance from public celebration to private cults like the Eleusinian in Athens, and finally to the Christian. The key to understanding tragedy for Nietzsche is the way at a certain moment one can no longer separate Apollonian and Dionysian and how *we, as audience members, through our vicarious involvement in the drama, experience that unity too.*

Winnicott, we saw, comes at this experience of unification through psychoanalysis. He wrestles with the inheritance from the late Freud and the work of Melanie Klein of a death instinct. He did not believe nor find experience justified their Eros vs. Thanatos dichotomy. It was at once too easy and a misunderstanding of the nature of the forces involved. Yet the power of destructiveness, of the negative side of the Dionysian ecstasy that sweeps away all in its path, is undeniable in human history and within our psyches. So Winnicott developed his unique answer to the problem of destructiveness in "The Use of an Object," a chapter in *Playing and Reality,* first read in New York in 1969. Some claim the baffled, hostile reception given it by the analytic society there was a material factor in giving Winnicott a heart attack; others discount the story, saying he was already an ill man.[11]

As we saw, Winnicott shows how the process of weaning gives rise to the transitional object, the baby's first toy that stands symbolically for the absent mother. It at once symbolizes absence and unity: through the transitional object the mother is still there. If unchallenged in its use, play arises through the use of the transitional object in an environment of trust, where the actual absence of the mother can be tolerated because she is known to return, which the transitional object represents. Once infants, then, can play on their own, they can play with others, and from play arises ultimately the cultural world in which we spend our lives, where we "play" with others, creatively responding to experience in a third area, the cultural area, the area of actual, everyday experience, neither wholly "me" or "not me" but made up of both. The Cartesian model fails because it does not deal with the very reality Descartes thought he was examining. He doesn't have to be disproved: he is simply irrelevant to understanding reality. By the same token Kant is answered, not through a monolithic Schopenhauerian will or a Nietzschean fusion of opposites, but by the same provision of a tripartite division of reality beyond our easy dualities. Drama goes farther, as we will see: the Kantian thing-in-itself, that ultimate point beyond which the "me" cannot go, is reached routinely in the dramatic experience.

Further, Winnicott viewed destructiveness through this tripartite experience of reality. One reason the transitional object must not be challenged, i.e., *subjected to a destructive effort by the mother,* is that then separation becomes intolerable and the maturation of the human personality necessarily collapses. Not only must the transitional object not be challenged, because its survival is so important, any subsequent object must survive destructiveness if it is to be felt/experienced as real. That, as we saw, is Winnicott's key insight, which brings us to the paradox of destructiveness as part of the very process by which something becomes real, in which destructiveness is an aspect of creativity, just as the Dionysian and Apollonian are aspects of one unity. Our perception of the *heavy* in drama is rooted in our recoil from destructiveness *for its own sake,* meaning *one without creative outcome.* That is the full measure of its repulsiveness to us, for the creative response to reality and life are synonyms insofar as we are talking about meaningful experience.

Now Campbell's perception of the ultimate unity of the slayer and the slain makes real psychological as well as mythological sense. In the mundane world, dualities are easily recognized and exploited, but those same divisions, when viewed from the point of view of the forces that produce the world of experience, appear as different facets of the underlying creative flow of reality. It has been and is a difficult concept for us to hold in mind. Our present culture and language work against something so at odds with the immediate polarities of experience, and we experience destructiveness so widely and with such dislike it is not appealing to see it *sub specie aeternitatis.*

Seeing reality truly, however, has always been our single greatest struggle.

There is a final aspect of the hero myth before we leave Campbell: the hero as saint. Here the hero overcomes his ego entirely and, once he finds ultimate reality, does not come back but moves out of the hero myth. Saints see the illusion of immediate experience, that all its "forms" or "truths" are corruptible. They move into God's realm, the realm of true being where creativity flows constantly into the world, creating it. In the rare case of a Bodhisattva in Buddhism, the saint returns and becomes the hero as avatar. In a sense this is Hamlet's dilemma in *Hamlet:* he has a saint's perception of the illusoriness of action and the corruptibility of the world of immediate experience but a hero's obligation to act.

Finally, the hero dies. The true mythological hero faces death without fear. He has seen past dualities like creativity vs. destructiveness, life vs. death, into the uniform, indestructible creative flow of existence.

Rites, ceremonies, even meditation, are all ways to handle the transitions individuals must make in life to embed them meaningfully in society and help them find the truth. The hero myth in a given society embodied its ideals and gave direction to the transitions in life: Alexander slept with the *Iliad* under his pillow, or at least beside him. But for Campbell in modern society, the old myths and gods are dead, the religious organization of experience supplanted by our modern economic-political system. Because all meaning is in the ever more atomistic Western individual, ever less in the group, the modern hero deed must be to "bring to light again the lost Atlantis of the coordinated soul," to render the "modern world spiritually significant."[12] In modern terms, we need to find the cosmic, creative power out of which the first gods emerged. *We* have become the modern mystery, and from our lonely *I* a *thou* must be found.

Drama is one of the places where we encounter this struggle as a community.

The Dramatic Hero

The fundamental story pattern in drama is a technical description of the pattern of the structural story development of the conflict. The Past (Part 1) contains all of the previous experience of the characters, including unresolved problems more or less unknown, preceding the immediate action. However the past is held in memory, a modus vivendi exists at the start of the immediate action in the Beginning, or Act 1 (Part 2), which embodies a false solution. Into that modus vivendi conflict-causing problems intrude, including sooner or later the inciting event, the problem whose solution will require the abiding problem from the past being resolved *necessarily* with the present, inciting problem. The protagonist initially makes false moves in dealing with that problem, then at the end of Act 1 settles on or is driven into a line of action she or he thinks will solve the problem. This is the Act 1 turning point into the Middle, or Act 2 (Part 3). Act 2 pursues that line of action until it reaches the *crisis* at the end of Act 2 when the attempted solution fails, or looks like it is about to fail, the emotional nadir for the hero. Thus the End, Act 3 (Part 4), represents the final climactic and intensely focused action on the part of the protagonist that succeeds in resolving the problem in the form it took in the *crisis*, or in tragedy fails. In any event, that problem with its fusion of past and present elements is solved, whether in a tale of moral redemption, as in *Schindler's List*, or in one of an action hero triumphing, as in *Raiders of the Lost Ark* and *Witness*. All is made clear, with the final values of the story asserted by its outcome. A New Beginning (Part 5) comes into view, which is the specific turn we imagine a story's "happily ever after" will take or the direction the community will take if the hero has been swept away in a tragedy.

Reviewing the fundamental story pattern this way makes clear just how dry, if typical, a description it is of dramatic action. You can guess only some of the nature of the dramatic journey we go on, as audience, through the hero and how the action plays within the context of the argument we are having with ourselves. The hero's journey, which every screenplay takes us on structurally through the fundamental story pattern, is not well described by the technical evaluation of action and character found in the various dramatic and screenwriting manuals going back as far as Aristotle's *Poetics*. There has been since the beginning of writing on drama the attempt to treat it as a structure within its own special bubble, but as I have been at pains to show throughout these essays, one element after another of that structure roots in the psyche and impacts our experience far beyond the realm of drama. We saw how the experience of fullness roots in the perception of human wholeness, while complexity implies a sense of the lack of integration of experience. The *heavy* we saw was the *raw* taken to the point of the experience of destructiveness without creative issue, while both moral substance and ambiguity are essential for story fullness and root in our innate ambivalence, while their lack leads to trivialization, until a drama becomes merely a moment in the history of entertainment. Slowness, we saw, arises from the sense of discontinuity in experience and our conscious inability to deal with more than one story at a time, while cause-and-effect writing is not just a sine qua non of good writing but implies the trustworthiness of experience, that one thing follows from another, whatever David Hume may say to the contrary. The difficult standard of necessary and probable makes that experience seem so real a screenplay becomes a convincing metaphor that *it is* reality, not its imitation. Our will to believe, if story elements are handled convincingly, is guided by these devices; our mythopoetic drive assembles the story elements into a coherent and revelatory experience.

Yet if structure can be discussed abstractly, and every specific story varies, what is the point, even in jest, of saying that drama is the story with a thousand faces? What is the underlying *heroic journey* being conveyed through the underlying *structure* the hero takes us on in each uniquely realized drama?

It falls into nine parts.

1. Arresting Life

Part 1 or the Past of the fundamental story pattern fits into this stage of the dramatic hero's journey. Here is that part of the protagonist's life—as well as those around him or her, whether in a narrow or broad community—that precedes the Beginning, the immediate action of the story. It is a retrospective time we learn of through the immediate action, as the need for its understanding and transformation becomes increasingly clear for the resolution of the immediate conflict that arises in a screenplay.

Much has happened here necessarily already. The prewar Schindler in *Schindler's List* is a business failure, his marriage a shambles. He is a fish out of water. Not even being a Nazi has provided the success he wanted. This is the Schindler whose relation to experience is amoral, a man prepared to exploit others ruthlessly at the start of the immediate action, as we see in his guilt-free taking of the Jews' apartment and manipulation through Stern of the Jewish businessmen.

Thus the behavior we see on the part of heroes at the beginning of the action is the continuation of how they have been in the past which, even worse, is based on a false adjustment to their problem(s). For Schindler, the false solution is the pursuit of greed.

Julie in *Blue* has lived unaware of her husband's infidelity, her own creativity submerged in his and her love for her daughter.

Terry in *On the Waterfront* has let himself be infantilized, bought off, and turned into a bum because of the dive he took for Charley and Johnny Friendly.

Book in *Witness* lives with a certainty about his milieu that is entirely wrong, surrounded by unperceived corruption in the police.

Hamlet in *Hamlet* is frozen in development by his perception of the pointlessness of action through the shock of his father's death.

The wife and husband in *Rashômon* betray in every version of the encounter with the bandit that they have spent their time together in ignorance of one another and themselves.

Michael Sr. in *Road To Perdition* has at once been a master hit man and lived as if another son for John Rooney; he is in for a rude awakening.

Isak Borg in *Wild Strawberries* has spent an entire life smugly self-satisfied, yet even at his end he must learn to see the lie he has been living and grow.

Heroes, then, stand in a false relation to the truth as fact, at the simplest; they may stand in a false relation to themselves, and possibly in a false relation to both the truth and themselves. They may stand in a false relation to morality. They may even stand in a false relation to God. Their lives are a lie, arrested in illusion.

2. Complying with the False

Now we can understand what establishing character, conflict, and milieu are about at the start of a screenplay, however labeled in a given manual. Whether or not we start off with a bang as in *Star Wars* or gradually as in *Rear Window*, we immediately settle into an initial stretch of action that lets us identify the nature of the reality of the story, whether magic realism, science fiction, romantic comedy, or any other style, and meet and identify with the key characters, in particular the heroine and/or hero. They behave as they are accustomed to. Their lives display the false modus vivendi with experience that is based on a false relation to truth or self, or both, as seen in *Arresting Life*.

As audience we don't immediately realize that falseness, any more than does the hero: *he thinks he is coping.* He, like ourselves, does not choose to live in conflict, illusion, or falseness, however often that turns out to be the case. We think we are living in accord more or less with the truth and with our selves, and are unhappy to discover that isn't the case. Lives are always solutions to their perceived problems, even if all too often those solutions in fact prove so unsatisfactory. The initial dramatic situation reflects this common human experience.

In *A Beautiful Mind*, neither we nor John Nash know he is mad; we accept Charles, for instance, as real. Time passes before we realize *we have been living the hero's error too.* The hero at the start of his journey, in a state of compliance with a false estimation of reality, places us through our identification with him within in the same experience of compliance with the false. His "false" may not be literally ours, yet it resonates with our own underlying sense that reality is not what it seems, nor are we as self-knowledgeable as we thought.

We are put, in other words, into Plato's cave and confuse shadows with reality.

In *Lantana* Val is under the sway of her daughter's death, while Leon and Sonja are caught in the failed marriage where Sonja craves passion and Leon feels numb. We see all this in the initial action, as they continue to live as they have been in response to their problems in the past. Terry lives in compliance with Johnny Friendly's expectations which *continues* to make him a bum, while Michael and the others in *The Godfather con-tinue* to act as if his destiny is separate from the family.

Jack in *The Importance of Being Earnest* lives a double life in ignorance of who he is and what his past is. Indiana has no idea the Nazis will show up that night in Nepal, as he catches up with Marion in *Raiders of the Lost Ark*, or that his nemesis is allied with them; he has no idea how much is going to be demanded beyond his usual resourcefulness.

Even in *Ran*, where the inciting event swiftly arrives, we see through the initial hunt, Ichimonji's dream, and the presentation of his decision to his sons a continuance of how he has been, of how he evaluates reality, self, and others, all of which will be proven thoroughly wrong.

Thus the stage of *Complying with the False* both allows the establish-ment of the story realm of the screenplay and draws us into the false re-lation of the hero to his experience *before he knows or admits or we know that it is false.* The nature of his compliance with falsity establishes what moral level the conflict is to be played out on, action-adventure to moral redemption. We eagerly go along with all this like proverbial lambs to the slaughter.

The initial phase of a screenplay, then, is always an exercise in irony.

This is the sense in which a screenplay begins in a *dumb* phase in plot-ting, as does the hero. The changes visible in the immediate action are illu-sory so long as the protagonist continues to comply with the false. Whether that will endure or change remains to be seen as the action unfolds.

We must remember that the hero has subverted his volition in both *Arresting Life* and *Complying with the False,* and *willingly* perpetuates his own self-deception.

3. Awakening

Into this initial *Complying with the False* phase of the action erupts the inciting event that leads to an *Awakening* of protagonists to their inner or outer false relations, or both. The inciting event cannot be solved in the immediate action unless the past falseness is also solved. That past falseness is a willing compliance with error mistakenly thought to resolve the conflict in the protagonist's life. The inciting event is a wake-up call, a bolt out of the blue as far as the hero is concerned, even if self-inflicted as with Ichimonji in *Ran*. Once this event appears it *must* be dealt with.

In *Kramer vs. Kramer* the inciting event comes as early as in *Ran*. Ted starts with the best day of his life, living as he has been throughout the years of his marriage, while Joanna has reached the breaking point. She breaks through his smugness when he returns home, refuses further *Complying with the False*, and leaves. That *forces* Ted into a reevaluation of his relation to Billy, parenting, himself, and his occupation, meaning his behavior in the world with others.

In *Lantana* the inciting event comes late in the form of Val's death, first misperceived as murder. This *forces* a collision between Leon and John where Leon continues *Complying with the False*; that is now isolated by the action and Leon slowly and reluctantly driven toward the truth.

The inciting event comes in the middle of the Beginning in *On the Waterfront*, with Edie's challenge to Terry's amorality and plea to help. In *Star Wars* the inciting event is late, near the end of the Beginning, as in *Lantana*, with the murder of Luke's uncle and aunt by stormtroopers; only after that does he join Obi-Wan Kenobi and begin to find his true nature. Similarly, the wake-up call is at the end of the Beginning for Schindler in *Schindler's List* as he watches Amon Goeth liquidate the ghetto; for Michael in *The Godfather* it comes as he promises to stand by his father in the hospital scene. For Jack in *The Importance of Being Earnest*, the inciting event is the deeply ironic command of Gwendolyn's mother to find a past as she denies his marriage proposal.

The hero's journey is the same in comedy and serious drama; how we relate to it differs only through the perspective given by the comic angle of vision.

The impact of this moment of *Awakening on us* jars us into a startled realization *of the price compliance exacts:* Terry is agonized by Edie's demand, Book stunned by the discovery of police corruption in *Witness*, and so on. This is only the beginning of the bitter cup the hero will have to drain: much more of the action must ensue and a deepening price for compliance with the false be exacted before he or we through him or her sees a way out. If the compliance has been with a false estimation of reality, then that will have to be corrected, though at the moment the wake-up call comes no one has any idea how to do that. It is the *necessity* for such action that is new for the protagonist. If the compliance has been to a false self, then a true self must be found. If the compliance has involved a false moral stance, as it does in our best stories, then establishing the *morally right* state of affairs becomes the story's focus.

For beyond the concordance with the inciting event in *Awakening,* the price of *Complying with the False* that begins to become apparent with the wake-up call is in proportion to the kind of damage and extent of compliance the hero has inflicted on himself and on his community, for the hero represents his community and his or her falseness to themselves falsifies their community, too.

Worse, the hero begins to become aware that the *nowness* of his life, the *presentness* of the action, is an illusion—that, in fact, he is caught up in a repetition of the past and not living in the present at all, however immediate the dramatic action may seem.

Romance offsets the absence of moral and "true/false self" dimensions in stories focused on a purely action level, even in Bond stories. Here the Campbellian "hero as lover" finding his other half comes into play: woman is most obviously symbolic on this level of storytelling and least developed as a person, whether Marion of *Raiders of the Lost Ark* or Jinx in *Die Another Day,* whom Bond goes back to save even though pursued himself.

It is in *Awakening,* finally, that characters begin to define whether they are going to pursue a *smart* development, which will entail both real transformation in story and character, or remain *dumb,* whatever the dramatic pressure may be, revealing character growth in terms of an ever greater deepening that is not, however, transformative.

4. Confused Growth—and the Pursuit of Error

If conscience has not characterized the hero before then it must be aroused, for we cannot change except through the perception of error, *of being wrong,* even in an action-adventure film as we just saw where gaining or regaining the woman stands in for this strand of development. Marion and Indiana's romance has failed in the past, and Marion is immediately reproachful toward him on his reappearance in her life in *Raiders of the Lost Ark.* Ambivalence is one thing, as we can see with Terry in *On the*

Waterfront with his complaining reaction to Joey's death, but ambivalence is our human condition and something with which we must necessarily live. Change is another matter, let alone growth, and the perception of error crucial for its motivation. *Complying with the False* is a *moral* error, which is the nature of Marion's complaint to Indiana; Jack is reproached for his having no past in *moral* terms in *The Importance of Being Earnest.* His failing may be amusingly put as an act of carelessness, but that act over which Jack had no control is made a matter of his volition by Lady Bracknell and faulted as a failure of character. He did the wrong thing. The case has already been made for Terry in *On the Waterfront.* For Schindler in *Schindler's List* the liquidation of the ghetto is decisive. Before this we see him betray a guilty conscience over the thanks of the one-armed worker; after the liquidation he begins to save Jews from Amon Goeth.

In the fundamental story pattern we speak of the false steps the hero takes after the inciting event occurs, as he becomes aware of the dimensions of the problem facing him and tries to find a solution. We see that the end of the Beginning is marked by his choosing or being driven into an attempted solution for the problem that has appeared with the inciting event. That "solution" makes up the developmental line of action in the Middle, Act 2.

This is true, but empty.

The hero, after the inciting event, finds himself unmoored from knowledge. He is not sure what is real or not, whom to trust, or what to do. He is like the man in the Platonic cave after he discovers the true nature of his shadows; how to behave after that is far from clear. Moreover, he is not at all happy about being enlightened. Life was easier before. So his first attempts represent a mix of half-hearted steps forward and a reluctance to let go of what he thought he knew, like Leon to an extreme in *Lantana.* The hero has the same reactions we would have in his position; he stands in for ourselves.

Consider the Middle in *Lantana* as Leon assumes John is guilty and discovers Sonja was a patient of Val's and then makes his ineffective confession, after finally listening to the tape. Leon thinks he has the answers even while his shortness of breath, unthinking violence, and declaration of numbness by now reveal only the extent to which *he fights to maintain a false relation to himself* even as he tries to solve his problems. He pursues error.

Schindler in *Schindler's List* is shocked by what happens to the ghetto and shown overlooking his empty factory. It's possible he is yet again about to fail: Amon Goeth at this point is a wholly unknown quantity. When Schindler goes to see him, he discovers Amon can be bought just like the other Nazi brass, yet Amon retains Stern in the camp, rightly understanding he is the key for Schindler and so for his own satisfaction through Schindler. Although Schindler regains his workers and resumes making money and now starts deliberately to save Jews, he is confused in conscience and still persevering in a course that at the End he will characterize as being a "war criminal." He is still far from the decision he will take in the *crisis* to spend his ill-gotten gains saving "his" Jews.

Jake in *Chinatown* is steeped in confusion until the *crisis*, when he finally learns the real relationship between Evelyn, her daughter/sister, and Evelyn's father, Noah Cross. He is not just duped in the beginning but allows himself to become romantically involved with Evelyn *and* consistently goes on misunderstanding what is going on. But a detective fascinates us because he must piece together reality, which is to say, *move from illusion to truth through error.*

Isak Borg in *Wild Strawberries* is stunned as the reality he seemed to have such a firm grasp on visibly unravels in his flashbacks and fantasies, while his efforts to interest Marianne are repulsed. His effort to change, his missteps, and his confusion are all palpable.

Terry's confusion is marked in *On the Waterfront* after Edie demands his help. He veers back and forth between Edie and Johnny Friendly until he takes Edie into his arms after being commanded to forget her. But then the path he pursues is an attempt to sort things out for himself, an illusion for any protagonist, and one which Johnny Friendly sees through instantly: Terry cannot be allowed to act as a free agent. No one can be so allowed by the holdfast character.

All this goes to show why if the initial confusion on *Awakening* over the inciting event gives way to a settled course of action that dominates the action of the Middle, that action in turn is betrayed in the *crisis* as a pursuit of error. Technically, if the problem were such the protagonist could solve it right away, there would be no ensuing action. But that solution is not deferred arbitrarily: it is deferred because it can only be discovered through error. The "testing" heroes are subjected to in the Middle is focused on this pursuit of error. Again, it is why the hero is able to stand in for us: he or she, like ourselves when we turn from the shadows and contemplate leaving the cave, must figure out how to do so while, just as in drama, *the hero's growth is always opposed by those whom it will most affect, namely, those presently in control of the story.*

For the story does not yet belong to the hero.

In *On the Waterfront* Terry almost loses Edie while Charlie is killed: now Terry's life is in danger. Failure stares him in the face in the *crisis.*

This is typical: Leon learns John is not guilty in the *crisis* in *Lantana;* Terry is reduced to futile rage; Julie's resolve in *Blue* to be involved collapses under Olivier's pressure. Will in *High Noon* ends up more alone than he would have been on the prairie before Amy abandoned him, for in the *crisis* he watches Amy and Helen leave. It is the nadir of his fortunes and felt as such, a pursuit of rectitude about to end in tragedy. All seem about to lose control of the story definitively.

The dramatic hero, unlike the mythological, is all too human. He will not journey to the father above, or below; his marriage, or lack of it, will not be sacred; he will, in the end, be alone, as even Harry Potter is in the Harry Potter films when he must face the basilisk and Tom Riddle in the second, or Professor Quirrell and Voldemort in the first.

The growth of the hero, then, is bound up in paradox. As he rises in awareness of the false and strikes out to find something better, he clearly begins a growth either *smart* or *dumb* in nature. But because of his all too marked humanity, that growth comes at the price of pursuing fresh error. His limitation in this regard goes right to the heart of our own as human beings. Terry in *On the Waterfront* typically grows greatly in the Middle: much as he rails against "conscience," he pursues it. His journey here represents the fact that all of us find our way in the dark with halting steps, glimpsing the truth like the proverbial light at the end of a very long tunnel, the escape route from Plato's cave. But that pursuit of error is purgative, for it strips the hero of illusion and to his true capacity, clearly seen at last, by finally revealing that the solution he has sought has been selfish, even as his capacities increase.

The selfish solution may persevere in life but must always fail in drama: the hero, when he acts truly, *acts for us.*

5. Failure of the False Solution

The failure of the selfish solution is only part of the story. Any solution that does not finally depend on the protagonist's *own* resources must also fail. This is what comes clear in the *crisis*—not just the failure of *Confused Growth and the Pursuit of Error* the hero embarks on at the end of the Beginning. What fails is an effort that in any way relies on others and yet at the same time isn't equally for others.

It's another paradox.

Terry leans on Father Barry and Edie in *On the Waterfront,* but what he discovers, as he survives the attempt to run him down and then in the End that testifying as Father Barry urges doesn't work either, is that his solution cannot be private or come from someone else.

Julie in *Blue* sees her effort to stand apart from life exploded in the *crisis,* and must face the reality that she must find a fresh solution *in engagement* with the others involved with her.

Schindler in *Schindler's List* has all the money he could possibly want as he learns in the *crisis* that the Jews are to be killed. But by pursuing both gain *and* saving Jews, his conscience has grown to the point this success is a failure. He realizes this as he wanders in his apartment and looks at his money. His solution has been selfish up to this point, and he could go as a success in his original terms and let his acts of mercy end up as transitory illusions. But he cannot do so.

The *crisis* reveals something else beyond the selfishness and erroneousness of the attempted solution to conflict. *The path pursued fails because it cannot undo the past.* Schindler won't be a *success* in his eyes if he leaves with his money. Terry won't act other than the way he has been as a bum, an animal, if he simply shoots Johnny Friendly in *On the Waterfront.* Julie in *Blue* won't solve the problems of her grief over her loss, or the misuse of her talent, or the misplacement of love with her husband rooted in the past, by trying to stand apart.

A curious thing happens with reference to *dumb* and *smart* character development through these last two phases of the hero's journey. *Dumb* characters are not affected at the moment of failure or by the preceding pursuit of error in the sense the pattern of their growth remains the same. The *crisis* may force a further revelation of character depth, as with Hamlet in *Hamlet,* or of capacity if an action-adventure hero, but though his situation may be critical such a protagonist's growth remains *dumb.* This is not true of *smart* characters. The pursuit of error and the moment of failure— actual or merely evoked as a possibility in the emotional nadir at the end of Act 2—bring the very question of such characters' success in transforming themselves into question. *Smart* characters have their essential drive in the story challenged. If *smart* characters fail, ultimately, then the entire transformative effort of their growth is wiped out in that failure, with all the implications of that for themselves and for all the others whose fate is dependent on them.

Imagine, if Terry fails in *On the Waterfront* he must flee with Edie or be killed. There will be no change for the community, and Friendly will remain in control on the docks. Terry's essay in living by conscience will be reduced to a daydream. Whether Terry flees or is killed in this exercise of the imagination, he leaves Johnny Friendly in possession of the story.

This would be a tragedy or, worse, a mishandling of storytelling descending from the *raw* into the *heavy*.

6. The Discovery of the True Solution

The true solution is for everyone, not just the hero. It may be immediately apparent, as when Shane in *Shane* must confront Ryker and Wilson, or Munny in *Unforgiven* confronts Slim and Little Bill. Or it may take a further stripping, as with Terry who futilely testifies against Friendly in *On the Waterfront* before he finally confronts his nemesis directly, as with Leon who makes a final misstep with Nick before finally seeing the truth.

Schindler has his money and negotiates the saving list with Amon, who is sure Schindler stands to gain, even though he can't figure out how in *Schindler's List*. Nonetheless, Schindler must still save the women and children from Auschwitz and survive the guards in his new factory.

Michael is in exile in *The Godfather* in the *crisis* ensuing on Sonny's death; he is brought back as the new don. But he must wait and proves capable of waiting, knowing the moment of reckoning must come, if not its date. That it must be against Barzini and his cohorts is knowledge he gains from the old don on his return.

Julie in *Blue*, after she gets over her shock that she cannot withdraw, realizes she must pursue a different course altogether, one of engagement. She begins by searching out her husband's mistress, whom she discovers is carrying his child.

Paul in *Analyze This* realizes he can't act as a thug any longer and must find a way to protect himself and his family, so he can withdraw from his criminal life. Jack in *The Importance of Being Earnest* prevents Cecily and Algy from marrying if he cannot; nonetheless, that act points the drama in the right direction, in that a solution must be found for all. The providential discovery of Miss Prism by Aunt Augusta and Miss Prism's story lead toward the general solution needed.

The *crisis*, then, represents not just an abstract failure of the line of action embarked at the end of the Beginning: it is the moment the selfishness of the protagonist's attempt becomes clear, i.e., when the *personal, moral inadequacy of her or his solution* becomes clear. Even in action-adventure films this moral element appears, if not directly flowing from the hero or heroine: Indiana has not been able to keep the Ark in *Raiders of the Lost Ark* yet cannot leave it in the hands of the Nazis: that is an obvious immorality he must rectify.

The Discovery of the True Solution thus leads directly into

7. The Heroic Deed

Terry in *On the Waterfront* at last *directly* confronts Johnny Friendly on the docks before the longshoremen over *the past*. The Campbellian holdfast in dramatic terms is the person who wishes to preserve the past unchanged that the characters were living at the Beginning who do not realize the delusiveness of their lives or that their *nowness* is only a repetition of past behavior. That is for the hero to make clear.

How creative Terry becomes when he finally confronts Johnny Friendly too! He speaks simply and eloquently but briefly with Charley in the taxi earlier; now he orates with increasing gusto before the fascinated longshoremen. He's glad now about testifying against Friendly. That wasn't ratting, as Friendly claims; he was ratting in the past when he sold himself out for Friendly, who sold out or killed anyone who didn't obey him. Friendly is the ratter, the betrayer. Friendly is reduced to challenging Terry to a physical fight, which gives Terry the chance to relive the past and bring it to a new conclusion. Beaten but successful, Terry leads the men to work.

The Heroic Deed asserts the true self for action-adventure heroes and in more substantive drama allows them to find their true self. This assertion and/or finding of the true self restores creativity and endows that quality on their immediate community.

Terry, through the play of drama, has restored his moral agency and thereby his ability to respond freshly to experience. In doing so, *he restores the creative flow of experience for everyone,* and by doing so, their individual and social health. In the hero myth the hero causes a return of the cosmic creativity; here a purely human return is established in terms of experience and psyche. The full self is found in playing, as Winnicott argues: the fullness of the self is what is restored for the triumphant hero or heroine, even if it takes a dark turn in Michael in *The Godfather* or Munny in *Unforgiven* or arouses our anger through the hero's limitation in *Witness*.

When Leon in *Lantana* breaks down and weeps, he at last overturns his numbness; now, because he can be creative again, he can meet *others'* needs, specifically Sonja's.

In *Ran* we see the positive solution for all take effect just before Saburo and Ichimonji die. *The Heroic Deed* here isn't facing down Johnny Friendly but Ichimonji's ability now to recognize Saburo as the true hero and successor, as the don does Michael in *The Godfather*. Lady Kaede is right to oppose this conjunction: if successful, it can only lead ultimately to a triumphant Saburo validated by the old hero and the perpetuation of the family success of Ichimonji and his heirs. By striking at them through Jiro, she dooms all connected with Ichimonji's family/clan; with the old and the new hero dead these fail and Lady Kaede triumphs in her vengeance, even in her moment of death. That *moves the story into her possession* and that of the subjugated allies, who now take their vengeance and resume what has been proven to be their rightful place.

Noteworthily, success in *The Heroic Deed* confirms a *smart* character's development as well as possession of the story. The success of a *smart* character, as we saw, transforms the social condition of his or her community. *Story transformation* embodies *social transformation*. That is *our experience* too through our identification with the hero as audience. His community stands in vicariously for our own, and the sensation we live through of a polity cleansed so that a New Beginning opens out we transiently and symbolically experience in the same manner. It is understandable now, parenthetically, why a breakdown in the will to believe is so fatal to drama. Our being forced to reflect on what otherwise happens as a matter of course through the story destroys a drama's ability to take us on any journey at all.

This transformation of social reality is central to the communal experience of drama in film and on stage. Even the TV audience, if solitary or no larger than a family unit, is multiplied into a group event through the numbers watching, although a group experience can only be implied by statistics. But drama in film and on stage is a journey undertaken within and ultimately for a renewed community.

What then is the hero's journey to this point?

The hero moves from a state of compliance with the false involving fact/truth or self or all three, a state he is comfortable enough with to override his guilt, one where change is more of a threat than going on compromised, whatever his ambivalence may be. He conspires with his own diminishment. His experience of this false modus vivendi as immediate and present in the Beginning, which we experience the same way through him, is an illusion. The truth is heroes are caught in a self-perpetuating, repetitive past. A key problem enters that begins a *necessary* process of *Awakening* that makes the falseness of the present in personal and factual terms increasingly apparent. The hero is confused and unsure what to do but finally chooses or stumbles into a line of action to solve his problem(s), aware that he has been living a lie that includes a truncated version of himself. Any step forward involves resistance from anyone whose life his actions challenge and change, especially the antagonist who is trying to preserve things as they are to maintain his grip on the story. That antagonist supports the false modus vivendi in which the creative flow of experience is stopped for it serves the antagonist's hold on power. Heroes are always the proponents of *Awakening* for all.

But the solution the hero pursues is also in error and fails, or at the least needs the tremendous refocusing provided by the *crisis*. All too often that solution is private and selfish up to the *crisis*. Selfishness in drama is a prescription to failure for him, for what might have worked initially for the heroine *Complying with the False* will no longer in the *crisis* and the End. His solution must work for all involved with him. Yet despite the pursuit of error he has grown in the process, incrementally recovering volition, which means his ability to act from conscience as a moral agent. The hero craves to act in truth with himself and strives to shed his false self. That final shedding takes place through the heroic act, which restores the fullness of self and the healthy creative response to reality both for heroes and their community, recognized as such by all in the *climax*.

That act overturns the grip of their opponent on the story. Herocs are the lens through which we focus our own growth to fullness as creative and morally responsible members of a cleansed community.

How is that so? By the commonplace I have so often previously referred to as identification, whether directly by identification, indirectly through empathy and sympathy, or through revulsion or fascination with evil or repugnant characters. These terms are the same, their apparent difference turning on a moral dimension allied to self-flattery in ourselves so that we say we identify with a hero of whom we approve, empathize or sympathize with one we are less sure of, or are fascinated or repulsed by one of whom we disapprove. Even though we refuse to say we identify with criminal protagonists, they too stand in for us. They too represent a path down which our nature can develop.

Identification is not a private "me" act in a "me vs. not me" reality: it happens in the cultural area, that area "you" and "I" share, where, as Winnicott correctly saw, most of our lives are spent. We are there together in both physical and imaginative interaction. The *imagination leaps the barrier between "me" and "not me," the dualism at the center of the argument we are having with ourselves, in that creative, existential area of cultural experience, Winnicott's "transitional area," the area where screenplays and drama occur.*

To say such an event is not real because it only occurs in the imagination is like saying a car is not real because it only works on land. Reality is a house with many rooms. Freud and Winnicott spent lifetimes exploring that house and trying to record what they saw as scientists: dramatists spend lifetimes going from room to room and conveying their insights with artistic passion within the demands of dramatic structure.

This act of identification is also a commonplace. Drama has always effected a union between separate psyches through identification. That is what Nietzsche evokes with his union of Apollonian and Dionysian in Greek tragedy. Freud sensed this malleability and potential of psyches to unify with his recognition of the similarity between the private and cultural superego in *Civilization and Its Discontents*. This unity of different psyches, if we can think beyond dualism, is not a mystery, any more than the slayer being the slain is mysterious in Campbell's mythological view, or Winnicott's struggle to show the profoundly creative impact of destruction on objects, meaning *fellow humans who survive;* that survival creates reality. In fact, the ultimate burden of Winnicott's third area of experience is that within the "transitional" space, the "me" and "not me" are already inextricably in contact.

Drama, through our identification with the hero, points to the same paradox, the union of the "me" of everyday life with the "not me" of the imaginary career of the dramatic protagonist.

In drama, what survives through the conflict is proven real *and* right. The resolution of conflict in the End and possibility of a new life glimpsed in the New Beginning *depends* on the continued effort to destroy the hero and what he or she stands for—on the creative effect of destructiveness, much as we balk at such language. That final reality, achieved through conflict, is what survives such testing, which as we have seen has deep implications for morality, creativity, the self, and the community of the protagonist's self. The all too human world created by dramatic heroes *is made whole through their journey.* Because we experience this through an act of the imagination, we require repeated such acts to renew the experience, for experience moves, caught in a space-time continuum that only stops in drama when the "villain" gains or holds the upper hand, for villains stand for some version of the frozen past; in life the flow of experience freezes when neurosis and psychosis overwhelm the self.

But this is not all.

8. Suffering

Heroes who pursue error in the present and complied more or less willingly with error and illusion in the past cannot lead until they atone for their past errors.

Aristotle recognized suffering as an essential ingredient in tragedy that flows naturally from tragic action. We accept suffering as such as a commonplace, whether the suffering of lovers, villains, or heroines and heroes. In Freud's view, suffering is inherent in human nature and civilization, such that much of how we behave can be understood as varying means by which we try to contain suffering. Yet the more civilized, the more we must suffer through the repression of instinctual satisfaction, of Eros and Thanatos, and so the deeper must be our sense of malaise and both unconscious and conscious guilt. Winnicott and modern psychoanalysis do not renounce this view; indeed, the presence of a constant stream of unconscious destructive fantasy with both the guilts and satisfactions it arouses is guaranteed to lend weight to Freud's traditional view. The very presence of the first transitional object, which Winnicott speaks of existing in a climate of trust and which represents the mother, *represents a denial of separation and hence of suffering.* The humorous tack taken by Aristophanes in Plato's *Symposium* doesn't hide the ensuing suffering of the "manwoman" separated by the gods into individual beings with an acute sense of loss and need to rejoin. As a comedic thinker he puts that suffering in a way to make us laugh, without any attempt to deny its presence.

The great religions of the world all speak of the suffering that is our lot, whether because fallen and living in a vale of sorrow, as in Christianity and Judaism, or bound to the corruptible wheel of reincarnation, as in Hinduism, or to deception and illusion, as in Buddhism, or to winning a cessation of suffering in heaven by obeying the Koran, as in Islam. The insights of the great religious figures have been hard won and caused all of them suffering. We have murdered some of them. In our own tradition, a smiling Christ who never mounts the cross seems inconceivable, for the suffering caused by our being caught up in error as to self and reality is the road to the truth; in religion, suffering is the road to the divine. Religious heroes are the ones who can take *our* suffering on their shoulders and atone for us, and guide us onto the path of righteousness *that relieves suffering.*

Thus we suffer through our need to atone for error, through our need to find the divine, and through the very nature of our need to live in a civilized manner, as well as from the inherent suffering built into human nature, with its impossible demands on reality and experience, for example, that "true love" should last forever. A hero who doesn't suffer would not be human to us. This takes us beyond the "testing" in the Middle, typically spoken of as trying the protagonist's resolve made at the end of the Beginning, as in the way Julie in *Blue* is systematically challenged in her effort to be uninvolved with life. It goes far beyond the testing inflicted on one lover by another, or a father on a daughter's suitor in a romance or romantic comedy. Suffering in heroes is inevitable because it results from testing, and testing is just a technical word for the destructive aspect of creativity in its attempt to destroy protagonists or their resolve in order to establish their reality. The responses and the accompanying alterations heroes go through in self and resolution are generated in reaction to that testing in the face of our inherent need to believe we rest in reality and truth.

Consider simple examples. Luke in *Star Wars* suffers because his uncle keeps delaying his leaving the farm: he is thwarted, frustrated, *and* compliant. When urged to take up the his true path as a Jedi knight by Obi-Wan Kenobi, Luke declines: there are chores to do at the farm; he's not free. When he returns to the farm there is the shock of his dead relations, whose death frees him to join Obi-Wan Kenobi *and* causes him additional suffering. He continues to suffer even while doing great deeds, most so when he thinks Darth Vader has killed Obi-Wan Kenobi, and later again as he sees his comrades destroyed in the attack on the Death Star. It is a constant thread in his experience.

Yet when he triumphs in the end he, for that time, *overcomes suffering.*

Or think of Paul in *Analyze This,* suffering because he cannot beat and kill, instead experiencing anxiety attacks rooted in a long-delayed coming to terms with his role in his father's death; or of Charlie in *Roxanne,* who suffers for his nose, as did his template, Cyrano, in *Cyrano de Bergerac,* and who helps give Roxanne to another man out of a sense of his own inadequacy. In the End, however, Paul and Charlie both triumph over suffering, the latter by "getting the girl," Paul by successfully exiting from the mob and cleansing himself of guilt over his father's death. Cyrano in Rostand's *Cyrano de Bergerac* moves down the path of romantic tragedy until the *climax* makes all clear and transforms Roxanne from a state of ignorance to truth.

Michael in *The Godfather* takes our understanding of suffering to another level. He is in error standing aside from the family: no sooner does he change than McCluskey hits him so severely he needs bandaging and even in Sicily shows a continuing bruising. It is a sign of suffering as outwardly telling as Ahab's ivory leg in *Moby Dick,* if on a smaller scale than that individual's engagement with the cosmos. Nor is Michael done suffering: he loses Apollonia in his false New Beginning, *in part because he has not yet atoned enough.* That biblical, Old Testament sense of proportion in dramatic writing is relentless in its drive to ensure that our heroes' suffering is proportionate to their error. Sonny has died: Michael must pay a life.

When we reach Terry in *On the Waterfront,* we see suffering as a constant thread from the beginning. He suffers over Joey's death, from love, from divided loyalties, from the sting of Edie's criticism, and then after he confesses to her, from her rejection. He suffers because his brother is murdered, and then because he is ostracized after testifying. Even Jimmy, one of the Golden Warriors, rejects him and kills all his pigeons, calling him one too. He suffers climactically as Friendly's thugs beat him so savagely he can't tell whether or not he is on his feet. No longshoreman comes to his aid: one remarks that Terry is one of Friendly's gang. Terry's atonement makes it possible for the longshoremen to follow him because he—just as importantly, at that moment—*survives*. So we can add a final and necessary path to suffering: *the creative effort to make real by the failure of destructiveness toward the hero and his transformations.* By the same token, Terry's walk leading the longshoremen to work is exhilarating: bruised and swaying, he has moved past Johnny Friendly's power and overcome suffering.

In the case of tragedy, suffering overwhelms protagonists *but dies with them* as the story moves to *others*. When the destructive side of creativity prevails, *time resumes for someone else than the hero*. In *drama,* we saw, we always end in affirmation for someone. This is the same destructive/creative testing that, when it results in a sense of destructiveness for its own sake without any creative final effect, drives us into a recoil from the *heavy.*

Isak Borg in *Wild Strawberries* by the End wants to change and atone. He wants to do something to help his son's marriage. His transformation through suffering is redemptive in our eyes; fortuitously, the power of Eros is such for Evald that he is driven to admit he cannot do without Marianne, and a film that seemed to look at the corruptible side of human experience with a religious intensity of expression ends on a positive note.

Suffering, in short, must burn out the erroneous part of the hero's character. That erroneous side must be seen to be what has not survived. The action through identification binds us with him and makes clear this element of his journey; consequently we accept his transformation and we experience it transiently as our *own*. Schindler's career in *Schindler's List* offers a final insight into the necessity of suffering. Those around Schindler suffer, whether Helen as Amon's maid or the many inmates in the camp in general and those Amon specifically torments or kills. Amon himself suffers, unable to carry through on his feelings for Helen except by beating her. Individuals Schindler saves often suffer first with Amon; finally Schindler himself suffers, first through losing his workforce as Amon wipes out the ghetto, then later, if briefly, when jailed for kissing a Jewish girl. But right up to the *climax* Schindler's suffering is implied, at best, and if overt, minor in emotional expression and consequence compared to the other major characters'. He seems instead a character of infinite resilience and resource, whether amorally putting his business together or later, moved by conscience, saving as many Jews as he can. He is not even rattled in Auschwitz as he buys the freedom of "his" women and children, even facing down a guard who wants to keep the children as he turns a girl's hand outward to display the softness needed, Schindler claims, to test shell casings for their smoothness.

Thus Schindler's breakdown as Stern and the Jews give him the ring in the *climax* is dramatically necessary if he is not to seem a kind of demigod we can watch with awe but not, finally, take as one of ourselves. As the inscription "Who saves one life, saves the world" is explained to Schindler, he at last completely breaks down, sobbing how he could and should have done more. He reproaches himself for keeping his gold Nazi party pin, his fancy car, and for his living so well on the money he made from the war, even though by now he has spent all of it for the sake of "his" Jews, bribing officials so they suffer no consequences from producing artillery shells that do not explode. Those reproaches strike home to our hearts, for who among us has not had similar feelings? That breakdown speaks to the essence of our experience as flawed human beings, to our unexpressed if powerfully felt suffering and guilt. That breakdown speaks to our depth of regret that we have failed ourselves and so failed the trust and need of those most dear and dependent on us. It speaks beyond our sense of failing our potential to falling too far short of "Love thy neighbor as thyself," that most impossible of injunctions and most moving expression of the creative urge toward universal love.

Suffering *creates us* human, and is the price we pay for our humanity. Suffering is the path to personal wholeness in the triumphant End in drama, to communal in the tragic; suffering is the road to the divine for the ultimate dramatic hero or heroine who, like Schindler, is finally a religious protagonist. They who survive their suffering or through their suffering make possible the renewal of the world around him *are* heroes, and because they are the ones we identify with, the path they take through suffering brings to our experience a sense of completion and fullness.

We cry we could have done more in *Schindler's List*; *we* stagger to our feet and lead the men in *On the Waterfront*; *we* annihilate our enemies in *The Godfather,* and kill the murderers in *High Noon.* We come to terms with our misunderstood life in *Wild Strawberries,* and effect a last minute change. We struggle to understand what has happened in *Rashômon,* and explore our variety in husband, wife and thief, and end with hope as the woodcutter takes the child at the story's end. *We* weep on the bed in *Analyze This* because we can no longer be evil. We rediscover our past at the end of *The Importance of Being Earnest* and, perhaps, lie about our name, in order to bring about a happy ending and a return to normalcy.

Now we can understand fully what it means to say that dramatic writing *always* ends with an affirmation of Eros and *always* overthrows Thanatos, even in film noir where the endings are so morally ambiguous. Morally volitional continuance, social and personal, is not just a matter of morality: it is the deepest expression of Eros.

Destruction as Thanatos is the nemesis of life and drama, of love in the broadest sense, however often it may prevail in life.

9. The New Life

What have heroes achieved, then, at the end of a screenplay and drama more widely? If they are action-adventure protagonists, they have proven their puissance; if more serious dramatic characters, they have achieved ego integration and wholeness; if comic heroes, they have achieved ego integration and wholeness and a redemption from the absurdity of life. The past is finally past, while the *present* opens as a *nowness* that is not an illusion. Schindler has led his flock to survival and himself to redemption; the circumstances that called forth his heroism are now past, and he and the others can move on to a genuine New Beginning also.

The New Life in the New Beginning, then, is another dramatic paradox: it is, simply, the true beginning. Until this point, action has repeated the past or challenged that repetition without final outcome; now these issues are settled. An interesting failure of a film like *Proof of Life* shows the price a film pays if the past is not adequately summoned into the immediate action and resolved along with the immediate conflict. A sense of loss and alienation is evoked for the Terry of that film, but his past has not been pulled into the action and explored and resolved. Consequently, the film feels that something is missing and is unsatisfactory. The relationship between husband and wife is evoked and resolved, although it too is problematic, for reasons having to do with credibility. Peter and Alice must change in relation to each other in each other's absence, even as Alice clearly falls for Terry, who is not so much heroic as impervious to Eros. Credibility suffers accordingly. *The New Life* for Alice and Peter does not convince; there is no *New Life* for Terry, no evocation and conciliation in the present with his past. Such an outcome cannot succeed in drama, whether substantively or commercially.

Thus the New Beginning with its *New Life*, which is always personal, can only be experienced if the old, failed beginning of the continuing past is fully evoked and dispelled. The movement of drama evokes the deepest of human dreams, that we can have a second chance *to do what we ought*. The personal, moral substance of the New Beginning is clear. That is why in *Ran* Kurosawa shows both Ayabe and particularly Fujimaki in a positive light at the start: they will be the true inheritors of the New Beginning.

I have stated the spiritual nature of drama strongly. But we are entitled to ask if this spiritual nature is an accident of the films reviewed here or simply of our particular times. Is it intrinsic to drama? Do we stand in profound error every time we evaluate or write a screenplay, or screenplay manual, or take a critical or aesthetic position that does not acknowledge this spiritual burden of drama? For it appears Campbell's belief that the modern task to return a sense of the spiritual to our lives and of brotherhood to our atomistic selves is exemplified by the nature of the dramatic hero's journey. It appears the true nature of dramatic action is from the unconscious to conscious, amoral to moral, destructive to creative, forgetful to remembering, divided to whole, absurdity to normalcy (comedy), and the deathtowardness of life (serious drama) to the possibility of a fresh, redeemed start where Eros triumphs over all that would divide, maim, debase, and murder the heart.

PART V

The Death and Life of Drama

CHAPTER 11

The Death and Life of Drama

D RAMA disappeared in the West from the early Roman Empire until its revival in the medieval church. Both births of drama in the West show it growing from religious practice. Drama's first great flowering in fifth-century Athens died when the religious impulse moved elsewhere in society, although a new form of comedy arose in the fourth century in Menander that influenced the Roman Plautus and Terence, and through them Shakespeare and ourselves. Menander took a great deal of inspiration from Euripides, the last great Greek tragedian, who also influenced Seneca, Nero's tutor. None of Seneca's plays were performed in his lifetime; they are the first "closet" dramas in history, although they too reach across the ages and influence us by being the model of tragedy for Shakespeare and the Elizabethans.

What we must recognize here is that drama can become so irrelevant it can literally disappear. The answer writers give to my hypothetical question about abolishing the dramatic enterprise in all its forms—namely, that if we did that enterprise would begin all over again—is disproved by history. Any earlier statement in these essays to the contrary must be amended in this light. There is indeed something in us drama impacts in its great moments, but those moments are transitory and we can be led down other cultural paths where drama cannot follow. A screenwriter who doesn't want to experience a "death of drama," even on the minor scale of his own efforts, needs to come to grips with what it is that gives drama its relevance and necessity.

We are certainly in one of the more protracted dramatic renewals on record, which begins in the late nineteenth century with the development of naturalism in response to the industrial revolution. Ibsen used naturalism to his own ends, and the writing conventions he created set much of the norm for what we take for granted in screenwriting today. With the advent of sound in film, which some lamented as the death of pure cinema, the dramatic impulse has gradually shifted from an increasingly moribund stage to film, reflected in the steadily growing stature of the screenwriters even in Hollywood, where their screen credit now lags just behind the director's. That too must change. We can refer to "Branagh's" *Much Ado about Nothing* because we know already it is Shakespeare's, but imagine if *Henry V* or *Hamlet* were new film scripts and Shakespeare was not given primary credit on screen but the director—the absurdity is obvious. There must first be the work before production can exist.

Let us begin with the first great birth of drama, rather than ourselves, in examining whether or not a spiritual burden is inherent and necessary to drama.

Prometheus in Athens, Gladiator in Rome

Tragedy is an Athenian achievement that was envied and admired throughout Greece, but it barely existed in the mid-sixth century BCE. Fifty years later, in 499 BCE, Aeschylus competed in the contests, or agons, between playwrights in the spring Greater Dionysia: we are looking, then, at a formidably fast development.

Everything happened at the same formidable speed in Athens from about this time. There had been some preliminary development toward tragedy starting about 600 BCE as Arion dressed men in goatskins to create a chorus of satyrs, the nature beings who celebrate the god Dionysus. Dionysus's worship was recent in Greece at that date, marked by mass, often lewd and riotous communal celebrations. Nietzsche derives his Dionysian impulse from this god whose worship passionately sweeps away the norms of behavior. Celebrants continued rowdy; women celebrants, maenads, flouted convention orgiastically in their ecstasies and sometimes turned lethal, as dramatized by Euripides in *The Bacchae*. Arion's action transformed this communal, celebratory worship into a performance by a special chorus of celebrants now attended by members of the larger community as spectators. The new celebratory choral songs were called dithyrambs, and competitions were now held to choose the best. From its beginning, then, tragedy develops as an Apollonian, form-giving effort to contain an actively oceanic impulse to dissolve all traditional social bonds in the name of religious transport to a god of resurrection.

Thespis wrote the first plays by creating the first actor, a man who stood out from the chorus to answer its questions. This actor used a mask, so could assume many roles: in fact, Thespis is said to have taken his show on the road, creating the first traveling theatre company on record. Nothing survives of his plays, although he received the first known prize for a tragic competition in 534 BCE: a goat. This theatrical development coincided with a burst of vigor after the long doldrums in Greece generally. Trade was stirring, and the populace: Athens took the lead in colonizing Ionia, today's Turkish coast. Other colonies were established widely too: Greece was again engaged with the larger world after the harsh impact of the Dorian invasions that swept away the Homeric world. In Athens the kings were overthrown by mid-sixth century and a dictatorship established by Peisistratus and his sons: it was Peisistratus who introduced the worship of Dionysus into Athens and associated the performance of tragedies with its spring festival, actively backing figures like Thespis and reinforcing the spiritual significance of this new form of drama. The interweaving of profound social and political reform, economic activity, entertainment, and religion is striking.

In fifty years, by 510 BCE, the dictators were gone, as Cleisthenes introduced a series of reforms that established direct democracy by adult male Athenians in the Assembly. It was something genuinely new in history, an experiment in self-responsibility that fascinated Greece and soon divided its city-states, some emulating Athens and others emulating more conservative models like Thebes or Athen's ultimate nemesis, Sparta. At the same time Greece was under increasing pressure from the Persian Empire, the greatest then ever known in the world, which conquered Ionia and was roused to anger against Greece when Athens actively aided an Ionian revolt the same year we first hear of Aeschylus. Aeschylus at his death requested that fighting at Marathon be mentioned on his gravestone, not that he was a tragedian. All the great tragedians were Athenian citizens, rulers of the city in the Assembly, and hoplites, meaning heavily armored soldiers; Sophocles was a general. A man like Socrates took his place in the fighting line. These Athenian men possessed a unity of life alien to us: an artistic career was not separated from a general involvement in society and being equally a politician and soldier.

Thus as we consider Athens we must see a political and social transformation simultaneous with a new religion rising to prominence, with all of which the first great burst of dramatic writing was intimately in-volved and embodied.

Athen's involvement with the Ionian revolt sparked the Persian invasion of Greece with its famous incidents: the death of three hundred Spartans at Thermopylae, the triumph of the Greek fleet at Salamis, and the destruction of the remaining Persian army at Platea in 479 BCE. Athens carried the war to the Persians in Cyprus, Ionia, the Middle East, and Egypt. It founded and then turned the Delian League into an empire, erected the Parthenon and other buildings on the Acropolis, and finally plunged into the Peloponnesian War with Sparta and its allies for dominance in Greece in a frenzy of self-destruction that went on for thirty years and devastated Greece. Only fifty years later an exhausted, divided Greece fell to Philip of Macedonia and his son, Alexander.

Within this transformative and violent background there was an intellectual and creative explosion in Athens that remains unsurpassed, if on some rare occasions matched. Now Aeschylus, Sophocles, and Euripides wrote dramas for the competitions in the Greater Dionysia that grappled with the "great questions" as their natural métier: the purpose of the gods, the nature of man, the inscrutable burdens of destiny, and the nature of justice.

Recently, Jacob Burckhardt's lectures on Athens and Greece in this period have been gathered up and published.[1] The young Nietzsche takes off from Burckhardt's thought in *The Birth of Tragedy*. Burckhardt's evaluation of Athens is revelatory for our purposes too.

He observes how well the fifth century BCE started. Athens was triumphant, the Persians on the run, and in the west, the Carthaginians defeated in Sicily. Ionia was free. Athens fascinated the Greeks; Burckhardt observes the city was a continual overachiever, undertaking projects seemingly beyond its ability and population base out of sheer esprit and daring. Even an exile could thrive there, unlike the case for the more traditional city states. Athens was Greece's great market and emporium, as well as undisputed center of intellectual and cultural life. The ideal of *kalokagatheia* predominated at the start of its great century, embodying a blend of wealth, nobility, and excellence which the male citizens strove to embody. The Athenians thought well of themselves too, certain they had created civilization itself. History *and* religion in the form of myth were continuous, living strands interwoven with politics and used as a matter of course in the great tragedies.

For myth, according to Burckhardt, although so shadowy a literary relic for ourselves, was alive and public in Athens, and reached the level of a publicly celebrated religion through the tragic dramatists. We need to remember that the renewal of life after winter was celebrated in the Greater Dionysia in the spring, and that Dionysus is a god who dies and is reborn, his return the creative root bursting into literal flower.

Three tragedies a day were performed in these competitions, with a bawdy, comic satyr play at their end. Performance started at dawn and ended at dusk, the same male, governing citizens from the military, political, and social worlds the participants and audience. Nor were the plays themselves offered in the droning, dull performance often satirized, as in Woody Allen's *Mighty Aphrodite:* they were sung and danced, with special effects like thunder, flying dragons, or gods appearing on stage. All these effects were carried out in a way adequate for the imagination then, as our own high tech productions meet our expectations. Then as now the sense of dramatic reality flows from the emotional persuasiveness of the action, buttressed by cause-and-effect and necessary and probable writing, not from the sophistication of production machinery.

But Greek tragedy was capable of effects we can only envy: so persuasive were some choral performances that on at least one memorable occasion the first rows of viewers were thunderstruck and fled the apparitions before them as if they were literally real. Those who led the city were in the first rows and the performance was Aeschylus's *Libation Bearers,* which begins with a chorus of Furies appearing, the dark goddesses of vengeance. Imagine a performance in Washington so compelling that the president and his immediate staff, the leaders of Congressional committees, the justices of the Supreme Court, and top brass from the Pentagon run in panic from the performers. Tragedy was the "last and grandest realization of myth," its playwrights nationally famous, their work literally shocking. Burckhardt remarks on the "passionate private will that drove these people on," whether in warfare, politics, culture, or religion.[2]

But a life lived on the edge came with a price that Burckhardt sums up as lawsuits, megalomania, and self-exhaustion. By the end of the fifth century, Plato felt embittered about Athenian society which executed his mentor, Socrates, after it lost the war with Sparta. Athens began its great century with an unforced morality, an almost impressionable, tender conscience, such that it felt criticism sorely even if it continued what it was doing, often quite brutally in warfare. By the end it was hysterical and self-destructive.

Athenian democracy itself was exhausting, and over the century natural eloquence gave way to oratory and rhetoric. These, by becoming techniques available to anyone, empowered the mediocre. After Pericles, there is a severe decline in Athenian leadership, with second-rates and demagogues leading the Assembly. Breeding gave way to money, modesty declined, and the urge to excellence became the urge to self-glorification, culminating by the century's end in a man like Alcibiades, wholly involved in his own glory like someone from the Renaissance, whether leading Athens, helping Sparta defeat Athens, or doing another turn as the would-be savior of Athens.

Homosexual love was common and not a feature of the decline: the most effective fighters in the next century before Alexander were the Theban Sacred Band of homosexual lovers who helped destroy Spartan predominance on the battlefield. But homosexuality does indicate how one-sided Athenian and Greek society was, for women were without political rights and heavily segregated. Some courtesans achieved great fame, like Pericles' companion Aspasia, but on the whole this was rare. Men were unpolished in love and untrained in love affairs, while Athenian literature is almost uniform in casting aspersions on the opposite sex.

The Greeks did like to talk, meaning men in social gatherings called symposia, where conversation emphasized wit and intelligence arguing great themes however much wine was drunk, something reproduced by Plato in his *Symposium.* Sociability seemed "inborn in Greeks."[3] Great themes were not restricted to the drama. These symposia continued all through the looming failure of the Peloponnesian War: "That this was possible at such a time supports Renan's belief that the stormy periods of history are actually favorable to the life of the mind."[4]

Burckhardt has an unusually positive opinion of the Sophists who entered into this feverish society over the course of the century, a group of men given a bad name by later philosophers but who had the role of teachers at the time, often imparting practical subjects as well as amorality, as embodied in their teaching that there are two sides to every issue, or that "might makes right." Crucially, the Sophists were skeptical about received religion and the myths, *as the Athenians became too as the fifth century wore on.* They led a widespread rejection of myth in favor of a lucid, rationalistic way of thinking. Euripides supported them and was Socrates' friend: he attacked the very myths he used in his plays, correcting them and giving voice to the demand the gods live by the same standards as men. The life went out of the myths, as well as the steel from the Athenian character, with the decay sparked by the war, rhetoric, self-aggrandizement, and rationalism. Athens never again emulated the military feats of the fifth century; we remember the city now for its cultural achievements.

Nietzsche spells out the consequences of this decline of myth tellingly in *The Birth of Tragedy*. As we have seen, he develops a view of tragedy as the ultimate joining of Apollonian and Dionysian impulses, such that at the climax "Apollo" gives shape to and communicates "Dionysus," unifying and giving voice to the impulses to order and to sweep away, to create and destroy, to blend with everything and speak from the self's heart, to join in the action of the characters and imagine ourselves part of the chorus, some of whose songs approach the power of the Psalms.

Consider this from the second choral ode in *Oedipus Rex:*

Let me be reverent in the ways of right,
Lowly the paths I journey on;
Let all my words and actions keep
The laws of the pure universe
From highest Heaven handed down.
For Heaven is their bright nurse,
Those generations of the realms of light;
Ah, never of mortal kind were they begot,
Nor are they slaves of memory, lost in sleep:
Their Father is greater than Time, and ages not.[5]

Or from *Oedipus at Colonus:*

Though he has watched a decent age pass by,
A man will sometimes still desire the world.
I swear I see no wisdom in that man.
The endless hours pile up a drift of pain
More unrelieved each day; and as for pleasure,
When he is sunken in excessive age,
You will not see his pleasure anywhere.
The last attendant is the same for all,
Old men and young alike, as in its season

> Man's heritage of underworld appears:
> There being then no epithalamion,
> No music and no dance. Death is the finish.[6]

Even Euripides in *The Bacchae* writes in this vein.

> Slow, yet unfailing, move the Powers
> Of heaven with the moving hours.
> When mind runs mad, dishonors God,
> And worships self and senseless pride,
> Then Law eternal wields the rod.
> Still Heaven hunts down the impious man,
> Though divine subtlety may hide
> Time's creeping foot. No mortal ought
> To challenge time—to overbear
> Custom in act, or age in thought.
> All men, at little cost, may share
> The blessing of a pious creed;
> Truths more than mortal, which began
> In the beginning, and belong
> To the very nature—these indeed
> Reign in our world, are fixed and strong.[7]

That is part of the last great spiritual trope from Greek tragedy in the last great play written by an old man in exile still married to reason and using, finally, the very form of Greek tragedy against itself to witness the perils of mass delusion and violence. All three quotes, if any were needed, make clear the spiritual burden assumed as a central thread in myth as given its last great turn by classic tragedy.

Nietzsche develops a detailed critique of Euripides' challenge to myth. For Nietzsche, Euripides is blind to the opportunity offered by tragedy of unifying primary human, apparently opposing drives, or how by doing so tragedy quite rightly belonged in a supreme religious festival and gave meaningful voice to human wholeness and transcendence. All this was as mysterious and doubtful to Euripides as to his friend Socrates and required a reform. Perhaps from a rational perspective tragedy and myth did. Psychological realism enters with Euripides—sentimental emotionality, and feminine passion as a motive power—as in the *Hippolytus* and *Medea*. Spectacle grows in importance, and a Euripidean development of plotting whereby the audience is told at the start of the action what to expect and at the end a god is flown in by a machine, the deus ex machina, to clear up any untidiness. Everything is rational and clear. The importance of the chorus fades, and with it music and dance.

> Yet the modish anti-Dionysiac spirit shows itself most clearly in the denouements of the new plays. In the older tragedy one could feel at the end the metaphysical solace, without which it is impossible to imagine our taking pleasure in tragedy.[8]

Instead there is now a new spirit:

> It believes that the world can be corrected through knowledge and that life should be guided by science; that it is actually in a position to confine man within the narrow circle of soluble tasks, where he can cheerfully say to life: "I want you. You are worth knowing."[9]

In other words, a rational view of life and a reduction of mystery to the knowable have been substituted in tragedy in place of a perception that combined often profound viewpoints concerning the great issues with an underlying act of unification of the warring parts of human nature through the dramatic action, the Nietzschean fusion of Apollonian and Dionysian. The new drama succeeding Euripides loses touch with the impossibility of avoiding conflict in self and society, as Freud might say, or the peculiarity of creativity that can be paradoxically destructive, as seen by Campbell and Winnicott, and loses the ability to spark the sense of tragic wonder or "metaphysical solace" Aristotle and Nietzsche saw as characteristic. Nietzsche, of course, may be right about the Greeks, but he is also looking about nineteenth-century Europe and taking issue with the new scientific, materialist optimism all around him embedded in the socialist dream of perfecting society. Painful as it has been, history has taught us to move from that dream too.

What is clear is how the loss of spiritual weight in the drama coincided inevitably with the decline of tragedy and drama generally in an exhausted, overwrought Athens, and with the quality of the writers drawn to the art. It hardly matters what we make out of Nietzsche's metaphysical solace or Aristotle's tragic wonder beyond noting their absence after Euripides' *The Bacchae* at the end of the fifth-century Athenian apogee. As Burckhardt pointedly writes, there was in fact no easy optimism or serenity in Greece in the fourth century but a general sense of malaise of which the famous Greek "serenity" could only be a denial. What succeeded tragedy was a comedy of *types* introduced by Menander, creating the dramatic repertoire of the nurse, ingénue, braggart-soldier, busybody, and so on that have been staples of comic writing ever since. Experience is stylized in such writing which, as we know, in comedic form enshrines a flight from reality. Comedy dies out too, after being given a last spin by Terrence and Plautus in Rome in the first century BCE.

Neither form of drama met the spiritual needs of its audience any longer; with that failure, it died.

Gladiator gives us a glimpse into the dominant entertainment that rose as drama declined and persisted for centuries after drama's death. Maximus falls from a great height by refusing to accept in a timely manner Marcus Aurelius's request that he restore the republic. Instead, his son Commodus kills Marcus and has Maximus's family murdered and attempts to kill Maximus when he refuses obedience. The wounded Maximus discovers his family's fate and despairs. A caravan nurses him to health and sells him as a slave to Proximo, a freed gladiator, who needs fodder for provincial gladiatorial shows. Maximus, however, won't fight. Proximo gives a speech before their first "performance," reminding his fighters that if they can't control their lives, then they can by fighting at least be remembered as men. Maximus fights, startled by the crowd's cheers as he triumphs. By the second time we see him fight he is the premier gladiator. He enters the arena alone first, slaughters a group of nervous opponents, then throws his sword into the crowd. "Are you not entertained?" he challenges them. He has learned a crucial lesson: killing men spectacularly is the ultimate expression of conflict and entertainment. He has become a star.

He returns to Rome as part of Proximo's "troupe": win the crowd, Proximo tells him, and you rule Rome, may gain your freedom and make a lot of money. Maximus, however, seeks vengeance on Commodus. So he does win the crowd in spectacular fight sequences and joins a plot against Commodus. The plot fails and Commodus wounds Maximus before facing him in the arena himself to win back the crowd. But Maximus kills him anyway. The hero's triumph may be for the community, but it is always won personally.

What chance is there for an art form like drama that has lost spiritual meaning and become merely a trivial entertainment against an entertainment that pits man against man and caters directly to our destructiveness? It is *raw* but not *heavy,* for there is a winner, while *we* as audience control the fate of the fallen with a thumbs up or down. We are made vicarious masters of life and death. Can a stage full of corpses that then rise for applause at the curtain compete with the emperor Claudius, who once famously staged a gladiatorial sea battle, ranting on the shore he would execute everyone if they didn't fight better? Can it match the confrontation of Roman and Carthaginian in *Gladiator,* the sacrifice of repressed minorities to wild beasts, the wholesale slaughter of Christian fanatics? *Gladiator* may be a film giving an entirely modern spin on this Roman "entertainment," but there were in fact gladiators in Rome and the provinces who provided regular "entertainments" of this kind, even in the Christian empire following Constantine's conversion in the fourth century. The answer is clear to the question starting this paragraph: drama could not, and historically did not, compete against such "entertainment."

Greek tragedy was the "last and grandest realization of myth," as Burckhardt points out and Nietzsche develops at length; both agreed that with its collapse the religious impulse hardly disappeared, but its public, penultimate spin of mythic belief gave way instead to underground religious cults like the Eleusinian Mysteries in Greece and later to the plethora of cults vying for supremacy in the Roman Empire, until finally Christianity prevailed. Nietzsche adds, "Every culture that has lost myth has lost, by the same token, its natural, healthy creativity. Only a horizon ringed about with myths can unify a culture."[10] This echoes Campbell's view that the traditional myths are dead in our culture and we have the burden of creating a new and unifying one out of ourselves. There is no guarantee we will do so. The emphasis on "healthy creativity" is particularly revealing, in view of Winnicott's view that the creative response to experience is characteristic of health. The death of drama in the ancient world indicates a spiritual confusion and loss and a growing debasement of public and private life, features the early church fathers attacked constantly. There is also an unexpected overlap with Freud's concluding thoughts in *Civilization and Its Discontents.*

But there is a question which I can hardly evade. If the development of civilization has such a far-reaching similarity to the development of the individual and if it employs the same methods, may we not be justified in reaching the diagnosis that, under the influence of cultural urges, some civilizations, or some epochs of civilization—possibly the whole of mankind—have become neurotic?[11]

Burckhardt closes his remarks on fifth-century Athens by observing, "For they were all being carried onwards and expected a violent end, without knowing what it would be."[12] Freud's last lines in *Civilization and Its Discontents* are:

And now it is to be expected that the other of the two "Heavenly Powers" [he refers to Thanatos and Eros], eternal Eros, will make an effort to assert himself in the struggle with his equally immortal adversary. But who can tell with what success and with what result?[13]

The final sentence was a last-minute addition as his attention turned toward the rise of Hitler. The spiritual impulse can go out of drama: an entire civilization can corrupt itself with a worship of Thanatos. There is no room for the creative flow that manifests itself in drama to endure in such a world, while its ultimate celebration of Eros must in such a context seem profoundly false.

Shakespeare in Elizabeth's London

Plato's cave is the key metaphor for the Greeks after the religious drive moved past the last flowering of myth in public celebration to private religious sects. The cave encapsulates a society in decline, no longer sure of its hold on the truth, nowhere better expressed than by Oedipus's cry of anguish in the climax of *Oedipus Rex* as the truth of his efforts to avoid the prophecy he would kill his father and marry his mother breaks in on him. In that moment he turns 180 degrees, so instead of the phantoms of his desire he now sees things according to a true light.

But the cave is not the key metaphor for the Elizabethans or for ourselves. For the Elizabethans it is the mirror provided by the magic of drama that shows time and character their true lineaments.

HAMLET

... for anything so overdone is from the purpose of playing, whose
end, both at the first and now, was and is, to hold, as 'twere, the
mirror up to nature; to show virtue her own feature, scorn her
own image, and the very age and body of the time his form and
pressure.[14]

Hamlet's antipathy in *Hamlet* to overemoting reminds me of Winnicott,
who points out that playing is its own reality but can be brought to a halt
if instinct is too aroused. Hamming it up is one way of thinking about this
overexcitation, for playing depends on its ability to convince in its own
terms. Hamlet's concern not to disrupt playing shows how profoundly
the ground has shifted from the Platonic view. In Shakespeare's words for
Hamlet, the truth is approached paradoxically through illusion through
playing, because reality is not apparent in everyday experience. We begin
to look at how our minds work when we look into the Elizabethan mirror. As eminent a critical thinker as Harold Bloom dates the creation of
modern consciousness to Shakespeare, specifically to Hamlet, and as a
dumb character he is particularly suitable for this inward turn, for Hamlet does not transform himself as he grows but instead steadily deepens
in insight.[15] Bloom is writing our own governing metaphor backward
into the Elizabethans: the inward look, with all the virtues of looking at
ourselves in depth combined with the solipsistic peril that angle of vision
entails. Yet that clearly starts with a mirror that reflects the inward condition of the viewer, his true "form and pressure."

How do the Elizabethans get to this mirror? Does drama play a spiritual role for them too?

They get to both through the immediate ability of political power to
spark a political, social, and religious transformation, and through a swift
capitalization of the heretofore long-term development of drama after its
rebirth within the church five hundred years earlier.

The Tudor monarchy begins in 1485 with Henry VII; his overthrow of
Richard III furnishes the material for one of Shakespeare's enduringly fascinating plays. The period of civil war Henry brought to an end furnishes
the material for Shakespeare's early history plays. But if Henry VII ended
a period of political upheaval, spiritually England was within the embrace
of the broad Catholic Church and the traditions of Europe; it has never
been so European since.

Henry VIII began handsome, dashing, and well-off. He even wrote a defense of Catholicism in response to Luther; Luther's epochal Theses were nailed to the cathedral door in 1517. But Henry for political reasons introduced a religious crisis. He wanted a wife who could bear him a son but could not get a divorce because the pope was in terror of Charles V of Spain, who ruled most of Western Europe and had just sacked Rome. Henry's wife, Catherine, was a member of Charles's royal family. This was the hard politics under Henry's famous romance with Anne Boleyn, Elizabeth the Great's mother. As a consequence, Henry turned his back on Rome.

In 1534 he pushed the Act of Supremacy through Parliament, which made himself head of the still Catholic English Church, although now his divorce of Catherine and marriage to Anne was legalized and accepted *in England.* But Henry had only started. As head of the Church in England he could now deal with his endless need for money, attend to the late medieval corruptions of the church that were endemic throughout Europe, and bind the English governing class to his new order. He dissolved the ancient monasteries and seized their great expanse of lands and wealth, keeping a good portion of these for himself but giving the rest to the nobility and what now became the gentility of England. They would be the backbone of the monarchy for centuries.

Anne of course lost her head; Henry still needed a male heir, dreading the return of the civil wars his father had ended, and Anne failed him. He finally achieved his goal with the birth of the frail Edward VI, although Edward's mother, Jane Seymour, died of natural causes. In 1544 Parliament recognized Mary and Elizabeth in succession to Edward; Henry died in 1547.

Trends as well as styles persevere: what began as a state power grab turned more religious under Edward, as England was now divided between Catholics and Protestants who in turn divided between Lutherans and Calvinists, both hostile to the other sects also multiplying. Catholics were caught ever more severely between their loyalty to England and Rome. When Hamlet half a century later laments in *Hamlet* that he was born to set right a time out of joint, his sentiments would have seemed all too pertinent to his audience. The abiding legacy of Edward's brief reign would be the *Book of Common Prayer,* which became the basis of the Anglican Church, the state religion evolving under the king and archbishop of Canterbury.

Mary tried to restore Catholicism in her equally brief reign. She married Philip of Spain who later gave the occasion for the Elizabethan apogee with the destruction of his armada in 1588. Mary earned her sobriquet, "Bloody Mary": her archbishop gained his position as the former Archbishop Cranmer was burned at the stake as a heretic. Religious divisions now attained profound and often lethal dimensions. Elizabeth herself was in danger under Mary because, while she observed Catholic rites, she was a Protestant. By the time Elizabeth ascended the throne in 1558, England was politically peripheral to Europe, in danger from the Catholicism as close to her shores as France and the Lowlands, modern Belgium and Holland, then under Spanish rule, impoverished, weak, and torn with religious dissension.

That's easy to say, but what does "torn by religious dissension" mean? Certainly, to some extent, it meant many *believed with increasing zealotry*, regardless of which faith they adhered to. The crisis of faith paradoxically deepened belief as it multiplied sects that divided the country and provided the fuel for destructive acts against one another. It is an instructive illustration of the way destructiveness can bind a group together *if* it turns its aggression against others, as Freud saw so acutely in *Civilization and Its Discontents*. The order of Elizabethan civil society was under as great a stress as our own has been under the pressure of great wars and the profoundest political, social, and technological changes in history.

The paradoxes continue. Other Elizabethans were not sure what to believe or so capable of changing belief from a lesser to a greater extreme. Some obeyed the laws and took their beliefs underground, hoping outward compliance would preserve them from persecution, particularly Catholics. For all the zealotry *there was no perceived governing spiritual order*, and *in consequence* the political and social order of the state was endangered from within and without. A thinking person could wonder what was the nature of reality and his or her role within it, and could ask, "What is the purpose of life, and what will happen to me at death?" Once the answers had been widely accepted; now they were not. An Elizabethan could live in an anguish of doubt akin to our own. The malaise Burckhardt notes in the Greeks appears as existential anxiety in the great Shakespearean tragedies.

This was not all. Elizabeth was excommunicated by the pope and legally became a target for Catholics aching to be martyred, while others held the view that as a woman she was unfit to reign, including John Knox in Scotland, who had to trim his views to maintain English favor for his efforts to transform Scottish religion. In response, Elizabeth developed a police state under Walsingham to contain internal and external plots and safeguard her life. Complicating everything was the absence of a direct heir: Elizabeth's death meant the ascent of the imprisoned Catholic Mary of Scotland to the throne until her execution in 1587, and a renewed, protracted civil war.

A religious upheaval is fundamental in understanding ourselves as well as the Elizabethans, for religion answers the great questions concerning the nature of reality, life's purpose and conduct, and our relation to the afterlife. For these to be unsettled means everything else occurs within an unsettled, uncomfortable sense of the world, where nothing finally feels sure.

English drama exemplified by Shakespeare rose within this context even more meteorically than Greek tragedy, regardless of the length of time that had passed since drama had been reborn. There is a quantum leap from late medieval drama to the Elizabethan stage.

Drama reappeared in the tenth century in the church as the "Quem Queritas Trope," where three women question the angel at Christ's sepulcher. As with Greek drama, the new drama's womb is religious, and medieval drama too at first was sung, as Gregorian chant. The trope soon had three episodes: the original questions, the apostles hurrying to the sepulcher, and an episode starring Mary Magdalene. Swiftly nativity plays developed that dealt with the dramatic events of Christ's birth. All was still sung, as with the Greeks. By 1175 these church dramatizations had grown into *plays* mundane enough the church forced them outdoors. A fluid, cinematic staging evolved, making use of church porticoes, so that the "stage" held multiple areas—designated hell, the terrestrial world, and heaven—between which the action could flow swiftly. Familiar stage effects like costumes, dramatic dialogue, and spectacle evolved. The plays moved into courts and marketplaces and coalesced into mystery cycles, some of which are still performed in Europe and run for weeks.

England developed five notable mystery cycles: the Chester (25 one-act plays), York (48), Wakefield (with the famous shepherds' plays), Coventry (3), and Ludus (43). Some of these may still have been around in Shakespeare's youth for him to see. Sometimes these were presented in great processional wagons with a stage above and dressing room below, each stage presenting a particular scene explained by mounted narrators to the crowds thronging narrow medieval streets as the wagons passed. Actors mixed with the audience, while the medieval guilds vied with one another to sponsor particular parts of plays—the bakers, "The Last Supper"; the shipwrights, "Noah's Ark"; and so on. The Greeks drew on living myth; medieval drama relied on the Bible. Production became ruinously expensive, but at least all saw the plays, commoner as well as nobility. All were edifying; however, the spectacular effects might overwhelm religious content, whether mechanical camels or lightning, the sacrifice of real lambs or a Judas nearly hung as a superrealistic effect.

But as Protestant "reforms" moved on in England, these mystery cycles were replaced by new morality plays. *Everyman* is a good example of these. The bawdier elements from the older plays split off into roving troupes performing secular farces. New elements entered in Elizabeth's reign with the revival of classical drama through the universities under Renaissance influence, which combined with the development of native romance. As if there wasn't enough change, the English language was in upheaval too, such that we can understand the Elizabethans today despite obscurities, while the fundamental rhythm of English developed into iambic pentameter, the blank verse created before Shakespeare by Surrey and Sussex. Shakespeare invented more words than anyone in the history of our language.

So we must think of the Elizabethans going through an upheaval in religion, politics, society, *and the language and art* through which to express themselves, all at once. The experience was at once exhilarating and frightening: great possibility coexisted beside great insecurity. *Everything* was up for grabs.

Elizabethan tragicomedy draws all these dramatic elements together: morality play, humor, the revival of classical forms and native romance. We accept the resulting blend to this day, believing a drama should have elements of humor and common characters as well as higher, even if the former start off in Elizabethan times as objects of ridicule; that there should be a happy ending, although tragedy is not ruled out; and that there should be a sense of weight, of existential/spiritual meaningfulness, even if some dramas seem hopelessly trivial or one-sided, as in some of the early comedies of Shakespeare. Earlier tragedies like Marlowe's *Doc-*

tor Faustus or *Tamburlaine* seem flawed because low in humor and high in bombast.

In 1561, only three years after Elizabeth becomes queen, *Gorbudoc* is staged at the Inns of Court in blank verse, patterned on Seneca, with horror piled on horror in the story. *Titus Andronicus* is the closest of Shakespeare's plays to Seneca. The more popular native romances and comedies were performed outside the cities, meaning across the Thames in London, under pressure from clerics and the early forebears of the Puritans among London's city councilors. After 1576 ten great theatres developed on the South Bank, where today the National Theatre stands and a rebuilt Globe. All were public and unroofed, untethered to any church and the Bible, secular and audience dependent, protected by the patronage of some great figure but nonetheless the first great flowering of commercial theatre in the West. Six acting companies dominated production and performance, and all roles were performed by men or apprentice boys; women actresses had to wait their chance another eighty years for the Restoration theatre of Charles II. Eventually four private enclosed theatres were erected for aristocratic winter performances. In 1603 James I put all the companies under royal patronage to control them. By then Elizabethan drama was at a peak, barely a quarter of a century after the first theatre was built in London.

A list of primary Elizabethan playwrights is revealing: Lyly, Peele, Greene, Marlowe, Kyd, Jonson, Beaumont and Fletcher, Heywood, Middleton, Dekker, Webster, Ford, and Shakespeare. It is a group of rare brilliance not surpassed by later English or American drama. As revealing is a list of Elizabethan eras of taste: high bombast, pastoral, antiquity, comedy, aristocratic comedy, domestic comedy, satire, comedies of manners, revenge plays, tragedy, plays governed by determinism. An "era" might be a few years or, with determinism, decades following Shakespeare. Burckhardt's summing up of the Greeks at the end of the fifth century bears here as England headed toward the civil wars in the seventeenth century that cost Charles I his head, elevated Cromwell, and shut the theatres: "For they were all being carried onwards and expected a violent end, without knowing what it would be." The expectation of a violent end may be overstating things for the English under the Stuarts at first, but the sense of being in the hands of fate and moving toward a climactic moment certainly is less distant to their experience.

Elizabeth simultaneously seeks to control this ferment and in part creates it. Simon Schama gives a useful overview here, largely echoed by Allison Weir.[16] Elizabeth was a master of public relations, "the first true woman politician in British history."[17] She knew she had to contain powerfully divergent impulses and somehow survive, so encouraged the cult of herself as Gloriana, the Virgin Queen, the model for Spenser's *Faerie Queen*. She deliberately assumed the attributes of the Madonna and magnified her impact through extravagance in palaces, jewelry, clothes, and pageantry. She was the biggest and longest running play of her reign.

In this sense, the film *Elizabeth* gets it right as it shows Elizabeth kneeling before a statue of the Virgin Mary. "What do they want," she demands of Walsingham, meaning everyone and no one in particular; she has just struck down her enemies on his advice. Walsingham tells her men need to be able *to touch the divine in this life*. That is what the cult of the Virgin Mary allowed believers to do, but her cult is repressed in Elizabeth's England. Elizabeth takes this to heart. She has her virgin locks shorn by her ladies-in-waiting, as they choke back sobs, and a white cosmetic applied to her flesh. Elizabeth tells them she has *become* a virgin, although we saw her to be anything but with her lover, Dudley, earlier in the film. Shortly after, she appears before her court as an apparition of divinity on earth—the awed courtiers stare, stunned, and fall to their knees, some grasping her hem as she passes to kiss it. Even the startled Walsingham kneels. No doubt her having just proved how lethal she is also influences their awe. She singles out the elderly Cecil, who tried to marry her off to foreigners, to declare she is now married to England.

This catches very well the awe the cult of Elizabeth engendered. Part of the purpose of her "progresses" around the realm from noble pile to pile was to be seen by the people, toward whom she could be remarkably generous in contrast with her usual tight-fisted attitude toward money. She so much became the *Virgin Queen* the nation forgot the dangers of succession because of a lack of a direct heir and was instead jealous of her final dalliance with the Duc d'Anjou, horrified at her belonging to anyone but themselves. She embodied the nation like Churchill at his peak, but unlike him, for decades.

They were troubled decades for all the reasons mentioned. Elizabeth tried with the Thirty-nine Articles in 1563 to make a "big tent" out of the Anglican Church, including all but Catholics and fringe Protestants. The romantic troubles of Mary of Scotland placed her in Elizabeth's hands for nineteen years; as a prisoner she too could be contained. The Dutch revolt against Spain made it impossible for the latter, a great power, to turn its attention fully to England, a revolt she abetted directly and through her sanction of the famous raids of Drake and his peers to bleed the Spanish treasury. For years she succeeded in this balancing act of containment and interference. Nonetheless, "it was a country in the throes of profound transformation" and only her resourcefulness kept that transformation from turning into a slaughterhouse like the Saint Bartholomew's Day massacre of Protestants in Paris in 1574.[18]

Not even excommunication in 1570 overthrew her; just as the theatre gained steam, the 1570s turned into golden Elizabethan years. Anyone knowledgeable knew how fragile was the nature of this success. When Philip finally sent the Armada in 1588, a year after Elizabeth had Mary executed, she appeared before the army like an Amazon queen, ready to fight with the body of a woman but "heart and stomach of a man." She wowed everyone—enemies, people, even the councilors who saw her up close and were periodically driven mad by her temporizing and stinginess.

She remained admirable into old age, defying public expectation that as a virgin she must wither. The Venetian ambassador wrote of her as having an unexpected appeal even then. Nonetheless, the sight of the gaudy old Elizabeth, bejeweled and bare-breasted, must have been trying. The war with Spain dragged on, the harvests failed, and inflation took off. London transformed itself from a city of barely 50,000 to over 200,000 by the end of her reign, as enclosure in the countryside broke up the medieval patterns of farming so great lords could assemble vast acreages to increase their herds and incomes. Added to all the other transformations going on, then, were an agricultural upheaval and an urban explosion. There was a proliferation of poor laws and of vagabonds, which brings us to Shakespeare.

So much has been imagined and written about Shakespeare that any summary must tread where angels fear to go. Here I largely follow the work of Anthony Holden, who points out Shakespeare's father was the equivalent of a mayor of Stratford before his fortunes declined later in life.[19] Shakespeare probably received a classical education as a youth in logic, rhetoric, and literature, something that provided a strand of connection to the university influence on drama, with its Renaissance attempt to revive classic tragedy by emulating Seneca. Shakespeare's was apparently a

Catholic family at a time of increasing suspicion and proscription of Catholics and Catholicism. Shakespeare's twenties are lost: he may have been a tutor to a Catholic lord's family. During this time he took an immense social leap and joined an acting troupe, when individuals in such troupes were thought no better than vagabonds. After a few years, he surfaced in London as an actor. By the late 1590s, Shakespeare was a part owner of his theatre, respected as a dramatist and poet and well enough off to buy a coat of arms for his father and be regarded as a gentleman. He bought one of Stratford's biggest houses and returned home in triumph.

Shakespeare carried out many functions as part of the Lord Chamberlain's Men which included the famous actors Kempe and Burbage, at first holding the horses of aristocrats, acting, and beginning to write, later rising to part owner. He averaged two plays a year, the first eight without credit. After that he was famous enough his authorship was given as a selling point. He was seen to outshine his competitors, yet he retired to Stratford in 1611 after a career in London of barely more than seventeen years.

As the greatest of the Elizabethans, what do the greatest of his plays have to stay about the spiritual burden of Elizabethan drama?

Consider this from *Hamlet*, as Hamlet picks up Yorick's skull:

HAMLET

Let me see. *(Takes the skull)* Alas, poor Yorick! I knew him,
Horatio; a fine fellow of infinite jest, of most excellent fancy: he
hath borne me on his back a thousand times; and how abhorred
in my imagination it is! my gorge rises at it. Here hung those lips
that I have kissed I know not how oft. Where be your gibes now?
your gambols? your songs? your flashes of merriment, that were
wont to set the table on a roar? Not one now, to mock your own
grinning? quite chop-fallen? Now get you to my lady's chamber,
and tell her, let her paint an inch thick, to this favour she must
come; make her laugh at that.[20]

The resemblance of the sentiments to the soliloquy starting "O what a rogue and peasant slave am I" is clear, as well as to the sentiments quoted from Sophocles. Othello says before he kills himself,

OTHELLO
. . . nothing extenuate,
Nor set down aught in malice: then must you speak

Of one that loved not wisely but too well;
Of one not easily jealous, but, being wrought,
Perplex'd in the extreme
. . . And say besides, that in Aleppo once,
Where a malignant and turban'd Turk
Beat a Venetian and traduced the state,
I took by the throat the circumscribed dog
And smote him, thus. *(Stabs himself)*[21]

These plays have a clear perception of mortality and a grappling with its meaning, but are very odd in what they leave out. *There is no reference to God or heaven* in any but the vaguest sense. Hamlet, as he considers suicide, stops from the fear that in death's sleep he may dream, and who knows what nightmares that may bring? Who, after all, knows anything about "the undiscover'd country," death?[22] Just about every Elizabethan, as a matter of fact; when you died, heaven or hell, God's grace or damnation, awaited your soul, with which you were intimately acquainted too. But in these plays we see no reference to a divine Christian order at all, for it was precisely the nature of that order that was under question. A mind like Shakespeare's, then, could consider an order *without* a received structure. Lear may refer to "gods" but takes a sharp view of man's nature without mythic or doctrinal swaddling:

LEAR

Why, thou wert better in thy grave than to answer with the
uncovered body this extremity of the skies. Is man no more than
this? Consider him well. Thou owest the worm no silk, the beast
no hide, the sheep no wool, the cat no perfume. Ha! here's three
on's are sophisticated. Thou art the thing itself: unaccommodated
man is no more but such a poor, bare, forked animal as thou art.[23]

Macbeth may make an occasional generic call of God but invokes no traditional religious solace after learning of his wife's death and, just before Birnam Wood appears to be on the march, soliloquizes:

MACBETH
Tomorrow, and tomorrow, and tomorrow,
Creeps in this petty pace from day to day,

To the last syllable of recorded time;
And all our yesterdays have lighted fools
The way to dusty death. Out, out, brief candle!
Life's but a walking shadow, a poor player
That struts and frets his hour upon the stage
And then is heard no more: it is a tale
Told by an idiot, full of sound and fury,
Signifying nothing.[24]

That is Hamlet's perception of the futility of action, which even such vigorous interpreters as Richard Burton or Mel Gibson were constrained to honor.

Shakespeare and the Elizabethan playwrights borrowed freely from one another and their sources. They turned all their characters into Elizabethans, put Elizabethan rhyme, slang, and blank verse in their mouths. They cannibalized the ages without our concern for historical accuracy. They used whatever they liked without our concern for such niceties as acknowledged borrowings. They didn't use what was of no interest to them. The omission of a received Christian viewpoint like that found in the morality plays only a little earlier is, then, deliberate and revealing. Man and his nature are up for grabs, and, in Shakespeare's vision, stoicism before inevitable suffering is the only recourse. It is as though he wrote from the center of Freud's world, where religion is dismissed and the bare facts of life must be registered and endured. Prospero does not thank God for his deliverance on his departure: he surrenders his magical powers and asks *our* indulgence to set him free. The truth seen through the prism of comedy in *Much Ado about Nothing* is that "man is a giddy thing" and can hardly be held responsible for his actions.[25] We are far from a Lutheran, Anglican, Calvinist, or Catholic vision of the redemptive power of grace, good works, or faith.

Shakespeare and Elizabethan tragedy stepped into a unique moment in history. Because no specific belief was generally held, all particular beliefs were subject to question. That need to wrestle with the burden of our behavior and our place in the cosmos inspired a generation to greatness in plays catering to general audiences consisting of many zealously held faiths. A play could not have taken any one of their versions of faith without causing a riot or losing some part of its audience, as well as entering an area subject to official repression. Yet plays did not reflect the official line either. Instead, and accepted by their audiences, they let their characters freely state their confusion and anguish and left it to ourselves as audience to draw our own conclusions. In so doing they implicitly stated: "*These conclusions concerning the great issues are ours to draw,*" something each sect accepted as true of itself if not of others. This tremendous legacy of Elizabethan and Shakespearean drama looms large and explains its continuing hold on ourselves. Imagine a current screenwriter with as many films to her or his credit as Shakespeare has through the constant stream of Shakespearean film adaptations: that would be success!

In this sense Bloom is right about the connection of modern consciousness with Shakespeare. Our modern consciousness grows from the spiritual freedom within the Elizabethan plays where the chief characters could be whatever they were capable of making themselves, for better or worse; where, looking within themselves, men and women could find what answers were possible *from their own resources,* however bleak they might prove, to the great questions of life, death, truth, reality, fate, morality, and self. The possibilities inspired the greatest outpouring of genius in dramatic writing since the Athenian apogee. When the Elizabethan noon was over and the ensuing civil wars concluded and the theatres reopened under a restored monarchy in the 1660s, the religious, social, and political issues that so troubled the Elizabethans settled into a broad, "Augustan" consensus, and drama fell deeply asleep.

The Argument We Are Having with Ourselves

Thus I can now culminate my remarks on drama's ultimate role in the argument we are having with ourselves. What the two preceding sections make clear is that dramatic apogees coincide with moments of intense social stress and transformations of belief. The spiritual element in drama at such moments is not there as a reflection of the time's social or religious concerns but as an integral part of what makes drama intensely relevant and calls to its service individuals of genius with moral and spiritual concerns. *Drama carries and embodies the spiritual concerns of its time.* One apogee hardly shares the outlooks of another; we live, as Winnicott emphasized, in a shared space-time continuum; we speak to our own times. But while our cultures may vary, *we* do so far less and speak to ourselves across the barriers of time insofar as we and our works endure in that shared "cultural area" that is Winnicott's third area, the transitional space where our mutual experience and culture transpire. What is present in that space is still alive and part of our ongoing dialogue. The argument over the relevance of "great white dead authors" is pertinent here: relevance is always under question. That the men disparaged as dead are being debated reveals that they are quite alive in the cultural area of our experience and part of our argument with ourselves.

What, however, can we say about modern dramatic writing?

Certainly it begins with a bang in the theatre of the late nineteenth century with naturalism and Zola, then is greatly influenced by Ibsen and those who follow. Those dramatists' stance vis-à-vis our culture has often been critical, taking one aspect or another of our social and economic behavior to task as we live through the enormous transformations of our industrial and technological revolutions, our wars of great isms, the materialism of our economic and social system's outlook, and our often apocalyptic, fractured religious sects.

Not surprisingly from the preceding analysis, we would expect to find we are living in an age of great dramatic writing—and we are with, at first, stage authors like Ibsen, Strindberg, Brecht, O'Neill, Beckett, Miller, and others, and now with a cinema that since World War II has overshadowed the stage in entertainment value and in dramatic writing that probes our experience and carries our spiritual quest. It is the era of Bergman, of Antonioni, of Fellini, of Truffaut, of screenwriters like Towne, or Schrader, or . . . We are in the midst of our own cinematic dramatic apogee, which makes it perilous to say for sure what we are striving for or where we are going; nothing so humbles one as reviewing his or her predictions or analyses after a few years have passed.

Campbell envisages the modern quest as our finding a new sense of "thou" in a new sense of community. Certainly in reaction to our Cartesian heritage, we have struggled ever more sharply against the division of experience into a simple "me vs. not me" framework; philosophers have struggled to escape that straitjacket, while Winnicott struggled in the language of modern psychoanalysis to indicate a place that is central to our experiencing where "thou" can be said to be embodied—that cultural, creative area where you and I mingle in our daily activities. It's so new a concept that we struggle to understand its meaning: how can the lonely

"I" of the self also be in some part a "you/me," an "us"? How is it possible that through creativity/playing, understood as cultural activity, we find the true self, not as a fixed quantity, but always *in process* and with some "other," for that is the nature of playing and experience? But we can understand why such a fleeting experience of wholeness requires repeated immersions in the mature playing of our creative response to reality, and how in such playing we continue to incorporate some part of an "other" into our self to continue.

A great paradox is that since we lost our unconscious relationship to nature, the "I" that is so private has always existed in relation to an "other": the "other" world of nature we separated from, and the actual "other(s)" we once unthinkingly moved among. The very fact we can objectify ourselves ("I" am speaking) reflects the presence of both this simultaneous separation and perception of the "other" in the heart of our self-conceiving. We recapitulate just this experience as infants in the process so clearly laid out in Winnicott as the mother, by separating herself from our omniscient illusion in the weaning process, brings us up against the perception of the "not me" and the "other" of the mother, whose separation from her infant simultaneously casts us into the first, lonely perception of ourselves as an "other" too.

I have said drama is caught up in this argument and takes sides. It has always taken sides. Curiously, drama is not found in simple societies, though storytelling and the rites that precede drama flourish. Drama excels in great civilizations in their moment of apogee and maximum stress; civilization, as Freud underscores, inherently causes profound conflict in the individual—how much more so when it is riding to a crest undergoing profound transformation. Even more curious *is the primitiveness of the immediate dramatic impact,* for screenplays quintessentially, as well as dramatic work more widely, appeal powerfully to our emotions from the beginning of an action, whether Schindler wowing the military brass in *Schindler's List* or the endangered Princess Leia being captured by Darth Vader at the start of *Star Wars*. Rachel is met in *Witness* at her husband's funeral; Will Kane in *High Noon* begins with a marriage, while in the *crisis* he drains the cup of abandonment. It is a truism of drama that *emotion makes real* within the milieu established at the start of a given work, developed in a cause-and-effect and more or less necessary and probable way. The paradox is as great as that involved in the appeal of music: for all the craft that goes into either art, their immediate impact goes straight past conscious reflection to the deeper layers of the self.

This paradox reveals some of its secret when we reflect it is precisely the conscious mind in times of great stress *that does not know what decision is right.* Greek Sophists may have taught there are two sides to every question, and Elizabethans wondered about the true nature of reality and religious solace. *We* wonder about all three and suspect a given question may have far more than two correct answers. Certain popularizations of science take this attitude further, like deriving relativism from relativity, where all is relative and so anything has a just claim, as in multiculturalism where any culture is held to be as valid as another, to the raising of quantum indeterminacy into the idea nothing can be known for sure. Earlier our mythopoetic instinct reared deism in the eighteenth century from Newtonian physics, with God as a distant clockmaker, and social Darwinism from the evolutionary theories of Darwin in the nineteenth century. We constantly and necessarily elaborate insights into explanatory systems to give a rational container to our social experience, even if paradoxically living in a system that denies ultimate knowledge and leaves us grasping hopelessly for a certain version of "the truth." In their succession these systems betray the extent and duration of the transformation we are undergoing, whose final outcome is so uncertain.

These are broad considerations but must be entertained to understand the role of drama at such times. Writing with urgent meaning is not an artificial importation into screenwriting and drama, weighing it with extraneous, unwanted concerns; on the contrary, stories that grapple with the central issues of the age *are what drama is for.* Avoid such undertakings altogether and the resultant work is not even entertainment but trivia. Trivia can indeed entertain but is soon forgotten; it has nothing to contribute to our needs.

Hence the emotional immediacy of drama. That emotionality recalls us from our conscious cerebral confusions to *the experience of a true self being found* through the hero's journey, the creative play of the screenplay or drama, however that "experience" or story may vary script to script, and however little writers need know this is what they are doing as they work out their stories. But, as we have seen, this is certainly one of the central achievements of the hero, realized on the level with which that story grapples with experience. It is as true of Jack in *The Importance of*

Being Earnest or Paul Vitti in *Analyze This* as for Schindler in *Schindler's List* or Michael in *The Godfather.*

Hence, too, the importance of identification touched on earlier in "The Nature of the Hero's Journey." Identification is as easy to talk about and as hard to understand in a "me vs. not me" universe as psychoanalytic discussions involving projection, introjection, and splitting that often become mind-boggling exercises in jargon in the psychoanalytic literature. What can all these terms mean beyond a parade of aspects of the self, for in a "me vs. not me" universe others in themselves are unknowable; we are left finally only with our own mental operations, as exemplified in the work of Klein. In such a view we cannot *actually* be another through identification, *actually* stand in another's shoes, nor can there *actually* be a union of Apollonian and Dionysian impulses outside a solipsistic reference: the self must *actually* always be lonely.

The difficulty of explaining actual experience through this approach has been apparent for a long time. Common sense has intervened for the most part and ignored these difficulties. Explaining shared experience is the issue at the heart of the struggle of psychoanalysis with itself, compounded with its nervousness over the reality of the imagination. Freud, we saw, begins and ends his great journey with the realization that both mental trauma and its cure can proceed from acts of the imagination, in the latter case justified by the curative efficacy of the imaginative act through a "construction" that lays bare the roots of the initial (imagined) trauma. If we are to some extent in a hall of mirrors, that merely reflects (no pun intended) a feature of our self-reflective human nature. Without realizing it, Freud guided analysis into the path of the late radical empiricism found in William James, where the truth is something we make and judge as truthful to the degree it is efficacious.

These assorted difficulties do not disappear in a "me–us–not me" universe, but they do begin to become susceptible to explanation. If part of us is inherently social, if part of who we are is *a shared experience* of other(s), then the need to use the language of introjection/projection or identification begins to evaporate. We are already an "us" in such a frame of reference, our "I" already a "thou." Facts do not alter age to age, only how we choose to approach and evaluate them. Admittedly, to see and act on this perception of an "I/thou" quality of the self would require a cultural earthquake. One can only hope that is the one we are heading toward.

Drama, without its practitioners being philosophers but almost their opposites, exists precisely in a "me–us–not me" universe. We can leave it to philosophers to wrestle over the implications of such a reality; as a matter of experience it is a commonplace. Moreover, this blending of "me" and "not me" is renewed every time we attend a drama and go through the various "forms" of identification with a heroine or hero. Drama's primitive, emotional appeal pushes reflection aside; its experience renews and exemplifies our bonds with one another. It brings our self once more to the simultaneous sense of self/other that characterized our unconscious relationship to reality far down the evolutionary ladder and characterizes us as a child; renewing this experience in the adult mind is at once, at its deepest, exhilarating and oceanic in nature. Nietzsche's "Original Mother" and "metaphysical solace" come to mind, and Aristotle's "tragic wonder."

Drama, if you will, by its questioning and through its action, returns us to the fullness of our "self" when the existing civilization around us has lost the ability to sweep up that self in a broadly accepted sense of relationship to the immediate, the other, and the eternal.

The happy ending reflects exactly that renewal, even on the trivial romantic level of "true love." Aestheticians and critics disparage the happy ending, but it is there in response to our own existential craving and need in times of stress. On profounder levels we see the possibility of the community ensured, as in the typical end of a western; the true self reaffirmed in its fullness, as in *On the Waterfront* and *Blue*; or a world-redeeming marriage attained, as in *Schindler's List*. Even the tragic ending brings us to a New Beginning. Thus is Eros always triumphant and Thanatos always the loser in drama.

This is the full meaning driven home by a contemporary film like *Ran*. But *Ran* is interesting in another light. We may be flies in Lear, sentiments echoed in *Ran*, but we are not the gods' playthings in our time, as we seem at times to be in Shakespeare's. In *Ran* we are instead told it is the gods who weep because they can't save us from ourselves. This has a curious echo in Campbell's belief the modern age is one in which the old myths and gods are dead and man is reduced to himself. That is the burden of the exchange over Saburo and Ichimonji's bodies in *Ran*. The gods cannot do more than weep, for if something else is to happen, we must create it. The very popularity of action-adventure heroes like James Bond and Indiana Jones resides in this "coming out of ourselves" need; they always find the answer, even if on the reduced level offered by such films. But what is important in drama is not so much the given story, as long as properly worked out, but the underlying pattern it manifests, which is always the complete hero journey.

Thus, at the end, when we identify with the hero it may well be an act of the imagination, but the imagination exhibits itself in the area of experience, of playing, of creativity, the area that predominates in our lives, the area where you and I are already mingled, the area of culture. We are far less apart from one another than we are accustomed to think, however we struggle to say that scientifically, i.e., materialistically. The journey the hero undertakes to the true solution and New Beginning through *The Heroic Deed* is, then, through identification of our own, *because it is already our struggle in our experience* unless we have undergone a spiritual death, unless we are the mother in *Blue* in the cave of her room watching images of life on television, incapable of recognizing her daughter or, any longer, being part of the creative flow of life.

It is in this sense, finally, that the metaphor of drama in which it claims to be reality is true: the screenplay, the drama, is reality, not an imitation; it is our search, however entertaining or chilling along the way, and our final goal. Good writing has always exemplified this hunger of the heart to be true, to live with truth, in love, in reality, in hope.

Appendix: A Case Study
Ingmar Bergman's *Fanny and Alexander*

F ANNY *and Alexander* is Bergman's farewell to film and contains his final views on human nature and the dramatic, cinematic art. It gives a very specific fleshing to the fundamental story pattern through the stages of the dramatic hero's journey as imagined in Alexander and Emilie's story: Arresting Life, Complying with the False, Awakening, Confused Growth—and the Pursuit of Error, Failure of the False Solution, The Discovery of the True Solution, The Heroic Deed, Suffering, and The New Life. Talking about these elements abstractly is a convenience, a set of buoys to mark the creative channel of a given outing, but not a formula; only the imagination of a dramatist can provide the material for a screenplay. But the imaginative breadth of *Fanny and Alexander* gives us a good opportunity to see in detail how the elements discussed earlier work.

The Past

Arresting Life

Alexander is a child hero under the care of his mother, Emilie, and his story is inextricably woven with hers. Nonetheless, even a child hero plays a crucial role, as Campbell points out is typical in the traditional hero myth. That certainly proves decisively true of Alexander in the *climax.*

Both he and Emilie share the same compromised past, if differently. Emilie yearns for something truer than her life in the theatre among the affluent, material Ekdahls. Yet she has complied with her role as lead actress, wife, and Ekdahl. Alexander's relationship to reality is infused with fantasy and insufficiently in touch with the truth. He fails to realize how unhappy his mother is, despite the frequent acuity of childhood perception with regard to a parent's emotional state and his own great sensitivity. Thus he is as compliant with the false as his mother *and* a cause of her own continuing falseness. Alexander's dependency is important here, for to see his mother's unhappiness must make him sense his childhood floats on quicksand and see/feel the necessity of corrective action that is for now entirely beyond him.

What we see, then, as the action begins is what *Arresting Life* means as a stage of the hero's journey: in *Fanny and Alexander* that means continuing in a pattern that demands a false relation to self and reality on the part of both Alexander and Emilie in terms defined by the affluent, theatrical Ekdahl lifestyle.

The Beginning—Act 1

Complying with the False

Emilie is part of the traditional Christmas performance presented by the Ekdahls, while at home Alexander drifts through the house and imagines a statue changes position. Reality is at once staged by the adults and imagined as fluid by Alexander, albeit conventionally on Emilie's part and in accord with childhood fantasy on Alexander's. His father, Oscar, is aware that the life of the theatre—for we are in a hall of mirrors in *Fanny and Alexander*—is a sheltered world. He says as much to the assembled company.

> OSCAR
> ... My only talent, if you can call it talent in my case, is that I love this little world inside the thick walls of this playhouse. And I'm fond of the people who work in this *little world.* Outside is the *big world,* and sometimes the little world succeeds for a moment in reflecting the big world, so we understand it better. Or it is perhaps that we give the people who come here the chance of forgetting for a while. ... (italics mine)[1]

These are not novel sentiments concerning the dramatic art but prepare the ground for Bergman's later views. Crucially, they identify the *theatre* as the little world. Nonetheless, the Elizabethan mirror is given its modern turn here: what the theatre reflects of the "big world" is its "form and pressure," for *our* playing in the theatre has the effect that we understand reality better, which opens the door to the modern concern with what the "self" is and can grasp.

At home, a luxurious Christmas festival is staged with Alexander and Emilie as full participants, climaxed for Alexander by his unhappiness with the pretty housemaid, Maj, who won't let him cuddle up in bed with her; Gustav Adolf will be visiting her instead. For consolation he puts on a magic lantern show for his sister after they are supposed to have gone to bed. His father Oscar's interruption only strengthens Alexander's stream of fantasy in response to frustration, as Oscar invents a story giving a chair a fabulous and amusing descent.

Later, when the festivities wind down and Helena and her old lover Isak talk, we begin to suspect how much is seething under the lavish Ekdahl surface. Helena laments that Emilie's relation with Oscar is sexless. The film doesn't explain Emilie's children, but the published version makes clear they were variously fathered with Oscar's quiet acquiescence and undiminished paternal feelings for "his" children. Oscar and Emilie are arrested in this pattern.

Similarly, his brother Carl and long-suffering wife, Lydia, are caught in another arrested repetition of behavior, a masochistic marriage and con- tinual running-up of debt for which they repeatedly ask Helena's help. Gustav Adolf is a merry satyr with girls like Maj, equably tolerated by his wife, Alma, as his flirtations do not diminish their satisfaction with one another, disconcerting as this may be to their daughter, Petra. The Ekdahls' is not an amoral but lax, self-indulgent lifestyle whose motto might be *Carpe diem*.[2]

Awakening

Alexander takes part in a production of *Hamlet* and sees Oscar have a stroke in rehearsal. At home Oscar does not rally; Alexander is horrified when he is summoned to his deathbed and breaks away, although his fa- ther tries to be reassuring. "Reality" could not come crashing in on Alex- ander any more viscerally. The shock to Emilie is as great. In a memorable scene after Oscar's death, Alexander is drawn from his room by strange screams filling the house; they are Emilie's as she paces back and forth, repeatedly letting loose a raw, inchoate scream as much rage and frustra- tion as grief. She has a lot suddenly to cope with: the lie of her life, as she has seen it, and now the loss of security, as represented by Oscar and the Ekdahls, for death cannot be ignored. Change, we know, is terrifying in itself; now for Emilie there is no reason any longer to defer finding her way to a truer life and undoing her sense of a lying past, even though that means tearing up everything she knows. No wonder she screams!

Confused Growth—and the Pursuit of Error

Oscar's death is the inciting event and forces out Emilie's unhappiness and ultimately forces Alexander to deal with the nature and power of the imagination. Later Emilie reveals the nature of her unhappiness to Helena, after she marries Edvard Vergerus:

EMILIE
. . . I was so thirsty—it sounds dramatic and overstrung, Helena, I know, but I can't find any other word—I thirsted for the truth. I felt I had been living a lie.[3]

The "lie" is the complaisant, life-loving lavish, material/theatrical life of the Ekdahls she felt was illusory and untruthful long before the beginning of the action. Emilie tells Bishop Vergerus:

EMILIE
. . . My life has been empty and superficial, thoughtless and comfortable. I have always longed for the life you live.[4]

She imagines his life to be the opposite of the Ekdahls', embodying the truth. Thus clear oppositions are developed for the Ekdahls vs. Bishop Vergerus: false vs. true, unreal vs. real, impure vs. pure, imaginary vs. actual.

Yet until Oscar's death Emilie persists in *Complying with the False,* however great her unhappiness. Her compliance has been simultaneously the condition for maintaining the illusion Alexander persists in, that life is known and comfortable and the imagination may be used without penalty. Alexander's persistence in imagination touches on *creativity* itself as a response to experience, and it is precisely on that level Edvard will try later to break his spirit. Emilie and Alexander, then, remain caught in their false modus vivendi until the *Awakening,* while the Ekdahls' initial modus vivendi is dependent on Emilie's continuing compliance with the false too.

But decisive change is foreshadowed both by Emilie's screams and when we see her with Bishop Vergerus at Oscar's funeral as Alexander curses under his breath. *Awakening* shades into *Confused Growth—and the Pursuit of Error*. Emilie, we discover, pursues a relationship with Bishop Vergerus that will prove profoundly wrong; while through Alexander the magic of the imagination merges with the affluent, realistic surface of the Ekdahls as he sees Oscar reappear at once corporeal, ghostly, and silent. Time's passage is elided: in short order Alexander finds himself confronted by Edvard, on his mother's behest, because he has told a story he was sold to a traveling circus. Step by step, a man hardly more than a stranger sanctimoniously browbeats Alexander, with his mother's encouragement, into apologizing for this "lie." The curious thing here is that Alexander begins in the wrong: he shouldn't have lied, even though the imagination is its own consolation and stories create existential spaces in which we can live. But the sight of an older man manipulating a child into compliance with his desires in such a fashion is revolting. Its effect is clear: "Emilie embraces the rigid Alexander and draws him down into her lap. He sits there like a puppet that has lost its strings."[5]

Then, deepening her new error, Emilie announces they will soon be one family. Alexander's adjustment to his father's loss must now collide with Edvard's insistence on factual truth and his intrusion into the Ekdahl realm as the new "father" authority. Alexander's reaction is to the point:

ALEXANDER
(Quietly to himself) Piss-pot, fuck-pot, shit-pot, sick-pot, cock-pot, cunt-pot, arse-pot, fart-pot . . .[6]

It doesn't help that the ghostly Oscar witnesses this sorry charade; he is as impotent as ever. The inevitable false steps after the jolt of *Awakening* now reach a decisive turn, in this case by the heroine on whom the child hero is dependent.

Act 1, then, through the hero and here the heroine's *Confused Growth— and the Pursuit of Error*, brings us to the point where they decide on or are driven into a course of action they think will solve their problems. Emilie's marriage to Edvard represents that turn in *Fanny and Alexander*, a turn as loaded with moral values as Edie and Terry's in *On the Waterfront*. But larger issues are involved in *Fanny and Alexander*: the nature of reality and the truth, and the use of the imagination. All are given a particular spin by Emilie's choice of the bishop as the representative of truth, purity, and reality.

Alexander already sees something of the price exercising his imagination will exact with Edvard. His being forced to accede to the bishop's will over the traveling circus story is a harbinger of the far more traumatic scene later over Alexander's story about the death of the bishop's first family. Alexander's secure world has been torn apart. It is his *mother's* doing; *what can he do?* Nothing, at first.

Emilie, however, sees something of the true reality she is going to encounter at the bishop's. Following her marital announcement she visits the bishop's palace and meets his repressive, repugnant family, including the monstrous Elsa. The palace is a bleak, stark contrast to the lush, red-hued Ekdahl comfort and furnishings. Moreover, Edvard wants Emilie to come with *nothing* from her and the children's past, a demand Emilie happily consents to, caught up in her dream of a pure life, but which she withholds for now from committing the children to. They, she explains, must make such a choice themselves. She imagines that choice will be only a matter of time. She openly yearns for Edvard's God, whom he explains is a God of love, unlikely as that already sounds. "He" is a challenge she desires, however, for her God has been "fluid and boundless and intangible, both in his cruelty and his tenderness. I am an actress; I am used to wearing masks. My God wears a thousand masks."[7]

As Edvard leads his new little family off from the Ekdahls as Helena and the others watch, Helena observes with a sense of foreboding, "I think we'll have Emilie back. Quite soon."[8]

Just as the heroine and hero complied with falseness in the Past and in the Beginning, in the false modus vivendi at the start of the action, they again comply with error at the end of Act 1. They *will* their mistakes, support and defend them. However, growth enters into this new error, which is made in response to a fuller awareness of the nature of the conflict in which the they are caught. But just as the immediate action has destroyed the initial false modus vivendi, which cannot bear the pressure of events released by the inciting event in *Awakening,* so will this new pursuit of error be subjected to destructive testing in the Middle, or Act 2.

What we see here is the destructive side of the creative response to reality in action. That destructiveness is the chisel taken to the stone of experience from which the final statue emerges. Michelangelo's famous view that he sought to release the form already within the stone applies with validity here: the proposed solution of the hero and heroine is an attempt to get to the truth that will finally end conflict. That can only be found through constant "revision," to use a writing term. All writers know what that means in terms of deletion, addition, and cutting and pasting.

Of course the hero and heroine do not realize *they have chosen error: learning that is what the ensuing action makes possible, the realization of which is the precondition of finding the solution that is true.* Act 2 development is particularly difficult for writers because of this paradoxical use of error to develop a true understanding of the conflict and find its true solution.

All we have said concerning a false modus vivendi applies also to Edvard. He has been a widower for years and craved Emilie yet thought she was out of his reach, married and successful. He has coped by becoming a hypocrite, something Alexander sees but which *neither Edvard nor Emilie recognizes.* Instead, in the palace whose bleakness as thoroughly echoes his character as the lavishness of the Ekdahls' home echoes theirs, he wishes Emilie and Alexander *to comply with his arrested life.* He in turn, in Act 2, will go through the pattern of development Emilie and Alexander suffer through in Act I *because of their resistance.*

Necessary and Probable, and Other Matters

I have said stories that earn our highest praise hit us as necessary and probable without qualification, and certainly *Fanny and Alexander* aspires to that level. In life much is unnecessary and improbable, although paradoxically probability and necessity give imagined stories a sense of ultrareality. The only caveat necessary for *Fanny and Alexander* regards the use of magic.

The world and relationships of the Ekdahls are compellingly detailed. Their moral laxness is startling yet clearly supported by the convincing characterizations of figures like Gustav Adolf and Maj. Placing the family in an entertainment context makes the laxness of standards seem less remarkable, although that plays to a popular prejudice not always true. But nothing in the Ekdahl world jars: Emilie's putting up with an impotent husband seems a cross to bear, while the film script's published version indicating multiple fathers of her children is left out of the film to avoid distraction. Emilie turning to Edvard after Oscar's death for both spiritual and physical solace makes perfect sense: that she makes an error does not undercut the probability of her behavior, while he, as we saw, has long yearned for her. He presents himself to her as tragically romantic through the loss of his earlier family, free of Oscar's impotence, and as the spiritual guide for whom Emilie has hungered. He seems solicitous. There is an inevitability about their connection, while Emilie's later recoil as she sees the truth is just as probable and necessary.

This convincing necessary and probable behavior holds up for the other characters too. Alexander is on a necessary collision course with Edvard, whom he sees through from the start. That collision is vividly dramatized when they collide over his story to Justine. Isak is a natural figure for Helena to turn to in the Middle, given their past connection and because he has access to the bishop, always apparently in need of money. Isak's otherness in the form of his Jewishness lets Bergman use him as a counterweight to the bishop. Emilie's climactic dosing of the bishop with a sleeping potion is just as probable and necessary if she is to leave. Almost all of the details of the film measure up to a necessary and probable standard without special allowances.

With one apparent exception: the use of magic. Magic is established as a feature of the Ekdahl world from the moment Alexander sees a statue move. We are in the realm of magic realism, Bergman style, as with *Like Water for Chocolate.* Unlike the latter, Bergman is at pains to give a realistic explanation for events that parallels the magical. Although it seems Alexander's wishes for the bishop's death magically are made real through the medium of Ismael, a realistic thread is offered also in which the bishop dies because, in his semistupor from Emilie's sleeping draught, he can't extricate himself from his burning sister. We can easily see the moving statue as an extension of Alexander's fantasy life. Only he sees the dead bishop at the end, accompanying his father: both can be seen as visualizations of his own inner split. Only when Helena also sees and talks to Oscar do we go beyond Alexander's imagination into what appears to be a convention in which magic is acceptable and established through Alexander at the start. We accept its presence as the established reality *of the film's reality,* but to that extent we are removed from our normal, taken-for-granted reality.

With that exception for the present, the fact that the screenplay so powerfully supports our perception of its actions as necessary and probable goes a long way toward persuading us, first through feeling and later through reflection, that it is true and real—as we come to feel *Hamlet* is

true and real, or *The Godfather,* however much a product of the imagination, however far removed from a precise historical-biographical existence. In *Hamlet* we accept the ghost: Oscar has his stroke playing the
ghost in *Fanny and Alexander.* We are not being asked to make anymore
of a leap than we are in the single greatest piece of drama in the canon.

Truth, we have repeatedly seen, is not just a quality of fact but of imagination. Bergman imagines with telling effect.

The *Cooked* and the *Raw, Smart* and *Dumb*

Emilie is a *smart* character: she renounces the Ekdahl world for the bishop's in the name of truth and reality. Then, chastened by experience, she
sees the Ekdahls' values come far closer to the truth than any religion or
ism ever can with a truncated version of reality. Alexander is handled
in a primarily *dumb* way, however, although Emilie draws him into the
pattern of her experiences. His growth pattern reveals ever more deeply
what makes him tick and the power of his imagination, although he too
is chastened by experience with the bishop. He does not go through his
mother's swings in evaluating reality, always prizing his Ekdahl world
and imagination. Inevitably Edvard comes into fatal conflict with Emilie and Alexander, for Edvard as the opposing force is also *dumb,* a man
who strives to hold on to his view of reality and force it on the others at
all costs *because of his own need to deceive himself.*

All the characters as the film goes through its initial phases seem *dumb,*
however. The burden of *Arresting Life* for the hero is the empowerment
of the past that the false modus vivendi at the start of the action allows a
screenwriter to dramatize through the initial conflicts, the phase of *Complying with the False. Smartness* in character as well as plot depends on
the response to the *Awakening* when the inciting event forces the past
into present awareness and consequently forces the protagonists to face
the falseness of their lives. Thereafter *smart* and *dumb* characters diverge.
Moreover, the plot develops inevitably in a *smart* way, even for a *dumb*
character, as it moves through the inevitable transformations in the action
that lead one way or another to the resolution of past and present conflict.
Thus, after the *Awakening* phase both *smart* and *dumb* refer meaningfully
only to character development.

Noteworthily, nearly everyone else in the screenplay is handled in a
dumb manner: Carl and Lydia, Helena, Isak, Gustav Adolf, Alma, Edvard's

family, Aron, and Ismael. The only exceptions are Maj and Gustav Adolf's daughter, who in the end wish to leave. Isak does not change in the sense of transform like a *smart* character in rescuing the children; he only reveals the extent of his resourcefulness and commitment to the Ekdahls. Why are these characters handled in this way in *Fanny and Alexander*? Because they represent meanings for Bergman between which the hero and heroine oscillate. In successful writing like *Fanny and Alexander*, they do not seem abstract embodiments but people convincing in themselves, fully rounded at least, developing in a *dumb* manner at best.

Conventionally, *"raw"* and "Bergman" seem synonyms. But this ignores his comedies and careful use of *cooked* effects. Magic in *Fanny and Alexander* is transparently a *cooked* effect. Remember, these terms refer to approaches to handling emotion, not the absence of emotion or its too great presence, which is reflected in the *heavy*. Alexander frequently manifests emotion through *cooked* means, whether in the moving statue or through the stories he tells, which reflect his unhappiness with life, like being sold to the circus, or show his inherent creativity, as in the magic lantern show in Act 1, or express the extent of his hatred of the bishop, as in the story to Justine. Even more vivid is Alexander's destructive rage against the bishop that Ismael at his Uncle Isak's lets Alexander see and vent as *imagined events that yet cause the death of the bishop* in a brilliant conjoining of fact and "fiction," for the bishop truly dies. It is just this consonance of reality and imagination that makes "magic" so telling in *Fanny and Alexander*. The view given earlier that the use of magic leads to a reservation in our sense of how thoroughly *Fanny and Alexander* seems necessary and probable now needs to be rejected. Bergman's use of magic *expresses the inner reality of the characters concerned* in the realm of "playing," i.e., of the screen*playing* which has our entire attention. It expresses how, in a basic Kantian and psychological manner, reality is always a construct rising from a stream of raw data that would overwhelm and disorient us unless structured for perception to begin with. Magic, then, expresses our relation to reality, however odd that sounds to our material, scientific minds: we make up reality, which is a constant stream in the space-time continuum of our experience, a steady *becoming* only prejudice makes us take for granted as something "solid" and "fixed."

Thinking, then, about the use of *cooked* behavior for Alexander reveals how Bergman's use of magic brings reality more intensely before our eyes through a character with whom we identify. That character makes a full use of our own faculties through his own *power of imagination.*

Alexander is involved in *raw* behavior only in extremis: at his father's death, which terrifies him, and with Edvard, with whom he never has a casual run-in, whether over the traveling circus story or when he faces the bishop over his tale concerning his first family. That confrontation is as direct and *raw* as anything Sophocles ever wrote, as Edvard forces Alexander to recant and then ask forgiveness before he beats and locks him in the dark attic. What is particularly insulting to us in this behavior *is Edvard's hostility to the imagination, to creativity,* because it is through our creative response to reality that we find the truth. We don't know if Alexander's tale about the death of the bishop's first family is true factually; we do know it is true spiritually.

The Meaning of Structure

We are too used to separating structure and meaning analytically. A story has a theme, we say, and a structure, Acts 1–3, through which it is more or less well expressed. Nothing could be farther from the truth. Structure and meaning are just different ways of speaking of our unitary experience of a screenplay through our identification with the protagonists. Structure is the expression of meaning: meaning is what is communicated by structure. In good writing everything tends to bear, we say, but in great writing everything bears absolutely, or as much as that is possible where human effort is involved. By Act 3, in effective drama, this relationship between structure and meaning becomes transparent.

Look again at Act 1. We see a lush, lax artistic and professional world but understand all is not well as we learn of Oscar's sexual failings and see the unhappiness of Carl and Lydia and fissure between Alexander and Maj. The Ekdahl glow is deceptive. Oscar's death splits the surface open: *this kind of life is wanting* is clearly communicated by Emilie's grief and turn to Edvard, even as the main body of Ekdahls persevere in their now challenged lifestyle.

In other words, the events are organized to communicate swiftly a set of meanings, just as less conventionally we could say the meanings are swiftly communicated in a sequence of events chosen for their thematic nature. So it is no surprise to see Emilie with the bishop; on the face of it, anyone she chose at this point would represent something *other* than the Ekdahl world and its values. It takes little to see he embodies opposite values of the Ekdahls' as he makes Emilie renounce everything from her previous life. What else can Alexander do but curse? The little family group walking away from the Ekdahl home at the end of Act 1 clearly points up the *meaning* of the action: *now* we will see if the bishop's world/values can survive the testing to follow. Our Act 2 expectation is of a clash of meanings to be tested, i.e., subjected to the destructive aspect of creativity as part of the effort to make the bishop's values real.

How will Alexander and Emilie cope now? We don't know, we're in suspense. Suspense in writing of this quality means *suspense over meaning*. Whatever is done we know will have different meanings, some good and desirable, some bad and undesirable. Urgent writing creates its own moral universe, and when that writing seems necessary and probable we identify wholly with that universe. The meanings that emerge and are defined from the conflict are defining for us through our identification with the heroine or hero. Those meanings are *pointedly* dramatized in *Fanny and Alexander*. In fact, as we reach the *crisis* with its rejection (failure) of the bishop's world, we understand that not just a place is being rejected, but an entire attitude toward and evaluation of human behavior. The *crisis* doesn't just point up the behavior involved in the conflict: *it points to that behavior's meaning.*

Structure is simultaneously this combination of events following a cause-and-effect chain we experience as more or less necessary and probable, and a set of ever more defined meanings. All action in good writing carries this kind of symbolic weight. The choices loom much more strongly at the end of Act 1 than at its beginning when they were merely incipient, and what marks the transition from Act 1 to 2 is this simultaneous sense of the action shifting decisively and the meaning of the action moving toward a new sense of definition at odds with the false modus vivendi we experience at a story's start.

The hero's journey falls within and communicates this structural drive. The initial action shows in what story-specific sense a compliance with a false past is involved, and to what extent that is based on an arrested life. Until Oscar's death, *Fanny and Alexander* concentrates on using structure to get this part of the journey out in the specific terms of Emilie and Alexander's lives. Once *Awakening* sets in with Oscar's death, structure and meaning move for Emilie and Alexander within the substance defined for their particular journey. The meanings expressed in structure are the meanings evolving from that journey's quest: for Emilie, it is the true way of living.

Confused Growth—and the Pursuit of Error clearly orients *Fanny and Alexander* toward the contest of meanings in the bishop's palace. We have a good idea of what that contest must involve, meaning in what direction the story must now move, although no sense of how the contest will end. Yet Emilie undertakes this pursuit of error as part of her quest for a true life. This is the only way the truth can be found. All our attention now flows with her toward finding *the truth,* which is where she has identified her true self is also to be found and, implicitly, Alexander's.

The Middle—Act 2

Confused Growth—and the Pursuit of Error, continued

The colloquial history of stage and film productions is full of stories of writers harassed by actors, directors, and producers to get the Middle of the story right, or else. "Or else" in film usually means bringing in another writer: in theatre, an out-of-town hotel window may simply be opened as an option for a playwright, to drive home the necessity of his going back to his room and trying yet again. It never does good to get too reverential about these matters, to forget, if you will, Shakespeare's inky hands. We shouldn't forget the way the mundane and inspired must work together, even if we end thinking a genius has been at work. Act 2 development is so hard because the imagination must pursue more deeply the line of action with its inherent and explicit meanings pointed to at the end of Act 1 *and*, as we saw, manage growth through error.

Bergman handles his Act 2 development powerfully. Things begin badly at the bishop's palace with a clash at dinner between the bishop's mother, Blenda, and Emilie over the traditional habits of the household. Blenda will not surrender her control over how things have been, while Emilie forbids her to interfere with her children. There is no milk of human kindness at the bishop's, no Christian sweetness or charity: *power* over others is nakedly at stake. Edvard tries to mediate but clearly intends that in time *things shall go on as they have* in the palace: not he or his family but Emilie and the children must change and conform. Alexander curses under his breath as he says grace. In their room Alexander and Fanny are blunt: "I don't want to live here," Alexander says, and Fanny: "I think we've got a horrid stepfather."[9] Fanny even has a foreboding in this room, which belonged to the bishop's first, dead children.

FANNY

One day when it's getting dark and I come into this room there will be two pale little girls dressed in black in front of the doll's house and they'll say in a whisper they've come to play with me.[10]

Actually, she and Alexander will be seen in a ghostly fashion by the bishop, with Emilie standing guard over them in the *climax* as Isak whisks away the actual children in the chest downstairs.

The children are not reassured by Emilie; in fact, next we see Helena talking over the phone with Isak, concerned about their well-being. She is worried and wants Isak to keep an eye on them; no one has heard from them in some time. Maj comes in equally worried about Gustav Adolf. At the same time, Justine comes into the children's locked room and provokes Alexander with her version of the accidental tragedy of the bishop's first family. Now Alexander spins his tale of how the bishop locked up his family and starved them and how they consequently drowned in their effort to escape. One of the drowned girls, he says, told him this story.

Alexander's story rings so true about the character of Edvard that Justine is not dismissive but horrified. Alexander, challenged by Fanny, quotes his Uncle Isak's reference to Hamlet about man: "There are more things in heaven and earth, Horatio . . ."[11] He admits he doesn't understand all the implications of these words, but will once he's grown. In the meantime he has justified the use of his imagination to reflect a reality so wide only the imagination begins to let us grasp it: a grown-up, which he is not, must use full creative capacity to respond to experience. Experience is what we have in the third area Winnicott identifies between the "me" and "not me," that area where we play, experience one another and culture, express our creativity, find our true self, and in drama encounter antagonists who for their own reasons try to stop the creative growth of heroes and heroines.

The story shifts again to Helena, who now engages Oscar in conversation. *He* too is worried about the children as Emilie arrives. Justine has carried Alexander's tale to the bishop, who summons the child. Alexander is frank: "I think the bishop hates Alexander. That's what I think."[12] Edvard insists he loves him and that it hurts to have to punish Alexander, *but Alexander must learn to tell the truth.* Even after Alexander caves in to the bishop's manipulation, Edvard insists on punishment, for "the punishment is to teach you a love of the truth."[13] He recites the various punishments available and canes Alexander. The boy is again threatened with the cane when he refuses to beg forgiveness, again caves in to the older man and begs forgiveness, yet still is locked in the attic.

Emilie bares her heart to Helena as this transpires at home. She had yearned for a purer life and "thirsted for the truth"[14] but now lives in dread and terror of the bishop. She is afraid to act because the law would be on his side. She is trapped, hates him viscerally, and dreads the collision between him and Alexander we have just seen happen. "We must find a solution," whispers Helena.[15] Emilie leaves and, once home, must force her way into the attic to save and embrace the shattered Alexander.

Act 1 feels relaxed in contrast to the drive of Act 2. But at this point the development has made clear the nature of Emilie's error. She has found a lie, not the truth, while Alexander has paid the price of her error more deeply than herself, for he is a child with only a child's resources, however imaginative. Love has been exposed as hate; truth, an immersion in falsity; forgiveness, condemnation in the bishop's world. Edvard may be a religious figure but stands for all the ideologues who have tormented our last 150 years with their doublespeak and tyranny and caused the deaths of countless millions in the historical world. Edvard Vergerus resonates with those figures of terror, none of whom presented themselves as bad: quite the contrary, they claimed the future and the right, as he does in *Fanny and Alexander.*

Here there is a telling consonance with the reason Aristotle rated tragedy over, say, history: history deals with confused, actual events, whereas tragedy *imagines an event that stands for all.* Read: drama imagines the essence of reality.

The Handling of the *Crisis*

Failure of the False Solution

What is the *crisis*? The *crisis* is not just a technical term connoting the failure of the concluding Act 1 resolve, accurate as such a statement may be. The *crisis* is the heroine and hero's failure to resolve their quest/journey, at once the culmination of the phase in which they pursue error and the moment where they both recognize *and feel fully*, and so make us feel fully, the consequence of their specific mistake.

That is what stares out at us with Alexander in Emilie's arms in the attic. That moment is so clear in meaning no dialogue is necessary. Both have failed, Emilie in her choice of the bishop's world as embodying the truth and Alexander in his mode of imaginative resistance. But if the bishop's world and values do not satisfy Emilie's quest for truth and purity, what will? We see how the *climax* must bring the answer to this question, must consummate the protagonists' journey one way or the other, in the terms given by the specific story imagined. After the attic scene, we know that whatever Emilie finds will not be anything offered by the bishop. We know from her meeting with Helena that it must involve a turn to the Ekdahls again. But first Emilie must emancipate herself and Alexander from the bishop. How is not apparent, but no climactic resolution was possible until this moment of *failure* was found and experienced, as that failure points toward and gives the specific context of meaning for the climactic action.

Emilie and Alexander's solution, moreover, must include a life that is *true for their community.* When Emilie went to the bishop's, she changed *communities* but did so for *herself.* Her choice to do so again also has profound social implications, then, as she turns now to the Ekdahls whose possession of the truth she rejected initially. Confirming their truth as hers also moves past the selfish solution that must always fail. So the *crisis* is not some technical need to maintain interest by preventing, through conflict, an easy resolution of the conflict that fans expect for some climactic chase sequence or its equivalent. The *crisis* reflects the essential purpose of drama to point through error toward whatever a given story will assert is "right" through the outcome of its *climax.* The crisis points up a given story's moral universe for the hero and heroine and their community in which they find that right.

Think how the *crisis* is handled in Kieslowski and Piesiewicz's *Blue.* Julie confronts Olivier and is forced to realize that her resolve of not being involved at all with life, announced at the end of Act 1, cannot be maintained. In *High Noon* Kane must begin the long walk toward the final shoot-out in total isolation, all efforts to depend on others to do the right thing having come to nothing. Princess Leia makes Luke and Han Solo in Lucas's *Star Wars* realize they have not escaped the Death Star but been allowed to leave so they can be tracked, while Luke is distraught over Obi-Wan's death: he had joined forces decisively with him at the turning point of Act 1. The corrupt police find Book and Rachel in *Witness,* ending their safety and Book's attempt to find a solution of his own for his problems which he initiated by his flight at the end of Act 1. Leon discovers John is not guilty in the *crisis* in *Lantana,* and that consequently his whole manner of approaching and understanding both Val's disappearance and his own life stand on equally false ground.

Julie searches out her dead husband's mistress as a first step in the End; Amy runs back to town in *High Noon* when she hears the first shots, while Helen controls herself and departs. Luke prepares for the climactic confrontation with the Death Star with the other rebel pilots; and Book begins a confrontation with Schaeffer and his men, while sending Samuel to get help from the Amish. Leon makes a last false step with Nick, then finally listens through to Sonja's tape. In each case the solution they begin to find through the *crisis* points the protagonists both toward a redefined sense of their community and toward the true solution of their problems.

As we look back over the second act of *Fanny and Alexander,* we see how tightly written it is, how clearly the past has connected with the present, and how powerfully the need to find the truth has connected with the communal life that goes with it. But while in the *crisis* we can only *feel* the depth of defeat. It is that feeling which motivates the action needed climactically.

Edvard makes the implications of Emilie and Alexander's defeat in the crisis abundantly clear. "Get it into your head once and for all that you must obey me, you must submit," he tells Emilie.[16] She must obey his "office." He adds: ". . . the slightest attempt on your part to rebel or get in touch with the outside world will affect your children's well-being." "Reality," he finishes, "is hell." He will confine her to her room. He is a man whose "slavery is his freedom." He may love Emilie more than anyone else, but her defiance is a form of insanity, much as defiance of the Communist regime in the USSR often landed one in a mental asylum. "All that must be suppressed. . . . (*Emilie screams. Edvard strikes her across the mouth*)."[17] The doublespeak and the power drive are transparent, and her despair. Equally clear is the extent to which Edvard's *dumbness* is *willed.*

A tyrant in the Campbellian sense *makes himself* by damming up the cosmic/Winnicottian creative flow of the universe/self and attributing his act to necessity, as Edvard does to Emilie. He is clearly a fallen hero in every sense. Normally we do not see villains' history in drama, only the effect of their fall which has typed them. But with Edvard we can see he is akin to a hero within his false modus vivendi at the start of a story *who refuses as the story develops to leave that falseness behind,* instead trying to impose it on others. He clots time: he stops others' creative response to reality, stifles their volition, and subsumes their moral agency within his own closure of their volition. Emilie understands this well,

EMILIE

I curse you. I curse the child I am carrying. I shall tear it out with my own hands and crush it as one crushes a poisonous animal. Every day, every hour I shall wish you dead. . . .[18]

The End—Act 3

The Discovery of the True Solution and the Heroic Deed

Now we see that the true solution to the hero's problem must be one that works for himself and his community. Edvard has made clear escape alone is not sufficient; he must be dealt with decisively, and a true reckoning made with Emilie and Alexander's Ekdahl connection.

Nonetheless, the physical safety of Emilie and her children are the prerequisite for the larger solution, as now Isak decisively enters the story. Bergman laid the groundwork for Isak's intervention with Helena in Act 2, and in Act 3 Bergman develops him first as the Jewish "usurer," the man with money for the "distressed" Christian, Edvard. Thus Isak is able to enter the bishop's household under the guise of interest in a chest he had once declined. Edvard's sister, Henrietta, treats him with contempt but seeks out her brother. As she leaves, Isak spirits the children with Emilie's connivance into the chest. A *cooked* element intrudes heavily here, capable of multiple interpretations: the bishop, suspecting a plot, opens the chest, and sees nothing. He rushes upstairs, only to find the children asleep on the floor, although Emilie prevents his touching them. They are apparitions. Isak succeeds in getting the real children to his home. Is it the bishop's guilt that blinds him or magic?

At Isak's, Alexander encounters a breathing mummy, has a run-in with a puppet "God" manipulated by Isak's nephew Aron, and meets his father who advises him to be charitable toward people. But Alexander regards his father as a weakling and reproaches him for not telling God on Edvard, which Oscar can't do because there is no God, Alexander adds half in anger, half mockingly. Then Alexander encounters Ismael, Isak's androgynous younger nephew.

Here Bergman develops the traditional otherness of the Jew in European society, given life in Shakespeare's *Merchant of Venice* and continuing now, as the repetitive spates of synagogue burning and defacements in France and Germany attest. That Isak is Helena's lover and a welcome member of the Ekdahl world is remarkable because so unlikely, but that world is actually an idealization of a tolerant reality on a par with its dark underside symbolized in the bishop's palace. Isak as a representative of all that is "other" in traditional society, ideal or darkly imagined, goes past the financial ability usually associated negatively with Jews *to all the other qualities not open to the more respectable world,* even one as tolerant as the Ekdahls'. Ismael embodies this aspect of otherness at the heart of Isak's realm, and it is through Ismael that the young hero manifests his true powers. He is the avenue to the unconscious realm, that reality which is not logical, not temporal in a linear sense, not Newtonian, a realm where far and near are the same, and "you" and "me" lose their polarity.

Alexander encounters this immediately with Ismael when asked to write his own name. Instead, he writes Ismael's.

ISMAEL
. . . Perhaps we have no limits, perhaps we flow into each other, stream through each other. . . . You bear terrible thoughts; it is almost painful to be near you.[19]

Ismael explains, "The truth about the world is the truth about God."[20] God just happens to be asleep and having nightmares. *In other words, God is at once creative and destructive;* these are different expressions of God's single being. Ismael won't let go of a now frightened Alexander, exploring instead the child's imagination in the service of his hatred of the bishop. What does Ismael-Alexander see?

Earlier, Carl and Gustav Adolf met with Edvard to try and ransom Emilie: they failed, and Edvard even has Emilie ask them to return her children. We know she hates and dreads the bishop and can only imagine what he has threatened her with to make her behave this way. But that night she gives Edvard a heavy sleeping potion and tells him she is going to leave. She hears him say,

EDVARD

You once said you were always changing masks, so that finally you didn't know who you were. (*Pause*) I have only one mask. But it is branded into my flesh. . . .[21]

His *dumbness* is congenital and recognized as such. Emilie easily eludes his drugged grasp. What Alexander sees follows his mother's departure. He sees the monstrous Elsa catch fire from the light Edvard moves closer to her on her night table, walk aflame into the hallway, summon Edvard with her cries, and then in his drugged helplessness envelop him in the fiery embrace of her great body.

Has Alexander killed the bishop, willing this fatal sequence of events? Later, the police superintendent's summary makes clear Edvard's death can be seen without reference to the imagination. You can take your choice as a viewer, a subtle piece of writing, while the fidelity of the magic to the truth, as touched on earlier, is transparent. This death is *The Heroic Deed* and culminates *The Discovery of the True Solution*. They are coterminous, the end of *The Discovery of the True Solution* coinciding with the carrying out of *The Heroic Deed*. Edvard put himself in opposition to Emilie and Alexander, creativity, and love: these can only move forward if he is removed. Alexander kills him.

The pattern of action in Act 3 both discovers the true solution for the hero and heroine's problems and makes possible its achievement *on an entirely personal plane of action*. This is the true reason two deeds are given, Alexander's magical and Emilie's accidentally realistic one.

Edvard's death restores the possibility of the cosmic, Campbellian creative flow, and the psychic, Winnicottian creative response to experience. Edvard makes sure we get both connections, with Emilie.

EDVARD

I have heard that the cosmos is expanding. The celestial bodies are hurtling away from each other at dizzy speed. The universe is exploding and we live at the very moment of explosion.[22]

Then follows his comment about the fixity of his mask. He has tried to stop the universe in himself. Alexander and Emilie's triumph at once solves their current need to deal with the bishop and the problem lingering from the past, Emilie's need to find a true life and Alexander's an understanding of the power of the imagination to alter reality.

Now Emilie realizes the very fluidity of reality that oppressed her is its true nature. Reality is a constant becoming, an unfolding of life in a space-time continuum, an action that *never* reaches ultimate resolution and clarity *except in drama which claims to be reality.*

Character, Suffering, and Expiation

Suffering

Suffering exists in drama as a precondition for the reality the dramatic metaphor asserts it is and substitutes for "everyday" reality. We may live through protracted periods of pointless suffering in the latter, but in drama *The Discovery of the True Solution* flows from suffering. Both realities join in understanding that suffering is the road to divinity, though few screenplays or dramas or lives take us there.

On the simplest level, both *Complying with the False* and *Confused Growth—and the Pursuit of Error* on the part of the heroine and hero cause suffering and must be expiated. That expiation, which is a subsequent and pointed additional suffering, leads to *The Discovery of the True Solution* and puts it into effect for others. Julie in *Blue* must be yanked back into life by Olivier, but finds his efforts make her suffer in the ways she has tried to avoid. But she is in the wrong *and must go through this suffering* to pay for her errors, if she is to have a renewed life. I said drama has a Old Testament, "eye for an eye" sense of justice where each misstep must be paid for. Terry in *On the Waterfront* cannot lead the longshoremen until he takes the beating at the hands of Johnny Friendly and his thugs and survives; then he can lead the men in. Suffering and expiation go hand in hand, the latter just a pointed version of the former. One of the implications of the *heavy* is that suffering comes to be indulged in without an expiation and hence of a point being sensed and achieved. The *heavy* brings us up against unrelieved suffering in everyday reality, unendurable to experience or the imagination.

But the survival of suffering is as important as suffering too: Terry by surviving his beating and Julie by surviving Olivier's recall to life display the creative essence of being a hero. They are the ones who survive the destructive side of creativity and show themselves to be both true and the source of the creative response to reality for others. Tragic heroes achieve the same end at the cost of their own future.

Thus Emilie has to suffer for misjudging first the past and then Edvard, and does so dearly. Alexander, though a child hero, must also suffer: he is full of undisciplined rage and fantasy. The bishop is wrong to attack him as he does, yet one thing Alexander learns from Edvard is the dangerous power of the imagination for both himself and others, as his wishes seem to cause Edvard's death. The imagination is a mighty tool *because it is most expressive of the true nature of reality,* as we saw, reflecting the creative, "becoming," changeable nature of our experience. The hero and heroine do not just survive, they grow—whether *dumb* or *smart*—through their experience and suffering into something more than what they seemed at the start: they grow into the truth.

The other characters dependent on the heroes' success cannot do anything but suffer along with them until they find the true solution. Until then *the hero's/heroes' are caught in the arrested life the Beginning reveals through the false modus vivendi.* The true solution, then, with the climactic occurrence of *The Heroic Deed,* is the great gift of the hero to whatever their community/society/civilization may be, whether the stripped-down one of the typical western, the Holocaust one of *Schindler's List,* or the longshoremen's of *On the Waterfront.* It is the finding of the true self and the restoration of the positive, creative flow of experience for that self's community.

The latter film gives a particularly clear demonstration of how the other characters hang helplessly on the hero's phases of *The Discovery of the True Solution* and *The Heroic Deed.* Neither Pop, Edie, Father Barry, nor the Crime Commission can do more than live in a continuing false modus vivendi despite all their efforts *unless* Terry succeeds against Johnny Friendly. When he does so climactically by taking the past away from Johnny Friendly and transforming its meaning, as well as expiating his errors through the savage beating, *everyone* is free to follow him into *The New Life,* or be appropriately sidelined, like Johnny Friendly.

In *Fanny and Alexander,* the thrust to find the true manner of living depends entirely on the affirmation Emilie and Alexander's experience brings to the Ekdahl lifestyle, which their affirmation transforms from one of convenience and privilege into an idealized vision of how things *should* be. Moral substance and/or ambiguity are always at hand in screenwriting, varying only with the level of ambition of a given drama.

The New Beginning and the New Life

In the End the restored Ekdahl clan gathers in as lavish and spectacular a manner as we saw in the Beginning at Christmas. Even Oscar is there in his corporeally ghostly way. Emilie is *willingly* present. Gustav Adolf makes very clear Emilie and Maj's infants are the cause for this family gathering as he emphasizes all are now together to celebrate the new babies: Maj's Helena Viktoria, i.e., *victory,* and Emilie's Aurora, i.e., *dawn.* He reminds them how terrifying the world can be, and that the Ekdahls are best suited to live in this "little world" represented by their gathering. The little world at first was the theatre but now is the tolerant, middle-class/artistic, protected, material world of the Ekdahls. If at first the little world meant the theatrical one of staged creativity, now it means the real world of creative response to experience. Where, then, is the "big world" Oscar spoke about at Christmas? Beyond this middle-class world that it menaces continuously, the true "other" reality where figures like Edvard with one mask embedded in their souls continually try to stop time and life and fix these in their own, unchanging likeness.

What kind of people are these Ekdahls? The kind that love what they can understand and enjoy their little lies that make life bearable, answers Gustav Adolf. The Ekdahls give a pointed representation to Nietzsche's idea that life can only be made bearable as an aesthetic experience. Without their little deceptions a man "goes mad and begins hitting out." Our white lies create a tolerable reality not from distortion but necessity, not from falsification but to serve a communal truth.

Bergman takes this one step further and presents the Ekdahl world as a kind of knowing dream, an Apollonian construct of the first order that has been put through a kind of Dionysian wringer by death and Emilie's *Confused Growth—and the Pursuit of Error* with Edvard, which threatened to sweep away the family by denying its self-valuation. We live in the meanings we create for ourselves. Bad times may be coming, but

GUSTAV ADOLF

. . . let us be happy while we are happy, let us be kind, generous, affectionate, *and good.* Therefore it is necessary, and not in the least shameful, to take pleasure in *the little world* . . . (italics mine)[23]

"To take pleasure in *the little world*" of our immediate experience, that "me–you/me–not me" tripartite reality in which we mingle and enjoy one another and our lives, and in which, implicitly, the presence of *the "other"* is a necessary element of our own wholeness. For Isak too is at this feast, as he has been with the Ekdahls all along. *Fanny and Alexander,* as a *play,* sees Emilie and Alexander find their true selves, and we vicariously share that experience by destroying Edvard and affirming Gustav Adolf. And just as the "other" embodied by Isak is part of the Ekdahl world, so too is Edvard part of Alexander's world, for Alexander is tripped up by Edvard's "ghost" who will now, with his father, haunt him as part of himself. Johnny Friendly ends *On the Waterfront* reminding the longshoremen he will be back. These "villains," the true antiheroes, can only be overcome, not expunged, because they are permanent parts of ourselves, expressions on the personal, psychic level of the destructive possibility of the creative nature of reality itself.

Gustav Adolf drives home the moral as he lifts his daughter.

GUSTAV ADOLF

. . . I am holding a little empress in my arms. It is tangible yet immeasurable. One day she will prove me wrong, one day she will rule over not only the *little* world but over—everything! Everything![24]

She is potentially the empress of the world, perhaps a world redeemer who will spread innocence and redemption everywhere. No profounder expression could be given the nature of The New Beginning in drama or as the final phase of the hero's/heroes' journey, *The New Life* in his/their renewed community.

Later that evening Emilie hands Helena a play she wants her to consider returning to the stage in, Strindberg's *A Dream Play.* It is Bergman's last clue for the journey world of *Fanny and Alexander:* through dream and nightmare a New Beginning has been reached, a true *Awakening* into *The New Life.*

Notes

Repetitive page references to key works are given for convenience as follows:

Aristotle: *Poetics*, trans. S. H. Butcher, ed. Francis Fergusson, 43rd printing (New York: Hill and Wang, 1995).

Bergman: *Fanny and Alexander* (New York: Pantheon, 1982).

Burckhardt: *The Greeks and Greek Civilization*, trans. Sheila Stern, ed. Oswyn Murray (New York: St. Martin's Press, 1998).

Campbell: *The Hero with a Thousand Faces, 2nd ed.* (Princeton: Princeton University Press, 1973).

Freud: *Civilization and Its Discontents*, trans. James Strachey (New York: W. W. Norton, 1989).

Hamlet: *Hamlet* (New Haven: Yale University Press, 1954).

Lee: *A Poetics for Screenwriters* (Austin: University of Texas Press, 2001).

Nietzsche: *The Birth of Tragedy*, trans. Francis Golffing (New York: Doubleday Anchor, 1956).

Rodman: *Winnicott: Life and Work* (Cambridge, MA: Perseus Publishing, 2003).

Schama: *A History of Britain, vol. 1: At the Edge of the World* (New York: Hyperion, 2000).

Schulberg: *On the Waterfront* (Carbondale: Southern Illinois University Press, 1980).

Winnicott: *Playing and Reality* (New York: Basic Books, 1971).

1. By the Ocean of Time

1. Thomas Mann, *The Magic Mountain*, trans. H. T. Lowe-Porter (New York: Heritage Press, 1962), vol. 2, p. 195.

2. Ivan Goncharov, *Oblomov*, trans. David Magarshack (London: Penguin Classics, 1954).

3. William Shakespeare, *Hamlet* (New Haven: Yale University Press, 1954), Act III, 2, ll. 124–130.

4. Rene Descartes, *Meditations on First Philosophy*, trans. Laurence J. LaFleur (New York: Liberal Arts, 1960), p. 24. The general reader may find *The Oxford Companion to Philosophy*, ed. Ted Honderich (Oxford: Oxford University Press, 1995), useful for quick summaries of the general work of the philosophers mentioned in the text.

5. David Riesman, *The Lonely Crowd* (New Haven: Yale University Press, 1953). This was for the 1950s the work that caught the public mind on the topic

of alienation, the subject explored in Hitchcock's *Rear Window,* specifically focused on the middle class.

6. David Hume, *A Treatise of Human Nature,* ed. L. A. Selby-Bigge (Oxford: Oxford/Clarendon Press, 1960). Hume's seminal work appeared in 1739 and has gathered readers and impact down the years.

7. D. W. Winnicott, *Playing and Reality* (New York: Basic Books, 1971), p. 50. The analysis of Winnicott's views on creativity is central to these essays, and found in large part on pp. 132ff. in "The Lost Poetics of Comedy."

8. The *Critique of Pure Reason* was first published in 1781, and the *Prolegomena to any Future Metaphysics* in 1783. Immanuel Kant, *Critique of Pure Reason,* trans., intro., and abridged by Norman Kemp Smith (New York: Modern Library, 1958).

Kant, *Prolegomena to Any Future Metaphysics,* trans. John P. Mahaffy et al., ed. Paul Carus (La Salle, IL: Open Court, 1955).

9. Jung differed in this from Freud, who was reluctant to ascribe anything positive to the unconscious until late in his career, and then minimally. Jung differed further in that he saw the unconscious as the seat of positive drives toward health as well as of neurosis and psychosis. It's better to consult a Jungian primer than search through Jung's work, given its breadth, diversity, and tendency to involve one in long, arcane passages followed by a few golden paragraphs.

However, Jung's Tavistock Lectures serve well as a general introduction: C. G. Jung, *Analytical Psychology, Its Theory and Practice* (New York: Vintage Books, 1968). The lectures were first given in 1935 in English by Jung in London, and editorial insertions update the material.

Swedenborg's thesis was that there is a correspondence between inner and outer nature, the physical and the ideal, immaterial world of the mind. What might be physically distant in one world could be near in another. Emerson used Swedenborg as his representative of "The Mystic" in *Representative Men.*

There is a good discussion on this in Robert J. Richardson, Jr.'s *The Mind on Fire* (Berkeley: University of California Press, 1995), pp. 197–199, among others.

A different perspective on relating inner and outer nature, with particular point for the subject of our own identification with the hero and heroine, is given by a series of studies published in *Science and Neuroimaging,* as reported in the *Los Angeles Times.* In one of these, a member of a couple was subjected to a shock; then, using brain-mapping techniques, the other member was given the same shock as the first looked on. Results showed the onlooker's brain "was a mirror of suffering, reflecting through many of the same neural circuits the pain that others feel, much as if the sensation were its own genuine torment." It's a nice instance of science and drama converging in the understanding of something as fundamental as empathy. See Robert Lee Hotz, *The Los Angeles Times,* The Nation section, February 20, 2004.

Recent experiments in Europe at the atomic accelerator at CERN reportedly show separated electrons echoing one another's behavior instantaneously.

Curiously, this quantum behavior was anticipated in fiction by Ursula K. Le Guin in *The Dispossessed,* among other works, where a device named an "ansible" is able to communicate instantaneously across light years with its mate. Arthur C. Clarke is the most famous of the "hard science" fiction writers, whose ideas have had a way of moving from conjecture to experiment and realization. Most recent is the idea of building elevators between a space station and Earth's surface: see Kenneth Chang, "Not Science Fiction: An Elevator to Space," *New York Times,* Science Times section, September 23, 2003.

10. Dennis Overbye, "E and mc²: Equality, It Seems, Is Relative," *New York Times,* Science Times section, December 31, 2002.

11. The *inciting event* is that event in the Beginning, or Act 1, that sets off the primary conflict by forcing the hero and heroine cumulatively to resolve the lingering problem(s) from the past preceding the immediate action within the immediate conflict. See "3. Awakening" in Chapter 10, "The Nature of the Hero's Journey," in these pages. See also Lance Lee, *A Poetics for Screenwriters* (Austin: University of Texas Press, 2001), pp. 75–76.

12. Andrey Tarkovsky, *Sculpting in Time,* trans. Kitty Hunter-Blair (Austin: University of Texas Press, 1986).

2. The *Heavy* as Opposed to . . .

1. Friedrich Nietzsche, *The Birth of Tragedy,* trans. Francis Golffing (New York: Doubleday Anchor, 1956), pp. 59–60. Here Nietzsche speaks of the way the Sophoclean heroes were like "luminous images" reflected back from "a deep look into the horror of nature." The selection of a narrow range of Greek myths for tragedy reflects this dramatic need for material strong enough to bare and break human nature for examination and finally tragic consolation.

2. Aristotle, *Poetics,* trans. S. H. Butcher, ed. Francis Fergusson, 43rd printing (New York: Hill and Wang, 1995), pp. 71, 109. Aristotle is at pains to make us understand tragedy ends in wonder, whether called "tragic wonder," Aristotle, p. 71, or "the wonderful is required in Tragedy," Aristotle, p. 109. Nietzsche means something of the same when he speaks of the need for a state of enchantment in which tragedy can transpire, Nietzsche, p. 56, culminating in the "metaphysical solace," Nietzsche, p. 50, and "metaphysical delight," Nietzsche, p. 102.

3. Sigmund Freud, *Civilization and Its Discontents,* trans. James Strachey (New York: W. W. Norton, 1989).

4. Sigmund Freud, *Analysis Terminable and Interminable,* in *Collected Papers,* vol. 5, trans. and ed. James Strachey (New York: Basic Books, 1959), pp. 316–357.

Freud, *Constructions in Analysis,* in *Collected Papers,* vol. 5, trans. and ed. James Strachey (Basic Books, New York: 1959), pp. 358–371.

Analysis Terminable and Interminable was written in 1937, two years before Freud's death; *Constructions in Analysis* was even later, 1938, a year before he died.

5. Harold Bloom, *Shakespeare: The Invention of the Human* (New York: Penguin Riverhead Books, 1998). The title pretty well speaks for itself; if

more is needed, try: "Consciousness is his salient characteristic; he is the most aware and knowing figure ever conceived," p. 404. Or, "We can hardly think of ourselves as separate selves without thinking about Hamlet," p. 405. Bloom is hardly reticent about his claim, nor of his admiration of Shakespeare; for him, there has been no post-Shakespearean dramatic achievement reaching similar, if different, heights. Shakespeare is definitive. See also Bloom's citation of Nietzsche's interpretation of Hamlet on p. 363. Our words may be different, but we share Nietzsche's opinion. See "The *Smart* and the *Dumb*," chapter 6 in this book.

6. Freud, p. 33.

7. Freud, p. 58.

8. Freud, pp. 64ff.

9. Freud, p. 69.

10. Freud, p. 82.

11. Freud, p. 107.

3. Moral Substance and Ambiguity

1. Budd Schulberg, *On the Waterfront* (Carbondale: Southern Illinois University Press, 1980), p. 71.

2. Aristotle, pp. 71, 109. It's worth also noting Aristotle on p. 117 rates tragedy as more pleasurable because it is so much more concentrated than other art forms. Uncomfortable as he is with the irrational, he knows this sense of wonder grows from the irrational, from the action issuing in pity and fear and yet being transformative and enrapturing, not depressing, which would be typical of the *heavy,* a state with which one hardly associates wonder.

4. Complexity vs. Fullness

1. Lance Lee, *A Poetics for Screenwriters* (Austin: University of Texas Press, 2001), pp. 20–29. These pages review both the will to believe we bring to drama and our mythopoetic drive by which we elaborate experience into meaning through stories.

2. Lee, pp. 17–20. The development of naturalism through Ibsen in the nineteenth century is reviewed here, including the naturalistic approval of slice-of-life writing because of the way it emulates actual life.

3. See the third part of "The Death and Life of Drama," chapter 11 in this book.

4. Aristotle, pp. 65–66. His *Poetics* are shot through with considerations of structure, action, and the nature of the imitation of an action. These pages review his specific elucidation of Beginning, Middle, and End.

5. Nietzsche, p. 102. The actual passage is, "That same nature addresses us through Dionysiac art and its tragic symbolism, in a voice that rings authentic: 'Be like me, the Original Mother, who, constantly creating, finds satisfaction in the turbulent flux of appearances!'" Our ultimate identification at the end of tragedy with "mystical Oneness," Nietzsche, p. 23, like the lyric of the lyric poet who "beholds the ground of being," Nietzsche, p. 39, or "genius in the act of creation merges with the primal architect of the cosmos," Nietzsche, p. 42, all speak to the nature of the transport tragedy takes us on, breaking down the individual ego, to put it in modern terms, in the name of an

oceanic identity with the becoming, creative nature of reality itself.

See the discussion on Winnicott in "The Lost Poetics of Comedy" in Chapter 7.

5. The *Cooked* and the *Raw*

1. When "climax" is italicized, the climactic action at the end of Act 3, or the End, that finally resolves the conflict is referred to. "Crisis" italicized refers to the *crisis* at the end of Act 2, or the Middle, in which we see the effort undertaken by the protagonist in Act 2, or the Middle, brought to a point of actual or apparently impending failure. It is the emotional nadir of a screenplay and drama.

2. Nietzsche, pp. 20–21. His definition of the Apollonian, repeatedly returned to and developed in his argument, begins here.

3. Schulberg, p. 128.

4. Arthur Schopenhauer, *The World as Will and Representation,* 2 vols., trans. E. F. J. Payne (New York: Dover Publications, 1966). Schopenhauer's key work is usually known as *The World as Will and Idea.*

The Freudian libido is generally thought of as the human sexual drive, but Freud means that fundamentally and broadly as our procreative urge and will to live and grow; only later did he erect it into Eros and oppose Thanatos to its life drive. See the discussions of Freud in chapter 2, "The *Heavy* as Opposed To . . .," and of Winnicott in chapter 9, "The Lost Poetics of Comedy," in this book.

5. Robinson Jeffers, *Selected Poems* (New York: Vintage Books, 1965), p. 104.

6. Winnicott, pp. 86–94. See discussion of Winnicott in chapter 9, "The Lost Poetics of Comedy," in this book.

7. Gotthold Ephraim Lessing, *Laocoön,* trans. Ellen Frothingham, 2nd printing (New York: Noonday, 1961). Lessing is in part concerned to show what is appropriate to achieve the effect of beauty in each medium: a cry may be evoked in Virgil's lines on Laocoön, while omitted with equal justice from the sculpture, and yet be enacted in drama. It is the loss of the individual in the general that is at root in much of what Lessing has to say, which, in terms of handling emotion, means achieving a *cooked* effect, or one that is naïve in Nietzsche's sense. Lessing specifically quotes Virgil's "clamores horrendos ad sidera tollit" (p. 20) which may express Laocoön's pain yet is fine *to hear*, an example of a language effect absorbing an otherwise direct expression of emotion.

The lack of necessity to beauty is a striking point in Lessing, and anticipates Freud's view of beauty as one of the essentials of civilization whose necessity isn't immediately apparent in terms of survival value. But that entire attitude only betrays a shockingly limited view of human nature, one, unfortunately, most of us subscribe to.

8. Geoffrey Chaucer, "The Miller's Tale," in *The Portable Chaucer,* trans., sel., and ed. Theodore Morrison (New York: Viking, 1960), pp. 133–154.

9. Norman Maclean, *A River Runs Through It, and Other Stories* (New York: Pocket Books, 1992), p. 112. I have cited Maclean's story here as well as the film: both refer to Paul as beautiful. But, interestingly, in the novella Norm goes

on to add, "He should have been—you taught him," referring to Paul being beautiful. That is left out of the film and would have detracted from our concentration on the paradox of beauty and early death through gambling in Paul and on the nature of fate; in a work of fiction it does not detract, adding an additional layering. It goes to the heart of the difference between drama, which concentrates and excludes, and fiction, which, like the epic, is comparatively inclusive.

6. The *Smart* and the *Dumb*

1. Nietzsche, pp. 51–42.
2. *Hamlet,* I, 2, ll. 129–159, p. 22–23.
3. *Hamlet,* I, 5, ll. 87–88, p. 46.
4. *Hamlet,* II, 2, ll. 609–610, p. 77.
5. *Hamlet,* II, 2, ll. 553–610, pp. 75–77.
6. *Hamlet,* III, 1, ll. 56–90, pp. 80–82.
7. *Hamlet,* V, 2, l. 361, p. 174.

7. The Lost Poetics of Comedy

1. Lee, pp. 117–122.
2. Aristotle, p. 59.
3. Winnicott, pp. 19, 40, 69. He first uses the phrase (p. 19) in the context of the threatening quality of the "not me" to the infant: such an object must be attacked, meaning mastered. He does not yet develop the use of destruction to create an object's reality, and does not follow through on the threatening quality of an object existing apart from our control, our "me" area of existence. One could argue civilization itself in part arises from the effort both to master and domesticate threatening—

because not subject to our magical control—natural phenomena.

His second use (p. 40) identifies play as a thing in itself. As play is directly expressive of ourselves and broadens into shared cultural experience, and is not the Kantian "thing in itself," an ultimate expression of the "not me," Winnicott's purpose in using that characterization is to indicate play's equivalence with other psychic phenomena, like the libido. It exists in its own right as a feature of mental structure and is not reducible to something else.

His third use of the phrase (p. 69) is within the context of the creative impulse as a thing in itself, meaning again a fact of psychic structure and, in the context here examined, as a feature of healthy living. Losing the creative response to reality makes it seem at once unreal and meaningless. Historically, it must be associated with the presence of an individual functioning as such, not identified with a given role or a natural phenomenon. Here Winnicott is in error, for our creative impulse is unlikely to have developed evolutionarily in the last thousand years or so but to have existed fundamentally and developmentally with other mental structuring elements for a very long time. Moreover, identification with a role or natural phenomenon does not indicate a lack of creative response but a fixity of creative response instead.

Finally, a word of caution. Although Winnicott speaks of the use of an object, and of how the destructive impulse creates the "not me," independent quality of that object through its failure to destroy the object, there is no implication that thereby reality is created out of an act of the imagination. Rather, such an act allows us to appreciate objective existence: that appreciation is created. This is not a minor creation but the attainment of sanity itself. In the case of cultural "play" activities, however, the other implication of the destructive impulse literally *creating* reality holds, where works of art/imagination or elements within these (like characters and their purposes in a screenplay) survive destruction and so achieve a reality apart from the private self, the "me" of the "me vs. not me" dichotomy. They do so, moreover, beyond the transitional or cultural third area, as artifacts.

4. The remarks following here thread through Winnicott's argument in *Playing and Reality*, cited above.

The following works are also of interest.

F. Robert Rodman, MD, *Winnicott: Life and Work* (Cambridge, MA: Perseus Publishing, 2003). Rodman's is an exhaustive, excellent work on Winnicott with useful chapters on Melanie Klein (pp. 106–131, 245–263) and an excellent review of Winnicott's great, late work, pp. 264ff. There is also an exhaustive listing of Winnicott's published work.

D. W. Winnicott's key works, in addition to *Playing and Reality*, for those interested are:

Collected Papers: Through Paediatrics to Psycho-Analysis (London: Tavistock Publications, 1958).
The Child, the Family, and the Outside World (n.p.: Pelican, 1976). It was first published in 1964.
Maturational Processes and the Facilitating Environment (London: Hogarth Press, 1965).
Therapeutic Consultations in Child Psychiatry (London: Hogarth Press, 1971). This is a masterful book recounting brief courses of treatment with child patients. It must be remembered Winnicott was a practicing pediatrician for over twenty-five years, and his work was grounded in profound familiarity with children.
The Piggle (London: Hogarth Press, 1977). This is certainly one of the most moving and touching case studies in the psychoanalytic literature.

The key works for Melanie Klein for interested readers are:

The Psycho-Analysis of Children (London: Hogarth Press, 1932).
Contributions to Psychoanalysis (London: Hogarth Press, 1948).
Envy and Gratitude: A Study of Unconscious Forces (New York: Basic Books, 1957). This work is at once electrifying to read and on reflection deeply repugnant, with its exposition of an instinctual death drive expressed through envy, evoking a psychoanalytic vision of "fallen man." It is perhaps a key to the frequent evangelical fervor of her devotees.
Narrative of a Child Analysis (London: Hogarth Press, 1961).

5. Kantian reality is essentially Freud's reality, where "me" becomes ego, superego, and id and "not me" the external world of objects. It is a view of

reality that for psychoanalysis leads into the elaborate language of introjection, projection, and the almost infinite and confusing variety these can undergo through schizoid operations, like Nash in *A Beautiful Mind* splitting off aspects of himself into what he perceives as other persons, like Charles. Any perusal of psychoanalytic papers will immediately involve the noninitiate in a bewildering hall of projective/introjective mirrors. Drama overlaps psychoanalysis here in speaking of *identification* without ever explaining *how* it could be, as opposed to *what* it is believed to be. Winnicott's third, shared area of experience both provides an escape from these psychoanlytic absurdities and has profound philosophical implications with regard to the true nature of reality.

6. Henri Focillon, *The Art of the West,* vol. 1: *Romanesque Art* (London: Phaidon, 1963), pp. 102–143. I am indebted to Focillon's discussion of the evolution of Romanesque decoration, which planted the idea firmly in my mind of the internal evolution of a style past its moment of maximum achievement into an increasingly telling loss of its initiating spirit, as if possessed of a life of its own.

7. Aristotle, p. 59.

8. Freud, pp. 33, 45ff.

8. The Weight of the Past

1. Aristotle, p. 104. The telling sentence is, "This [metaphor] alone cannot be imparted by another; it is the mark of genius, for to make good metaphors implies an eye for resemblances." The resemblance involved is that we say, metaphorically, that one thing *is* another, not *like,* as in a simile. Moreover, the recognition that this is a "mark of genius," meaning an innate gift, gets at a further implication that, however a writer may have an eye for resemblances, he either has a gift for metaphor, or the identification of the seeming different, or does not. The implication is fatal for the idea of imitation, of one thing being like another; that way lie talent and commonplace and not particularly telling writing. The other way implies the creative gift to a high degree, the ability to erect another reality through the imagination we recognize as our own as well as stun us with unities we had not been able to see for ourselves.

A second implication for Aristotle is as revealing: what "cannot be imparted by another" cannot be taught, nor can it be imbibed through a "how to" literature. Understandably, the author of the first *Poetics* didn't pursue these implications. Good writing instructors know that they don't create writers: they bring experience to bear for someone already a writer but at the beginning of his or her efforts. The only amelioration of the truth is the other truth: that creativity is far more widespread than commonly asserted, at once Winnicott's point and observable in the special setting of a writing class, however few in there actually have the inclination to bend their creativity into a professional writing career.

I might add I understand genius in an Emersonian light of our common humanity writ large.

9. The Weight of the Wrong Decision

1. Schulberg, p. 133.

10. The Nature of the Hero's Journey

1. Joseph Campbell, *The Hero with a Thousand Faces*, Bollingen Series 17, 2nd ed. (Princeton: Princeton University Press, 1973), p. 246.
2. Campbell, p. 246.
3. Campbell, p. 245.
4. Campbell, pp. 317–318.
5. Ralph Waldo Emerson, "The Oversoul," in *Essays, First and Second Series* (A. L. Burt Co.), pp. 190–213. A key expression of this belief is, "Meantime within man is the soul of the whole; the wise silence; the universal beauty, to which every part and particle is equally related; the Eternal One," pp. 191–192. As we introspect and come to know ourselves most thoroughly, we find we become in touch with this under/overlying divine spark/common soul, so that simultaneously when we are most universal in our selves we are most individual.

Campbell pursues a very similar line of thought in *The Hero with a Thousand Faces* when he writes, "The way to become human is to learn to recognize the lineaments of God in all the wonderful modulations of the face of man," Campbell, p. 390, and, "The modern hero-deed must be that of questing to bring to light again the lost Atlantis of the coordinated soul," Campbell, p. 388. This is part of the modern hero's task of returning spiritual significance to our experience of the world/self.

The profoundest questing is into oneself to find the common self; the simplest level of the questing is the action-adventure variety, the sort in which the hero as warrior indulges in *The Hero with a Thousand Faces* and which we see reflected in film in the literal action-adventure genre and our various heroes of external deeds as they take us on the dramatic hero's journey outlined in these pages.

6. Campbell, p. 362.
7. Campbell, p. 336.
8. Campbell, p. 337.
9. Campbell, p. 342.
10. Campbell, p. 388.
11. Rodman, pp. 323–348.
12. Campbell, p. 388.

11. The Death and Life of Drama

1. Jacob Burckhardt, *The Greeks and Greek Civilization*, trans. Sheila Stern, ed. Oswyn Murray (New York: St. Martin's Press, 1998). The text is based on the famous lectures delivered in Basel in 1872 but not published until now. They present a radically unromantic and hardheaded view of Greek achievements, particularly Athenian, through the Hellenistic Age by Burckhardt, who is most famous for his *Civilization of the Renaissance in Italy*. The young Nietzsche was deeply influenced by Burckhardt, even as he leaped past him with regard to understanding the nature of classical tragedy and its dual religious and entertainment roles in Athens in the fifth century, and in the philosophical depth he could bring to his reflections.

2. Burckhardt, p. 226.
3. Burckhardt, p. 264.
4. Burckhardt, p. 262.

5. Sophocles, *Oedipus Rex,* in *The Oedipus Cycle,* trans. Dudley Fitts and Robert Fitzgerald (New York: Harvest Book, Harcourt Brace, 1949), p. 44, first strophe.

6. *Oedipus at Colonus,* in ibid., p. 145.

7. Euripides, *The Bacchae,* in *The Bacchae and Other Plays,* trans. Phillip Vellacott (Baltimore: Penguin Books, 1965), p. 209.

8. Nietzsche, p. 107.

9. Nietzsche, p. 108.

10. Nietzsche, p. 136.

11. Freud, pp. 109–110.

12. Burckhardt, p. 281.

13. Freud, p. 112.

14. *Hamlet,* III, 2, ll. 20–25, p. 87.

15. See note 5, chapter 2, above.

16. Simon Schama, *A History of Britain,* vol. 1: *At The Edge of the World* (New York: Hyperion, 2000). Schama is a distinguished historian, and his popular BBC program, *A History of England,* was broadcast in 2000–2001. Prior works includes the Dutch Golden Age, the French Revolution, and Rubens and Rembrandt (*Rembrandt's Eyes*). *Landscape and Memory* is a brilliant examination of how culture, history, and landscape intersect in certain key, modern myths to create and reveal national psyches.

His work on the Elizabethans spreads over several chapters. For a more detailed look at Elizabeth, the reader could try Alison Weir's *Elizabeth the Queen* (London: Pimlico, 1998), or the readable older biography by J. E. Neale, *Queen Elizabeth* (London: Reprint Society, 1942). There is no lack of material on the Elizabethans or Elizabeth. Alison Weir has some unusual conjectures, such as a suspicion the elder Cecil was behind the suspicious death of the first wife of Robert Dudley, Elizabeth's favorite.

17. Schama, p. 332.

18. Schama, p. 369.

19. Anthony Holden, *William Shakespeare: The Man behind the Mask* (Boston: Little, Brown, 1999). Holden is a noted writer and biographer but not a Shakespearean scholar in the sense of devoting a lifetime to that single topic. This is at once his strength and weakness, allowing him to draw together academic strands impartially, while without an academic standing to put him on a par—in their own minds—with Shakespearean specialists. Nonetheless, he takes issue with Harold Bloom that there is "not enough to know," p. 1, to write a revealing life of Shakespeare, although Bloom does admit we can learn to recognize Shakespeare's "temperament, sensibility and his cognition" (Holden, p. 3).

For my purposes, Holden presents an entirely readable and conjecturally solid outline of Shakespeare's life, reasonably filling in the "lost years" before Shakespeare shows up in London. He puts the events we are sure of in a clear Elizabethan context, whether concerning Shakespeare's early education or later status as a gentleman. I think we are unlikely to go further, as the sense of mystery about Shakespeare is so canonical that it is likely to endure until technology allows investigative time travel.

20. *Hamlet,* V, 1, ll. 189–201, p. 154.

21. William Shakespeare, *Othello,* in *The Complete Works of William Shakespeare,* Cambridge Edition Text

(Garden City: Garden City Publishing, 1936), V, vi, ll. 346–350, 356–361, p. 979.

22. *Hamlet,* III, 1, l. 79, p. 81.

23. William Shakespeare, *King Lear,* in ibid., III, iv, ll. 102–107, p. 1005.

24. William Shakespeare, *Macbeth,* in ibid., V, v, ll. 19–28, p. 1053.

25. William Shakespeare, *Much Ado about Nothing,* in ibid., V, iv, ll. 108–109, p. 628.

Appendix: A Case Study

1. Ingmar Bergman, *Fanny and Alexander* (New York: Pantheon, 1982).

2. "Take advantage of today," Horace, *Odes,* I, xi, l. 8.

3. Bergman, p. 26.

4. Bergman, p. 141.

5. Bergman, p. 100.

6. Bergman, p. 94.

7. Bergman, p. 101.

8. Bergman, p. 104.

9. Bergman, pp. 110–111.

10. Bergman, p. 110.

11. Bergman, pp. 122–123.

12. Bergman, p. 135.

13. Bergman, p. 137.

14. Bergman, p. 141.

15. Bergman, p. 142.

16. Bergman, p. 156.

17. Bergman, p. 157.

18. Bergman, pp. 157–158.

19. Bergman, p. 199.

20. Bergman, p. 200.

21. Bergman, p. 188.

22. Bergman, p. 188.

23. Bergman, p. 207.

24. Bergman, p. 208.

Film and Drama List

The author is given for each work referred to in the preceding chapters; a "D" indicates he or she also directed the work. Adaptations are given due credit; an asterisk indicates either an unfilmed work or no specific film adaptation (as with Shakespeare) is referred to. Grateful acknowledgment is made to Tom McWilliams for preparing this list.

An Affair to Remember, 1957 Leo McCarey D, Mildred Cram, Delmer Daves
    Donald Ogden Stewart
Analyze That, 2002 Peter Steinfeld, Harold Ramis D, Peter Tolan
Analyze This, 1999 Based on the story by Kenneth Lonergan and Peter Tolan
    Peter Tolan, Kenneth Lonergan, Harold Ramis
*Antigone Sophocles
*The Bacchae Euripides
A Beautiful Mind, 2000 Based on the novel by Sylvia Nasar
    Akiva Goldsman
Beckett, 1964 Based on the play by Jean Anouilh
    Edward Anhalt
Blue, 1993 Krzysztof Kieslowski D, Krzysztof Piesiewicz
Born Yesterday, 1950 Based on the play by Garson Kanin
    Albert Mannheimer
Born Yesterday, 1993 Based on the previous film
    Douglas McGrath
Breaking the Waves, 1996 Lars von Trier D, Peter Asmussen, David Pirie
Chinatown, 1974 Robert Towne
Chocolat, 2000 Based on the novel by Joanne Harris
    Robert Nelson Jacobs
City Slickers, 1991 Lowell Ganz, Babaloo Mandel
Cyrano de Bergerac, 1990 Based on the play by Edmond Rostand
    Jean-Claude Carrière D, Jean-Paul Rappeneau
Dave, 1993 Gary Ross
Die Another Day, 2002 Neal Purvis, Robert Wade

Dirty Harry, 1971 Based on the story by Harry Julian Fink and Rita M. Fink
    Harry Julian Fink, Rita M. Fink, Dean Riesner
*Doctor Faustus Christopher Marlowe
Elizabeth, 1998 Michael Hirst
Fanny and Alexander, 1983 Ingmar Bergman D
La Femme Nikita, 1991 Luc Besson D
Friday the 13th, 1980 Victor Miller
Gladiator, 2000 Based on the story by David Franzoni
    David Franzoni, John Logan, William Nicholson
The Godfather 1, 2; 1972, 1974 Based on the novel by Mario Puzo
    Mario Puzo, Francis Ford Coppola D
*Gorbuduc Thomas Morton, Thomas Sackville
*Hamlet William Shakespeare
Harry Potter and the Chamber of Secrets, 2002 Based on the book by J. K. Rowling
    Steven Kloves
Harry Potter and the Sorcerer's Stone, 2001 Based on the book by J. K. Rowling
    Steven Kloves
*Heartbreak House George Bernard Shaw
*Henry V William Shakespeare
High Noon, 1952 Carl Foreman
*Hippolytus Euripides
The Importance of Being Earnest, 2002 Based on the play by Oscar Wilde
    Oliver Parker D
*King Lear William Shakespeare
Kramer vs. Kramer, 1979 Based on the novel by Avery Corman
    Robert Benton D
L.A. Confidential, 1997 Based on the novel by James Ellroy
    Curtis Hanson D, Brian Helgeland
Lantana, 2001 Based on the play by Andrew Bovel
    Andrew Bovel
Lethal Weapon 1, 1987 Shane Black, Jeffrey Boam
Lethal Weapon 2, 3; 1989, 1992 Jeffrey Boam
*The Libation Bearers Aeschylus
Life Is Beautiful, 1997 Vincenzo Cerami, Roberto Benigni D
Like Water for Chocolate, 1992 Based on the novel by Laura Esquivel
    Laura Esquivel
*Macbeth William Shakespeare
Married to the Mob, 1988 Barry Strugatz, Mark R. Burns
The Matrix, 1999 Andy Wachowski D, Larry Wachowski D
*Medea Euripides
Memento, 2000 Based on the story by Jonathon Nolan
    Christopher Nolan D
Mighty Aphrodite, 1995 Woody Allen D

Much Ado about Nothing, 1993 Based on the play by William Shakespeare
    Kenneth Branagh D
The Name of the Rose, 1986 Based on the novel by Umberto Eco
    Andrew Birkin, Gérard Brach, Howard Franklin, Alain Godard
No Way Out, 1987 Based on the novel The Big Clock by Kenneth Fearing
    Robert Garland
*Oedipus at Colonus Sophocles
*Oedipus Rex Sophocles
On the Waterfront, 1954 Budd Schulberg
*Othello Shakespeare
Pale Rider, 1985 Michael Butler, Dennis Shryack
The Pianist, 2002 Based on the novel by Wladyslaw Szpilman
    Ronald Harwood
Prizzi's Honor, 1985 Based on the novel by Richard Condon
    Richard Condon, Janet Roach
The Professional, 1994 Luc Besson D
Proof of Life, 2000 Based on the novel The Long March to Freedom
    by Thomas Hargrove
    Tony Gilroy
Raiders of the Lost Ark, 1981 Based on the story by George Lucas
    and Philip Kaufman
    Lawrence Kasdan
Ran, 1985 Based on King Lear by William Shakespeare
    Akira Kurosawa D
Rashômon, 1954 Akira Kurosawa D
Rear Window, 1954 John Michael Hayes
The Return of the Jedi, 1983 George Lucas, Lawrence Kasdan
*Richard III William Shakespeare
A River Runs through It, 1992 Based on the novella by Norman Macean
    Richard Friedenberg
Road to Perdition, 2002 Based on the graphic novel by Max Allan Collins
    and Richard Piers Rayner
    David Self
*Romeo and Juliet William Shakespeare
Roxanne, 1987 Based on Cyrano De Bergerac by Edmund Rostand
    Steve Martin
*Saint Joan George Bernard Shaw
Scarface, 1983 Oliver Stone
Schindler's List, 1993 Based on the novel by Thomas Keneally
    Steven Zaillian
Shadowlands, 1993 Based on the play by William Nicholson
    William Nicholson

Shane, 1953 Based on the novel by Jack Schaefer
    A. B. Guthrie, Jr.
Sleepless in Seattle, 1993 Jeffrey Arch, Larry Atlas, David S. Ward, Nora Ephron D
Smiles of a Summer Night, 1955 Ingmar Bergman D
Star Wars, 1977 George Lucas D
A Streetcar Named Desire, 1951 Based on the play by Tennessee Williams
    Tennessee Williams
Suddenly Last Summer, 1959 Based on the play by Tennessee Williams
    Gore Vidal
*Tamburlaine Christopher Marlowe
*The Tempest William Shakespeare
*Titus Andronicus William Shakespeare
Tootsie, 1982 Larry Gelbart, Murray Schisgal, Don McGuire
The Unbearable Lightness of Being, 1988 Based on the novel by Milan Kundera
    Jean-Claude Carrière, Philip Kaufman D
Unforgiven, 1992 David Peoples
The Usual Suspects, 1995 Christopher McQuarrie
Wild Strawberries, 1957 Ingmar Bergman D
Witness, 1985 Earl W. Wallace, William Kelley
The Year of Living Dangerously, 1982 Based on the novel by C. J. Koch
    Peter Weir D, David Williamson